Abstracts of the
TESTAMENTARY PROCEEDINGS
of the
PREROGATIVE COURT OF MARYLAND

Volume XXXVIII: 1771-1772

Liber: 44 (pp. 203-596)

by
V. L. Skinner, Jr.

CLEARFIELD

Printed for Clearfield Company by
Genealogical Publishing Company
Baltimore, Maryland
2012

ISBN 978-0-8063-5586-3

Made in the United States of America

INTRODUCTION

Purpose of the Prerogative Court.

The Prerogative Court was the central point for probate for Provincial Maryland. It was mirrored after the Prerogative Court of Canterbury. There was a judge as well as clerk(s) of the court. Initially, all probate was brought directly to the Prerogative Court, located in the Provincial Capital. As the Province became more populous, all documents were still to be filed with the Prerogative Court; however, administration of probate was delegated to the various county courts. Even so, there are documents only in the Prerogative Court and not in the appropriate county, and vice versa.

Documents filed in the Prerogative Court.

The following documents were filed in the Prerogative Court: administration bond, will, inventory, administration accounts, and final balances. The testamentary proceedings contain the administration bond and the docket for the court. If the administrator is lax in filing documents, then a summons is also recorded.

Equity Court

The Prerogative Court was also the court for equity cases--resolution of disputes over the settlement and distribution of an estate. The case was brought before the judge and could take several years to resolve. Often depositions were taken and recorded in the minutes.

Notes on the Abstraction.

1. The left hand column contains the liber/folio number. The folio numbers are presented just as they appear in the actual document, e.g., 32a, 78½.
2. The right hand column contains the abstraction text.
3. Various libers specify a particular session for the Prerogative Court, e.g., 1678; or, September Court 1742. This information is presented as "Court Session:" followed by the appropriate session. Should no session have been specified, then the phrase "no

date" is used.
4. An ellipsis (...) is used to indicate a
    continuation of the previous information,
    but no relevant genealogical information is
    present.
5. The following symbols are used in the
    abstraction:
    • ? - difficult to read.
    • # - pounds of tobacco.
    • ! - [sic].

Abbreviations.

The following abbreviations have been used
throughout this abstraction:

AA - Anne Arundel Co.
ACC - Accomac Co.
BA - Baltimore Co.
CE - Cecil Co.
CH - Charles Co.
CR - Caroline Co.
CV - Calvert Co.
dbn - de bonis non
DE - Delaware
DO - Dorchester Co.
ENG - England
FR - Frederick Co.
g - gentleman
GB - Great Britain
HA - Harford Co.
IRE - Ireland
JP - justice of the
    peace
KE - Kent Co. MD
KEDE - Kent Co. DE
LaC - letters ad
    colligendum
LoA - letters of
    administration
LoD - list of debts

MA - Massachusetts
MD - Maryland
MO - Montgomery Co.
NE - New England or
    "non est"
NEI - "non est
    inventar"
NPN - no page number
NY - New York
NYC - New York City
p - planter
PA - Pennsylvania
PG - Prince George's
    Co.
PoA - power of
    attorney
QA - Queen Anne's Co.
SM - St. Mary's Co.
SMC - St. Mary's City
SO - Somerset Co.
TA - Talbot Co.
VA - Virginia
WA - Washington Co.
WO - Worcester Co.

This volume is a continuation of the series,
covering 1771 to 1772. Most of the entries for
the docket involve situations where the personal
representative has not filed the proper
documents.

Beginning with the March 1772 Court session, the
format of the court changes. Three court
sessions (6 months) are presented at the same
time.

44:203 24 June. Walter Hanson (g, CH) exhibited:
- bond of Henry Hagen executor of Clear Sympson. Sureties: Thomas Semmes, Charles Goodrick. Date: 6 May 1771.
- bond of Mary Kersey administratrix of Thomas Kersey. Sureties: Philip Magrah, Alexander Hambleton. Date: 18 May 1771.
- bond of Sarah Hagan administratrix of Henry Hagan. Sureties: William Coombs, Sr., William Coombs, Jr. Date: 13 May 1771.
- inventory of William Joy.
- inventory of Alexander Smith Hawkins.
- inventory of Elisabeth Warren.
- inventory of George Thomas Sparr.
- inventory of John Smallwood.
- accounts on estate of Elisabeth Dade.
- accounts on estate of Richard Elms.
- accounts on estate of John Bowers.
- accounts on estate of Basil Hagan.
- accounts on estate of Robert Mastin.
- accounts on estate of Jacob Clement.
- accounts on estate of James Nailor.
- accounts on estate of John Givan.
- accounts on estate of James French.
- accounts on estate of Leonard Burch.

44:204 Thomas Bowles (g, FR) exhibited:
- bond of Elisabeth Vennemon administratrix of John Vennemon. Sureties: Jacob Gripe, John Ulrich. Date: 11 May 1771.
- bond of Joseph Hunt & Levi Mills administrators of Thomas Mills. Surety: Isaac Baker. Date: 23 May 1771.
- will of Catherine Malot.
- will of Catherine Tom.
- inventory of Conrod Sharer.
- inventory of William Thomas.
- inventory of Sam Case.
- inventory of Paul Boyer.
- inventory of Godfrey Thiphart.
- inventory of James Perry.
- accounts on estate of Samuel Perry.
- accounts on estate of Lodowick Boyerly.

Court Session: 1771

- LoD on estate of Meredith Davis.
- accounts on estate of Samuel Bowman.
- accounts on estate of Thomas Hawkins.
- LoD on estate of Michael Hofner.

44:205 1 July. Col. William Young (BA) exhibited:
- will of Barnet Johnson, constituting Hester Johnson executrix. Said executrix was granted administration. Sureties: Thomas Johnson, John Johnson. Date: 24 June 1771.
- will of David Morgan, constituting Lydia Morgan executrix. Said executrix was granted administration. Sureties: Job Barnes, John Morgan, Jr. Date: 25 April 1771.
- bond of Robert Saunders executor of Jacob Shortell. Surety: John Roberts. Date: 13 May 1771.
- bond of Elisabeth Graham executrix of Daniel Graham. Sureties: James Anderson, Edward Harris. Date: 13 May 1771.
- bond of Charles Harryman administrator of Isaac Raven. Sureties: Robert Duy, Thomas Davis. Date: 13 May 1771.
- bond of George Myer, Michael Swoope, & Frederick Eichelberger administrators of George Myer. Sureties: Jacob Myers, Jacob Eichelberger. Date: 21 April 1771.
- bond of John Hart administrator of Alexander Valles. Surety: Jacob Myer. Date: 3 June 1771.

44:206
- bond of Jane Gardin administratrix of James Gardwin. Sureties: Nicholas Smith, Charles Hissey. Date: 21 June 1771.
- bond of Alexander Stenhouse administrator of John Gough. Surety: John Macnabb. Date: 21 April 1771.
- LoD on estate of John Hall.
- LoD on estate of John Hall [!].
- inventory of Jonathan Massey.
- inventory of William Mattox.
- inventory of William Johnson.

- inventory of Luke Wyle.
- accounts on estate of William Jenkins.
- accounts on estate of David Harvey.
- accounts on estate of John Hill.
- accounts on estate of John Hall.
- accounts on estate of John Wallis.
- accounts on estate of John Murra.
- accounts on estate of Elisabeth Trotten.
- accounts on estate of John Meek.
- accounts on estate of John Pawnall.

44:207 25 June. Deputy Commissaries to examine accounts of:
- QA: Charles Blake administrator of Sarah Blake.

28 June.
- CH: Butcher Frankling & his wife Cloe executrix of William Douglass.
- CH: Margaret & Thomas Reeder executors of Benjamin Reeder.

1 July.
- BA: John Mercer administrator of Hans Rudolph.
- QA: Richard Small & James Small executors of Richard Small.
- CV: Young Parran administrator of Elisabeth Parran.
- CV: Young Parran administrator of Phillip Parran.
- CV: Ann Elt administratrix of Benjamin Elt.
- CV: James Sewell administrator of Francess Harriss.
- TA: Elisabeth Harwood & Robert Harwood administrators of William Harwood.
- TA: Mary Brown administratrix of Adam Brown.

6 July.
- BA: Rebecca Wheeler executrix of Benjamin Wheeler.

9 July.
- KE: Ann Smith executrix of Nicholas Smith.
- KE: Nathaniel Comegys administrator dbn of Alexander Kelley.
- KE: James Welsh & his wife Milcah administrators of Thomas Sappington.

10 July.
- SO: Ephraim King administrator of

John Flewellin.
- DO: Thomas Noel & his wife Sarah executrix of Alexander Frazier.
- DO: James Payton & Sarah Thomas executors of Henry Thomas.
- DO: William & Abner Lecompte executors of Philemon Lecompte.
- DO: Jane Farguson administratrix of Thomas Farguson.
- DO: Mary Phillips & Richard Phillips executors of Reuben Phillips.

4 July.
- petition of John Maddox (FR). Administration bond on estate of Grove Tomlinson assigned to petitioner.

11 July.
- QA: Samuel Brown administrator of Esther Hall.
- QA: Samuel Brown administrator dbn of Andrew Hall.
- QA: Elisabeth Wiggins executrix of William Wiggins.
- BA: David Dixon executor of James Dixon.
- BA: Jacob Bond & Benjamin Green executors of David Thomas.
- DO: Elisabeth Wheeler & Benjamin Wheeler executors of Thomas Wheeler.

44:208 10 July. John Goldsborough (DO) exhibited:
- will of William Gray.
- will of Henry Hooper.
- will of James Fargusson.
- inventory of William Green.
- inventory of Thomas Wheeler.
- inventory of William Phillips.
- inventory of Abraham Clark.
- inventory of Mary Jones.
- inventory of Philemon Lecompte.
- LoD on estate of Priscilla How.
- accounts on estate of Philemon Lecompte.

11 July. Thomas Wright (g, QA) exhibited:
- bond of Sarah Meredith administratrix of John Meredith. Sureties: Nathaniel Wright, William Wrench. Date: 27 May 1771.
- bond of Rachel Imbert administratrix

Court Session: 1771

of Thomas Imbert. Sureties:
Philemon Murphy, Robert Tate. Date:
16 May 1771.
- bond of Elisabeth Herring
administratrix of David Herring.
Sureties: John Peters, Daniel Jones.
Date: 23 May 1771.
- bond of Ann Coursey administratrix
of William Coursey. Sureties: John
Sayer Blake, Clement Sewel. Date:
27 June 1771.

44:209
- bond of William Stevens
administrator of William Chalmers.
Sureties: Samuel Blunt, John Sliney.
Date: 27 June 1772 [!].
- inventory of Thomas Cook.
- inventory of James Dolan.
- inventory of George Spry.
- inventory of Margaret Cox.
- inventory of Henry Darnall.
- inventory of Abraham Delahunt.
- inventory of Samuel Whiting.
- inventory of John Pratt.
- additional inventory of Nicholas
Clouds.
- additional inventory of William
Jacobs.
- additional inventory of Thomas
Clayland.
- accounts on estate of Henry Darnall.
- accounts on estate of Gideon Swift.
- accounts on estate of James Gould.
- accounts on estate of William
Jacobs.
- accounts on estate of David Nevill.
- accounts on estate of Sweatnam Burn.
- accounts on estate of Thomas
Clayland.
- accounts on estate of Thomas Hewet.
- accounts on estate of John Downes
the elder.
- accounts on estate of Joseph Tolson.
- accounts on estate of Nicholas
Clouds.
- accounts on estate of James Tolson.
- accounts on estate of Isaac
Leverton.
- accounts on estate of Frances
Walters.
- accounts on estate of George Powell.
- accounts on estate of William
Tarbutton.

- accounts on estate of Edward Crapper.
- accounts on estate of Isaac Tippins.
- accounts on estate of Abram Delehunt.
- accounts on estate of Thomas Lee.
- accounts on estate of Thomas Kemp.

44:210 13 July. Thomas Holbrook (g, SO) exhibited:
- will of James Nairne, constituting James Nairne executor. Said executor was granted administration. Sureties: Isaac Dickeson, William Hall. Date: 11 June 1771.
- will of Thomas Ricards. Also, bond of Thomas Ricards administrator. Sureties: Levin Moore, Daniel Phillips. Date: 19 June 1771.
- bond of William Moore administrator of Thomas Moore. Sureties: Benjamin Scott, Levin Beauchamp. Date: 18 June 1771.
- inventory of Joseph Hitch.
- inventory of Michael Cutler.
- final accounts on estate of William Shores.
- accounts on estate of John Robertson.

15 July. George Scott, Esq. (PG) exhibited:
- will of Mordecai Jacobs, constituting Jemima Jacobs, Benjamin Jacobs, & Mordecai Jacobs executors. Said executors were granted administration. SUreties: Robert Tyler, Thomas Macgill. Date: 8 May 1771.
- will of Hugh Wilson. Also, bond of Elisabeth Wilson administratrix. Sureties: Jos. Beall, Josias Shaw. Date: 18 June 1771.
- inventory of Thomas Williams.
- inventory of Richard Bowes.
- inventory of Richard Blues.
- inventory of Mary Thompson.
- accounts on estate of John Clagget.
- accounts on estate of Jane Goddart.
- accounts on estate of Alexander Fraiser.

44:211 24 July. Joseph Nicholson (g, KE) exhibited:
- bond of George Sanders administrator of William Sanders. Sureties: Mathew Smith, Thomas Smith. Date: 26 June 1771.
- bond of Henrietta Wallis & Henry Wallis administrators of John Wallis (son of John). Sureties: Aquila Page, Henry Hurt. Date: 5 July 1771.
- bond of Hannah Miles administratrix of Nathaniel Miles. Sureties: Isaac Spencer, George Vansant Mann. Date: 22 July 1771.
- additional inventory & LoD of William Wilmer.
- additional inventory of William Hollingsworth.
- additional inventory of Nicholas Smith.
- inventory of James Hacket.
- inventory of Philip Rasin.
- inventory of Samuel Corse.
- LoD on estate of James Claypole.
- accounts on estate of William Hollingsworth.
- LoD & final accounts on estate of Isaac Harrisson.

29 July. John Bracco (g, TA) exhibited:
- bond of Joshua Clark administrator of John Scott. Sureties: Henry Clark, Caleb Clark. Date: 22 June 1771.
- bond of James Beall administrator of Thomas Beall. Sureties: Alexander Beall, Samuel Nichols. Date: 26 June 1771.

44:212
- bond of Elisabeth Bullen administratrix dbn of Peter Cox. Sureties: Thomas Stevens, William Sharp. Date: 16 July 1771.
- will of William Parrott.
- inventory of James Donellan.
- inventory of Stephen Ratcliff.
- inventory of Thomas McCleland.
- LoD on estate of Thomas McCleland.
- final accounts on estate of Samuel Abbot.

John Goldsborough (g, DO) exhibited:

- will of Thomas Wall, constituting John Russel executor. Said executor was granted administration. Sureties: William Wall, Thomas Wilson. Date: 13 June 1771.
- bond of Elisabeth Howarth executrix of John Howarth. Sureties: Edward Thompson, Joseph Thompson. Date: 11 June 1771.
- bond of Mary Vickars administratrix of John Vicars. Sureties: John Wheeler, William Vickers. Date: 5 June 1771.
- bond of Rosannah Robinson administratrix of James Farguson. Sureties: Thomas Creighton, Joseph Robinson. Date: 22 May 1771.
- will of Frances Stevens.
- inventory of Henry Thomas.
- inventory & LoD of Robert Griffith.
- inventory of Mary Edmondson.

44:213
- inventory of John Parkerson.
- inventory of Christiana Wallace.
- inventory & LoD of Reymour Land.
- inventory & LoD of David Pollock.
- inventory of William Whiteley.
- inventory of Solomon Trego.
- inventory of John Jobson.
- inventory of Abel Grace.
- LoD on estate of James Sherwin.
- inventory of John Hicks.

8 August. Thomas Holbrook (g, SO) exhibited:

- will of John Killum, constituting William Badley executor. Said executor was granted administration. Sureties: William Nutter, Thomas Handy. Date: 17 July 1771.
- will of William Robertson. Also, bond of William Badley administrator. Sureties: Thomas Connelly, William Wright. Date: 1 August 1771.
- will of Mary Fullerton. Also, bond of Charles Fullerton administrator. Sureties: John Watkins, Joshua Fullerton. Date: 26 July 1771.
- will of Elijah Conner, constituting Isabella Conner executrix. Said executrix was granted

administration. Sureties: William Lankford, David Lankford. Date: 23 July 1771.

- inventory of William Kibble.
- inventory of Thomas White.
- inventory of Jonathan Bounds.
- inventory of James Trehearn.
- inventory of Chr. Piper.

44:214
- accounts on estate of Philip Murray.
- accounts on estate of Thomas White.
- accounts on estate of Benjamin Franceway.
- accounts on estate of William Brown.
- accounts of estate of Joseph Wheatherly.
- accounts on estate of Esther Tull.
- accounts on estate of William Stevens.
- accounts on estate of Christopher Piper.

24 August. Walter Hanson (g, CH) exhibited:
- bond of William Farr administrator dbn of John Farr. Sureties: John Farr, Jos. Thompson. Date: 9 August 1771.
- bond of William Thornton (VA) administrator of Richard Scoggin. Sureties: Samuel Love, Theo. Hanson. Date: 23 July 1771.
- bond of Sarah Brooke administratrix of William Brooke. Sureties: Hugh Hamil, John Brooke. Date: 5 July 1771.
- bond of Elisabeth Speake administratrix of John Speake. Sureties: Robert Wade, Jr., Jo. Hatton. Date: 20 June 1771.
- bond of Mary Warder administratrix of Walter Warder. Sureties: William Warder, William Fairfax. Date: 24 June 1771.
- bond of Eleanor Warder administratrix of John Warder. Sureties: William Warder, William Fairfax. Date: 24 June 1771.
- will of Basil Hamersley.
- inventory of Henry Hagan.
- inventory of Charles Rock.
- inventory of Robert Sennett.
- inventory of Thomas Stromat.

44:215

- inventory of Thomas Gordon.
- inventory of John Cole.
- inventory of Maximilian Mathews.
- inventory of John Montgomery.
- inventory of Thomas Higdon.
- inventory of Francis Semmes.
- accounts on estate of Whitten Wallace.
- accounts on estate of William Douglass.
- accounts on estate of Thomas Morris.
- accounts on estate of Barton Hungerford.

30 August. Col. William Young (BA) exhibited:
- bond of Jane Butler administratrix of Peter Butler. Sureties: John Stevenson, James Gray. Date: 30 July 1771.
- bond of Ruth Fitch administratrix of Henry Fitch. Sureties: William Fitch, Thomas Bailey, Jr. Date: 5 August 1771.
- bond of Thomas Logan administrator of William Robertson. Sureties: John Macnabb, James Charshe. Date: 1 August 1771.
- bond of Benjamin Howard administrator of Ann Howard. Sureties: Isaac Daws, John Wilson. Date: 30 July 1771.
- will of Daniel Graham.
- inventory of Benjamin Wheeler.
- inventory of Thomas Wheeler.
- inventory of Martha Garretson.
- inventory of James Dixon.
- inventory of Robert Dunn.
- inventory of John Hatton.
- inventory of John Murra.
- inventory of George Myers.
- LoD on estate of George Myers.
- accounts on estate of Benjamin Wheeler.
- accounts on estate of Jethro Lynch.
- accounts on estate of Aquila Nelson.
- accounts on estate of James Philips.
- accounts on estate of Charles Beck.
- accounts on estate of John Wheeler the younger.
- accounts on estate of John Hatton.

44:216 18 July. Deputy Commissaries to examine accounts of:
- KE: Mary Garnett administratrix of Thomas Garnett.
- QA: John Young executor of John Young.

19 July.
- CH: John Evans, Jr. & his wife Victoria executrix of Thomas Nelson.
- CH: David Lindsay Ward executor of Abraham McLoad.
- WO: Rhoda Henderson & Ephraim Henderson administrators of John Henderson.

24 July.
- KE: Charity Pratt administratrix of Philemon Pratt.

25 July.
- BA: Evan Phillips administrator of James Phillips.
- KE: Mary McHard administratrix of Samuel McHard.

27 July.
- SM: Aaron Milbourn & Augustus Milbourne surviving executors of Stephen Milbourne.
- SM: Joshua Watts executor of Thomas Watts.
- TA: Lambert Booker & Alexander James executors of Lambert Booker.
- TA: Ann Bowman executrix of Samuel Bowman.

29 July.
- petition of Charles Tims (CH) & Jane Parsons (CH). Administration bond on estate of Daniel Wright assigned to petitioners.
- TA: John Blythe & his wife Sophia executrix of Lawrence Porter.

30 July.
- DO: James Shaw & his wife Mary & Abner Lecompte executors of John Lecompte.

2 August.
- DO: Solomon Camper & his wife Philadelphia executrix of Stephen Sherwin.
- DO: John Curmeen & his wife Anne administratrix of Ambrose Aaron.
- DO: Jabus Pritchett executor of Phunback Pritchett.
- DO: John Wheeler executor of Thomas

Wheeler.
- DO: Mary Smith administratrix of Edward Smith, Jr.
- DO: Esther Blades & George Blades executors of Joseph Blades.
- DO: Susanna Mcfarlin executrix of John Mcfarlin.
- DO: Edward Broadus & his wife Elisabeth administratrix of William Trego, Jr.
- CV: Mary Dixon administratrix of Benjamin Dixon.
- CV: Francis Lawther & Hugh Hopewell executors of Elick Parran.
- CV: Margaret Brown administratrix of George Bourne.
- BA: Elisabeth Bond executrix of William Bond.
- SO: Abigail Collins executrix of John Collins.
- SM: Stephen Milbourne & Sarah Thomas executors of John Thomas.
- SM: John Fenwick, John Manning, & Margaret Manning executors of James Manning.
- SM: Aaron Milbourn & Austen Milbourne surviving executors of Stephen Milbourne.

44:217 3 August.
- SM: William Bayard & his wife Eleanor executrix of Alexander McFarlane.

7 August.
- SO: William Stewart executor of Rebeccah Dashiel.
- SO: Sarah Harris administratrix of James Harriss.
- SO: Isabella Cox administratrix of John Cox.
- CH: Josiah Hawkins administrator of Henry Hawkins.

8 August.
- CE: Andrew Welsh executor of William Callender.

9 August.
- petition of Nicholas Maccubbin (AA). Administration bond on estate of William Kirkland assigned to petitioner.
- TA: Ann Feddeman administratrix of Daniel Feddeman.

21 August.

Court Session: 1771

- DO: John Creighton executor of Robert Creighton.

22 August.
- petition of Susannah Key (SM). Administration bond on estate of Phillip Key assigned to petitioner.

23 August.
- FR: Ann Cheney & Richard Cheney executors of Ezekiel Cheney.

24 August.
- QA: Charles & Hovel Warner (?) executors of Richard Warner.
- CH: Kenlem Truman Stoddart & Walter Stoddart surviving administrators of Richard Stoddart.
- CH: Charles Brandt executor of Mary Wood.
- CH: John Wright executor of John Wright.

26 August.
- PG: Margaret Miles administratrix of William Miles.

28 August.
- QA: William Ruth executor of Christ. Brown.
- WO Pharahe Munroe administratrix of John Francey.
- WO: Elijah & Benjamin Purnell executors of Joseph Purnell.
- WO: William Bartlet Townsend administrator of Comfort Atkinson.

29 August.
- FR: Catharine & Benjamin McInnely executors of John McInnely.
- KE: John Kennard executor of John Kennard.

3 September.
- QA: Joseph Beall executor of Joseph Beall.
- QA: John Smith executor of John Smith.

5 September.
- TA: William Lavall executor of Thomas McCleland.
- TA: Peter Hunt executor of Peter Hunt.

9 September.
- SM: Wilfrid Neale & his wife Elisabeth, Eleanor Diggs, Raphael Neale, & George Slye executors of Edward Diggs.
- CE: Jane Strawbridge & John

Strawbridge administrators of John
Strawbridge.

44:218 10 September.
- BA: John Anderson administrator of
  Edward Flanagan.
- BA: Mary Magdalane Tripolete
  administratrix of Abraham Tripolete.
- BA: Elisabeth Pain administratrix of
  William Pain.
- CE: Isaa Vanbebber & Pineas Chew
  executors of Sarah Chew.

11 September.
- KE: Rachel Blackiston administratrix
  of Michael Blackiston.
- WO: Hannah Conoway executrix of
  Phillip Conoway.
- SM: Robert Holton administrator dbn
  of William Holton.
- QA: Gideon Emory executor of Thomas
  Emory.
- DO: Benjamin Keene, Jr. executor of
  Benjamin Keene.
- DO Ann Green administratrix of
  William Green.

11 September.
- appointment of William Turner Wooten
  (PG) as Deputy Commissary (PG), in
  room of George Scott, Esq. (dec'd).
- SO: Job Gastineaux executor of
  George Lewis Gastineaux.

12 September.
- DO: John Pagan administrator of
  William Pagan.
- DO: Rachel Bozman executrix of
  Philemon Bozman.

13 September.
- SO: Sarah Bouth administratrix of
  William Bouth.
- DO: Betty Todd executrix of Benjamin
  Todd.
- QA: Sarah Massey administratrix of
  John Massey.
- WO: Powell Patty administrator of
  John Patty.
- WO: John Campbell executor of Elisha
  Evans.

14 September.
- DO: Betty Stewart & John Travillion
  Stewart executors of John Stewart.
- QA: Ann & Arthur Emory executors of
  John Emory.
- QA: Mary Saterfield administratrix

of William Saterfield.
- QA: Lodman Elbert executor of Hawkins Downes.
- TA: Frances Gibson administratrix of Francis Gibson.
- KE: Mary & William Lynch administrators of Nicholas Lynch.
- WO: Joshua Hitch executor of John Talbot.
- WO: Ann Smith executrix of John Smith.
- WO: Tabitha Tilghman administratrix of Gideon Tilghman.
- SO: Mathew Kemp administrator of Richard Stevens.
- SO: Isaac Green executor of Richard Green.
- WO: John Campbell administrator of Elisha Evans.

44:219 17 September.
- CE: Thomas Williams surviving executor of Robert Williams.
- SO: Joseph Kenney executor of William Kenney.
- CE: Ann Armstrong administratrix of Archibald Armstrong.
- CE: Andrew Wallace, John Brown, & Mary Parker administrators of Isaac Parker.

18 September.
- WO John Parker executor of George Parker.

21 September.
- DO: Comfort Parish administratrix of Richard Parish.

23 September.
- KE: William Mobey & his wife Rachel executrix of William Hynson.
- KE: Peter Body administrator of John Body.

24 September.
- CE: John Ward surviving administrator of Henry Ward.
- CE: John Ward executor of Hannah Ward.

25 September.
- TA: Abner Turner administrator dbn of William George Thompson.

26 September.
- CH: James Maddox (son of Notly) & his wife Sarah executrix of Notley Warren.

27 September.
- WO: Purnel Bowen administrator of Littleton Bowen.
- KE: John Williamson executor of George Williamson.
- petition of Jane Roberts (QA). Administration bond on estate of Benjamin Roberts assigned to petitioner.
- petition of Abraham Freeman (SM). Administration bond on estate of Jacob Freeman assigned to petitioner.

28 September.
- SM: John Hatton Reed executor of John Reed.
- SM: Catharine Wilson Thomas administratrix of James Thomas.
- CH: William Lindsay & his wife Jane administratrix of Francis Adams.
- CH: Elisabeth Kerrick administratrix of Hugh Kerrick.
- QA: Lydia Costin administratrix of Henry Costin.
- SO: Adam Anderson & his wife Elisabeth administratrix of Thomas Bond.
- BA: David Dickson administrator of James Dickson.
- BA: Ann & William Bond executors of Joshua Bond.

1 October.
- BA: Lydia Morgan executrix of David Morgan.
- QA: Honour Elliot administratrix of William Elliot.
- KE: Benjamin Howard administrator of Benjamin Howard.
- KE: Benjamin Howard administrator dbn of Charles McCubbin.
- CE: Esther Bateman administratrix of William Bateman.

7 October.
- FR: Mary & Nathan Haines executors of Daniel Haines.

9 October.
- QA: Thomas Emory 3rd & Arthur Emory, Jr. administrators of Nathaniel Wright.

44:220 3 September. Thomas Wright (g, QA) exhibited:

Court Session: 1771

- will of William Hughlet,
  constituting Thomas Hughlet
  executor. Said executor was granted
  administration. Sureties: William
  Haslet, Robert Dixon. Date: 1
  August 1771.
- bond of William Clarke administrator
  of John Price. Sureties: William
  Simmonds, Richard Arescott. Date:
  18 July 1771.
- bond of Susannah Smith
  administratrix of Richard Smith.
  Sureties: William Purnel, William
  Smith, Jr. Date: 15 August 1771.
- bond of Edward Coursey administrator
  dbn of William Coursey. Sureties:
  R. Tilghman, Robert Browne. Date:
  18 July 1771.
- inventory of Nathaniel Comegys.
- inventory of Richard Small.
- inventory of Thomas Imbert.
- inventory of Mary Hadley.
- inventory of James Clough.
- LoD on estate of Christ. Plummer.
- 2nd additional accounts on estate of
  Christ. Plummer.
- accounts on estate of Mary Hadley.
- accounts on estate of William
  Wiggins.
- accounts on estate of Richard Small.

9 September. Exhibited from TA:
- inventory of Daniel Feddeman.
- inventory of Peter Hunt.

44:221 10 September. John Goldsborough (g, DO)
exhibited:
- LoD on estate of Mary McKeel.
- accounts on estate of Mary McKeel.
- accounts on estate of Nehemiah
  Lecompte.
- accounts on estate of Robert Rowe.
- accounts on estate of Priscilla
  Howe.
- accounts on estate of John Handy.

Thomas Holbrook (g, SO) exhibited:
- bond of Sarah Hitch & Robert Hitch
  administrators of Joshua Hitch.
  Sureties: Joshua Hitch, Benjamin
  Hearn. Date: 23 August 1771.
- bond of Sarah Ann Messeck

administratrix of Covington Messeck. Sureties: William Stewart, William Dashiel. Date: 28 August 1771.
- inventory of Thomas Humphris.
- inventory of Thomas Moore.
- inventory of Mary Fullerton.
- inventory of James Pusey.
- inventory of Ezekiel James.
- inventory of James Quatermus.
- accounts on estate of John Collins.
- accounts on estate of James Harriss.
- accounts on estate of John Cox.
- accounts on estate of Thomas Giles.
- accounts on estate of James Treaharn.

44:222 11 September. Appointment of William Turner Wootton (g) as Deputy Commissary (PG), on demise of George Scott, Esq. (dec'd).

Court Session: 14 July 1771

Docket:
- WO: summons to Betty Corbin executrix of Mary Sheldon to render accounts.
- WO: summons to Purnell Bowen administrator of Littleton Bowen to render accounts.
- WO: summons to Samuel Smiley administrator of Andrew Smiley to render accounts.
- WO: summons to Samuel Brittingham executor of Elijah Brittingham to render accounts.
- WO: summons to Alexander McKallan executor of Arthur McKallan to render accounts.

44:223
- WO: summons to Hannah Sterling & James Bennett executors of Joseph Sterling to render accounts.
- WO: summons to Hannah Connoway executrix of Phillip Connoway to render accounts.
- WO: summons to Levi Noble executor of James Noble to render accounts.
- WO: summons to Milby Atkinson administrator of Levi Atkinson to render accounts.
- WO: summons to Hannah Massey executrix of Joseph Massey to render

accounts.

- WO: summons to Tabitha Tilghman administratrix of Gideon Tilghman to render accounts.
- WO: summons to Sarah Hall administratrix of Stephen Hall to render accounts.
- WO: summons to Leah Caldwell administratrix of William Caldwell to render accounts.
- WO: summons to Southey King administrator of William King to render accounts.
- WO: summons to Ezekiel Green executor of Ezekiel Green to render accounts.
- WO: summons to Magdalene Burn administratrix of Solomon Burn to render accounts.

44:224
- SO: summons to Mathew Piper administrator of Christopher Piper to render accounts.
- SO: summons to John Merine administrator of William Merine to render accounts. Renewed to DO.
- SO: summons to Frances King administrator of Nehemiah King to render accounts.
- SO: summons to Isabella Cox administratrix of John Cox to render accounts.
- SO: summons to Mathew Kemp administrator dbn of Richard Stephen Bounds to render accounts.
- SO: summons to Isaac Green executor of William Green to render accounts.
- SO: summons to Abigail Collins executrix of John Collins to render accounts.
- SO: summons to Ellis Shores administratrix of William Shores to render accounts. Final accounts exhibited. To be struck off.
- SO: summons to Elisha Worrick administrator of Arthur Worrick to render accounts.
- SO: summons to Job Gastineax executor of George Lewis Gastineaux to render accounts. Renewed to DO.

44:225
- SO: summons to Sarah Harris administratrix of James Harris to render accounts.

- SO: summons to Stephen Garland administrator of John Robertson to render accounts. Accounts exhibited. To be struck off.
- SO: summons to Adam Anderson & his wife Elisabeth administratrix of Thomas Bond to render accounts.
- SO: summons to William Stewart executor of Rebecca Dashiel to render accounts.
- SO: summons to Isaac Green executor of Richard Green to render accounts.
- DO: attachment to Sarah Hicks executrix of John Hicks to render accounts.
- DO: William Minor (QA) vs. John Stevens executor of Priscilla Howe. Summons to defendant to render accounts.
- DO: summons to Ann Traverse, Levin Traverse, Henry Traverse, & John Hicks Traverse executors of Henry Traverse to render accounts.
- DO: summons to Christopher Nutter & his wife Eleanor administratrix of William Nutter to render accounts.
- **44:226** SO: summons to John Pagan administrator of William Pagan to render accounts.
- SO: summons to William & Abner Lecompte executors of Philemon Lecompte to render accounts.
- SO: summons to Lurana Spedding executrix of Hugh Spedding to render accounts.
- TA: J.T. 3rd for James Pett vs. Abner Turner administrator of George Thompson. Summons to defendant to show cause why he conceals said estate.
- TA: summons to John Roboson administrator of Israel Cox to render accounts.
- TA: summons to Mary Elston administratrix of William Elston to render accounts.
- TA: summons to John Sherwood, Jr. administrator of Thomas Sherwood to render accounts.
- TA: W.P. for Luke Chevers & his wife Susa, Clement Sales, & Gabriel Sales vs. John Cox & his wife Jane & John

Studdon & his wife Elisabeth.
Libel.

- TA: summons to Frances Gibson administratrix of Francis Gibson to render accounts.

44:227
- TA: summons to John Goldsborough & Nicholas Goldsborough administrators of Nicholas Goldsborough to render accounts.
- TA: summons to Elisabeth Holmes administratrix of Nicholas Holmes to render accounts.
- TA: summons to Mary Harwood administratrix of Peter Harwood to render accounts.
- TA: summons to Elisabeth & Robert Harwood administrators of William Harwood to render accounts.
- TA: summons to Mary Smith administratrix of Simon Steven Smith to render accounts.
- TA: summons to Charles Bullen administrator of Rachel Cox to render accounts.
- TA: summons to William Levell executor of Thomas McChanon to render accounts.
- TA: summons to William Harrison administrator of John Harrison to render accounts.
- TA: summons to Ann Feddeman administratrix of Daniel Feddeman to render accounts.
- TA: summons to Henrietta Maria Carslake administratrix of John Carslake to render accounts.

44:228
- TA: summons to Mary Brown administratrix of Adam Brown to render accounts.
- TA: Thomas Barron surety on estate of James Chapman vs. Jane Chapman executrix of said James Chapman. Summons to defendant to render accounts.
- TA: summons to Jean Scott administratrix of John Dobson to render accounts.
- TA: summons to Hannah Turner executrix of Edward Turner to render accounts.
- TA: summons to John Blythe & his wife Sophia executrix of Laurence

Court Session: 14 July 1771

Porter to render accounts.
- TA: summons to Hannah & Harman Knote (QA) administrators of Nathaniel Knotts to show cause why they conceal said estate.
- QA: summons to Ann & Arthur Emory executors of John Emory (surveyor) to render accounts.
- QA: summons to William Ringgold administrator of Edward Brown to render accounts.
- QA: summons to John Nabb executor of Elisabeth Nabb to render accounts.

44:229
- QA: summons to Susannah Tolson executrix of Joseph Tolson to render accounts.
- QA: summons to Mary Clayton executrix of Solomon Clayton to render accounts.
- QA: James Bordley vs. Charles Blake administrator of Sarah Blake. Attachment to defendant to render accounts.
- QA: Benjamin Kirby vs. Ruth Clouds executrix of Nicholas Clouds. Summons to defendant to render accounts. Final accounts exhibited. To be struck off.
- QA: summons to Giles Hicks executor of Cornelius Dailey to render accounts.
- QA: James Holliday vs. John Sutton & his wife Mary administratrix of John Mumford. Summons to render accounts.
- QA: summons to John Brown (son of John) administrator of Joseph Meaner to render accounts.
- QA: summons to Sarah Price administratrix of William Price to render accounts.
- QA: summons to Vinson Benton administrator of David Nevill to render accounts. Final accounts exhibited. To be struck off.

44:230
- QA: summons to Sarah Fowler executrix of John Birstall to render accounts. Final accounts exhibited. To be struck off.
- QA: summons to John Culbreath administrator dbn of William Culbreath to render accounts.

Court Session: 14 July 1771

- QA: summons to Christ. Cox & William Price administrators of Thomas Cox to render accounts.
- QA: summons to Edward Clayton administrator of Abraham Delahunt to render accounts. Final accounts exhibited. To be struck off.
- QA: summons to Thomas Yewell administrator of Mary Hadley to render accounts.
- QA: summons to Samuel Brown administrator dbn of Andrew Hall to render accounts.
- QA: summons to Samuel Brown administrator of Esther Hall to render accounts.
- QA: summons to Robert Wood administrator of David Robertson to render accounts.
- QA: summons to Absolom Sparks administrator of Sarah Reed to render accounts.

44:231
- QA: summons to James Miller administrator of John Clayland to render accounts. To be struck off.
- QA: summons to Susannah Clayland executrix of Thomas Clayland to render accounts.
- QA: summons to Tabitha Bryan executrix of John Bryan to render accounts.
- QA: summons to John Seeders administrator of Frances Walters to render accounts. Final accounts exhibited. To be struck off.
- QA: summons to John Ferrill & his wife Mary administratrix of Thomas Hewett to render accounts. Final accounts exhibited. To be struck off.
- QA: summons to Christ Cross Routh administrator of Henry Darnall to render accounts. Final accounts exhibited. To be struck off.
- QA: summons to Andrew Hennessey (TA) administrator of John Hennessey to render accounts.
- KE: summons to John Gleaves administrator of John Gleaves to render accounts.
- KE: summons to Benjamin Howard administrator of Benjamin Howard to

Page 23

render accounts.
44:232 • KE: summons to John Osborn
administrator of Henry Osborn to
render accounts.
• KE: summons to William Crabbin
administrator of Meredith Walton to
render accounts.
• KE: summons to Joshua George
executor of Hannah George to render
accounts.
• KE: summons to William Freeman
executor of Laurence Strainer to
render accounts.
• KE: summons to Thomas Smith
administrator of William Hollis to
render accounts.
• KE: summons to William Pearce
administrator dbn of Mary Watkins to
render accounts.
• KE: summons to James Chiffin
executor of James Chiffin to render
accounts.
• KE: summons to William Pearce
administrator of Beatrix Johnson to
render accounts.
• KE: summons to John Chapple
administrator of Sarah Kelley to
render accounts. Issue in CE.
• KE: summons to Jerutiah Barrett
executrix of John Barrett (QA) to
render accounts.
44:233 • KE: T.J. for Stephen Bordley, Esq.
(KE) & his wife Hannah vs. S.C. for
Ebenezar Reynour & Jonathan Turner
executors of Thomas Perkins (g, KE).
Text of petition of plaintiffs.
Said Hannah is widow of said dec'd.
Dec'd made will on 16 February 1768.
44:234 By: Thomas Johnson, Jr., James
Tilghman 3rd.
Ruling: widow to recover her 1/3rds.
• KE: summons to James Sweeney &
Elisabeth Sweney administrators of
Catharine Maccatee to render
accounts.
• KE: summons to John Crew
administrator of Edward Drugan to
render accounts.
• KE: summons to John Lambert Wilmer
executor of Simon Wilmer to render
accounts.
• KE: summons to Peter Body

Court Session: 14 July 1771

administrator of John Body to render accounts.

- KE: summons to William Sluby & his wife Rachel executrix of William Hynson to render accounts.

44:235
- KE: summons to James Smith executor of Thomas Sealy to render accounts.
- KE: summons to Joyce Smyth administrator of Charles Ringgold to render accounts.
- KE: summons to Dean Reed executor of John Reed to render accounts.
- KE: summons to Andrew Hickman & his wife Hickman Rachel administratrix of Isaac Wilson to render accounts.
- KE: summons to Rachel Anderson administratrix of William Anderson to render accounts.
- KE: summons to Ann Hutchison administratrix of John Hutchison to render accounts.
- KE: summons to Hannah Smith administratrix of Jonathan Smith to render accounts.
- CE: summons to Catharine & Thomas Williams executors of Robert Williams to render accounts.
- CE: summons to Mary Mercer administratrix of Robert Mercer, Jr. to render accounts.

44:236
- CE: summons to Samuel & Thomas Tigart administrators of Cardiff Tigart to render accounts.
- CE: summons to Sarah Abbott executrix of William Abbott to render accounts.
- CE: summons to Edward Daugherty administrator of Joseph Chissell to render accounts.
- CE: summons to Adam Vance administrator of James Vance to render accounts.
- CE: summons to John Ward administrator of Henry Ward to render accounts.
- CE: summons to Ann & Samuel Miller executors of Thomas Miller to show cause why they conceal said estate.
- CE: Nathan Sedgwick vs. Sarah Sedgwick & Fran. Boyd executors of Richard Sedgwick. Libel. Summons to defendants to render accounts.

Page 25

Plaintiff is husband off Sarah one of executors.

- CE: J.H. for Thomas, George, John, Sarah, Esther Betty, & John Heron & his wife Martha vs. Jen for Sarah Sedgwick & Fran. Boyd. Libel, answer, demurrer.
- CE: summons to Jonathan Hollings administrator of Abigal Hollings to render accounts.
- CE: summons to Rebecca & Thomas Cooper executors of John Cooper to render accounts.

44:237

- CE: summons to Richard Oldham executor of Ann Oldham to render accounts.
- CE: summons to Amos & George Alexander executors of Theophilus Alexander to render accounts.
- CE: summons to Sarah Pennington & William Withers administrators of Abraham Pennington to render accounts.
- CE: summons to Susannah Elliot administratrix of Benjamin Elliot to render accounts.
- CE: Jos. Earle vs. Sarah Cunningham administratrix of George Cunningham. Summons to defendant to render accounts.
- CE: summons to Rebecca Ellsbury executrix of Frederick Ellsbury to render accounts.
- CE: summons to Archibald Ankrim executor of George Ankrim to render accounts.
- CE: summons to Isaac Vanbebber & Phineas Chew executors of Sarah Chew to render accounts.

44:238

- CE: summons to James Corbit executor of James Corbit to render accounts.
- CE: summons to Andrew Welsh executor of William Callender to render accounts.
- CE: summons to Augustine Beedle executor of John Beedle, Sr. to render accounts.
- CE: summons to Jane & John Strawbridge administrators of John Strawbridge to render accounts.
- CE: summons to Thomas Chandler & his wife administratrix of Peter Jones

- to render accounts.
- CE: summons to John Anderson & William Glasgow executors of John Glasgow to render accounts.
- CE: summons to James Scott & Thomas Witherspoon executors of John Scott to render accounts.
- CE: summons to Alexander Moore & his wife Margaret executors of John Callender, Jr. to render accounts.
- CE: summons to Jonathan Humberstone administrator of George Humberstone to render accounts.

44:239
- CE: summons to John Donohoe & his wife Mary administrators of John Anderson to render accounts.
- CE: summons to Sarah Lewis administratrix of John Lewis to render accounts.
- CE: summons to Elisha Terry administrator of William Terry to render accounts.
- CE: summons to Zarah Zuile administratrix of Mathew Zuile to render final accounts. Final accounts exhibited. To be struck off.
- SM: J.T. 3rd for James Biscoe (son of Basil) by Kenelm Harrison his next friend vs. Bennett, James, Mary Biscoe, & Thomas Crawley & his wife Ann. Attachment to following to testify for plaintiff: Ann Williams, Robert Clark.
- SM: summons to William Bayard & his wife Eleanor administratrix of Alexander Mcfarlane to render accounts.
- SM: summons to John Goldsborough administrator of Ignatius Goldsborough to render accounts.
- SM: summons to Eleanor & John Johnson executors of John Johnson to render accounts.

44:240
- SM: Thomas Dashiel (SO) vs. Ann Rawlings & Charles King & his wife Susannah administratrix of Thomas Coode. Summons to defendants to render accounts.
- SM: summons to Leonard Briscoe one of executors of John Theobalds to render accounts.

Court Session: 14 July 1771

- SM: summons to Elisabeth Chesley executrix of John Chesley to render accounts.
- SM: summons to Charles Sewell executor of Francis Goodrick to render accounts.
- SM: summons to John Manning administrator of Joseph Manning to render accounts.
- SM: summons to Annastatia Norris administratrix of William Norris to render accounts.
- SM: summons to Catharine Wilson Thomas administratrix of James Thomas to render accounts.
- SM: John Ford & Luke Mattingly vs. Mary Ford executrix of Peter Ford. Attachment to defendant to show cause why she conceals said estate.
- SM: John Heard one of administrators of Richard Heard vs. said John Heard & Barbara Heard administrators of said Richard Heard. Attachment to defendants [!] to render accounts.
- 44:241 SM: summons to Catharine & Thomas Spalding executors of Thomas Spalding to render accounts.
- SM: summons to Joshua Watts executor of Thomas Watts to render accounts.
- SM: summons to William Paltry administrator of Mildred Jordan to render accounts.
- SM: summons to Jane Stone administratrix of John Stone to render accounts.
- SM: summons to John Smoott administrator of Joseph Thomas Granger to render accounts.
- SM: summons to Elisabeth Heseltine administratrix of Charles Heseltine to render accounts.
- SM: summons to Robert Holton administrator dbn of William Holton to render accounts.
- SM: summons to Robert Holton executor of Elisabeth Holton to render accounts.
- SM: summons to Martha Edwards & William Guither executors of Richard Swan Edwards to render accounts.
- 44:242 SM: summons to Hezekiah Burroughs executor of Richard Burroughs to

render accounts.
- CH: summons to Henrietta Nowland administratrix of Daniel Nowland to render accounts.
- CH: attachment to William Bryan surviving executor of William Bryan to render accounts.
- CH: attachment to James Edelin & his wife Susanna executrix of Basil Hagan to render accounts.
- CH: summons to Ann Hasty administratrix of Clement Hasty to render accounts. To be struck off.
- CH: summons to Margaret Carrico administratrix of Peter Carrico to render accounts.
- CH: summons to Zachariah Johnson administrator of Robert Johnson to render accounts. To be struck off.
- CH: attachment to Charles Sanders administrator of Jane Doyne to render accounts.

44:243
- CH: summons to James Johnson administrator of John Johnson to render accounts. To be struck off.
- CH: summons to Edward Boarman executor of John Gardiner to render accounts.
- CH: summons to William Smallwood administrator of Lucy Herbert Stoddert to render accounts.
- CH: summons to Priscilla & William Smallwood administrators of Bayne Smallwood to render accounts.
- CH: summons to Henry Smith Hawkins & Thomas Hawkins executors of Alexander Smith Hawkins to render accounts.
- CH: summons to John Wright executor of John Wright to render accounts.
- CH: summons to Margaret & Thomas Reeder executors of Benjamin Reeder to render accounts.
- CH: summons to Richard Elson & Ann Turner administrators of Thomas Turner to render accounts. Accounts exhibited. To be struck off.
- CH: summons to Elisabeth Grove administratrix of Ebsworth Grove to render accounts.
- CH: summons to Grace Harman administratrix of John Harman to

render accounts.

44:244 • CH: summons to William, Kenelm, & Walter Stoddart administrators of Richard Stoddart to render accounts.

• CH: summons to Warren Dent administrator of William Bowie to render accounts.

• CH: summons to Hugh Hamill executor of John Hammill to render accounts.

• CH: summons to Mary Hawkins executrix of Rudolph Morris Hawkins to render accounts.

• CV: Thomas Holland administrator dbn Jos. Isaacke, Sr. vs. Samuel Goslee. Summons to defendant to show cause why he conceals said estate.

• CV: summons to Edward Wood executor of Eleanor Slye to render accounts.

• CV: summons to Mary Smith administratrix of Joseph Smith to render accounts.

• CV: summons to John Weems, Jr. administrator of James Fleet to render accounts.

• CV: summons to Rebecca Arnold executrix of David Arnold to render accounts. To be struck off.

44:245 • CV: summons to Mary Bond executrix of Benson Bond to render accounts. Accounts exhibited. To be struck off.

• CV: summons to Ann & Driver Greeves administrators of John Greeves, Jr. to render accounts.

• CV: summons to Elisabeth Williamson executrix of James Williamson to render accounts.

• CV: summons to Ann Gray executrix of John Gray to render accounts.

• CV: summons to Mary Duke administratrix of James Duke to render accounts.

• CV: summons to Margaret Bourne administratrix of George Bourne to render accounts.

• CV: summons to Rebecca Arnold administratrix of Harrison Dowell to render accounts. To be struck off.

• CV: summons to John Hutchison & his wife Elisabeth executrix of William Deaver to render accounts.

Court Session: 14 July 1771

- CV: summons to Thomas Reynolds, Thomas Holland, & Edward Reynolds (witnesses to will of Josias Sunderland) to prove said will.

44:246
- PG: summons to Elisabeth Eastwood executrix of Benjamin Eastwood to render accounts.
- PG: summons to John Marloe administrator of John Smallwood to render accounts. To be struck off.
- PG: summons to Stephen West administrator of Capt. Archibald Johnson to render accounts.
- PG: summons to Margaret Miles administratrix of William Miles to render accounts.
- PG: summons to John Cook, Esq. administrator of Thomas Lee to render accounts.
- PG: summons to Edward Swann administrator of Thomas Swann to render accounts. To be struck off.
- PG: Jen for Samuel Selby, et. al. vs. S.C. for John Dorsett, et. al. Libel, answer, general refirmation.
- PG: summons to Marjory Lyles administratrix of Zachariah Lyles to render accounts.
- PG: Henry Jameson vs. Walter Pye administrator of Edward Queen. Attachment to defendant to render accounts. Renewed to CH.

44:247
- PG: Philip Fennally (son of William) vs. Christopher Lownds administrator of said William Fennally. Summons to defendant to render accounts.
- PG: summons to Elisabeth Osborn administratrix of Robert Osborn to render accounts.
- PG: summons to Ann Clagett executrix of John Clagett to render accounts.
- PG: summons to Mary & Leonard Waring executors of Francis Waring to render accounts.
- FR: summons to Catharine Mock administratrix of George Mock to render accounts.
- FR: summons to William Aldridge executor of Nicholas Aldridge to render accounts.
- FR: summons to George Smith & John

Page 31

McCorcle executors of Teter Tanner to render accounts.

- FR: summons to Philipania Bonsom administratrix of Laurence Bonsom to render accounts.
- FR: summons to Robert Harper & Thomas Hawkins executors of Josias Harper to render accounts. Final accounts exhibited. To be struck off.

44:248

- FR: summons to Ann Williams administratrix of Charles Williams to render accounts.
- FR: summons to Andrew Williams administrator of Ann Davis to render accounts.
- FR: summons to Andrew Owler administrator dbn of Jacob Shiviner to render accounts.
- FR: summons to Catharine Norris administratrix of William Norris to render accounts.
- FR: summons to John Hoffner & Lodowick Byerly administrators of Michael Hoffner to render accounts. Final accounts exhibited. To be struck off.
- FR: summons to Isabella Richardson executrix of William Richardson to render accounts.
- FR: summons to Margaret & Jacob Rop administrators of Nicholas Rop to render accounts.
- FR: summons to Sarah Johnson administratrix of Thomas Johnson to render accounts.
- FR: summons to Edward Perkinson administrator dbn of Joseph West to render accounts.

44:249

- FR: summons to Margaret Keller administratrix of Abraham Keller to render accounts.
- FR: summons to Sarah & William Watson executors of David Watson to render accounts.
- FR: summons to Amos & John McGinley executors of James McGinley to render accounts.
- FR: summons to Mary Laurence executrix of George Laurence to render accounts.
- FR: summons to David Hunter

administrator of Anthony Hunter to render accounts.

- BA: summons to William Harriott administrator of Susannah Harritt to render accounts.
- BA: summons to Thomas Bond (son of John) administrator of Daniel Thorn to render accounts.
- BA: summons to Andrew Stigar administrator of Jacob Rock to render accounts.
- BA: summons to Philemon Deaver executor of Richard Miller Cole to render accounts.

44:250
- BA: summons to John Hammon Dorsey administrator of William Gough to render accounts.
- BA: summons to Benjamin Jones administrator of Charles Jones to render accounts.
- BA: summons to Margaret Brown administrator of Absolom Brown to render accounts.
- BA: summons to Mary Skipton administratrix of John Skipton to render accounts.
- BA: summons to John Sergant administrator of James Sollers to render accounts. In custody. To be struck off.
- BA: summons to Henry Oram & Ann Statia Oram executors of Daring Haws to render accounts.
- BA: summons to Daniel Chamier administrator of Rowland Carnan to render accounts.
- BA: summons to Magdalene Tripolete administratrix of Abraham Tipolete to render accounts.
- BA: summons to John Anderson administrator of Hugh Orrs to render accounts.
- continued to f. 267.

Court Session: 1771

44:251   23 September. Benton Harriss (g, WO) exhibited:
- will of Baxter Bennett, constituting James Bennett executor. Said executor was granted administration. Sureties: George Martin, Charles

Bennett. Date: 5 July 1771.

- will of Robert Melvin, constituting Robert Melvin executor. Said executor was granted administration. Sureties: Solomon Webb, Elijah Burnet. Date: 26 April 1771.
- will of Samuel Hall, constituting John Hall executor. Said executor was granted administration. Sureties: Hadrick Hall, Daniel Elloiot. Date: 12 April 1771.
- will of Ephraim Christopher, constituting Hannah Christopher executrix. Said executrix was granted administration. Sureties: Jethro & Jesse Bowin. Date: 7 August 1771.
- will of Isaac Brittingham. Also, bond of Samuel Ennis acting executor. Sureties: Isaac Brittingham, John Ennis. Date: 26 April 1771.
- will of Benjamin Melson, constituting Jos. Melson executor. Said executor was granted administration. Sureties: Daniel Clifton, Robert Hopkins. Date: 20 May 1771.
- bond of Tabitha Nicholson executrix of Samuel Nicholson. Sureties: Parker Rodgers, Charles Nicholson. Date: 17 May 1771.
- bond of Mary Truitt administratrix of William Truitt. Sureties: Charles Parker, Jethro Bowin. Date: 10 May 1771.
- will of Rachel Piper.
- accounts on estate of Elisabeth Holland.
- accounts on estate of Arthur McCallan.
- accounts on estate of John Johnson.
- accounts on estate of William Long.
- accounts on estate of Reyley Truitt.
- accounts on estate of George Toadvine.
- accounts on estate of William Miller.
- accounts on estate of Mary Bennett.
- accounts on estate of Levy Atkinson.
- accounts on estate of Joseph Sterling.

44:252
- accounts on estate of Thomas Timmons.
- accounts on estate of Thomas James.
- inventory of Solomon Taylor.
- inventory of Arthur Jehosaphat.
- inventory of A. J. McAllen.
- inventory of Thomas James.
- inventory of Selby Hickman.
- inventory of Solomon Milbourn.
- inventory of John Flint.
- additional inventory of John Flint.
- inventory of Benjamin Melson.
- inventory of Angelo Atkinson.
- inventory of Catharine Mumford.
- inventory of George Toadvine.
- inventory of Elisabeth Hart.
- inventory of James Fookes.
- inventory of John Mumford.
- inventory of Samuel Hall.
- inventory of Mary Bennett.
- inventory of Robert Davis.
- inventory of Robert Melvin.
- inventory of John Kilpatrick.
- inventory of William Hayman.

25 September. Joseph Nicholson, Sr. (g, KE) exhibited:
- bond of Ann Tuckerman administratrix of Joseph Tuckerman. Sureties: Thomas Woodal, Nicholas Slubey. Date: 5 September 1771.
- bond of William Bordley & Arthur Bordley administrators of Stephen Bordley, Jr. Sureties: Thomas Wilkins, James Claypole. Date: 4 September 1771.

44:253
- bond of Sarah Kennard administratrix of Thomas Kennard. Sureties: Robert Buchanan, Stephen Kennard. Date: 3 September 1771.
- inventory of John Carvill, Jr.
- inventory of William Haley.
- inventory of Nathaniel Miles.
- inventory of Mary Wilson.
- inventory of George Williamson.
- inventory of Andrew Toalson.
- LoD on estate of Isaac Wilson.
- LoD on estate of Nicholas Smith.
- LoD on estate of Hen. Talbot.
- LoD on estate of Andrew McIntee.
- accounts on estate of Andrew McIntee.

Court Session: 1771

- accounts on estate of Henry Talbot.
- accounts on estate of Nicholas Smith.
- accounts on estate of Isaac Wilson.
- accounts on estate of James Claypole.
- accounts on estate of Benjamin Parsons.
- accounts on estate of Draper Lusby.
- accounts on estate of William Wilmer.

Exhibited from SO:
- will of Thomas Dashiel, constituting William Allen executor. Said executor was granted administration. Sureties: David Polk, Esme Bailey. Date: 9 September 1771.
- will of Michael Dorman, constituting Chase & Esayah Dorman executors. Said executors were granted administration. Sureties: Isaac & Thomas Newman. Date: 10 September 1771.
- will of Joseph Burt.

44:254   John Allen Thomas (g, SM) exhibited:
- will of William Locker, constituting Elisabeth Locker & Thomas Locker executors. Said executors were granted administration. Sureties: Thomas Griffin, William Jenkins. Date: 3 September 1771.
- will of Nehemiah Griffin, constituting Ann Griffin executrix. Said executrix was granted administration. Sureties: Thomas Griffin, Joseph Biscoe. Date: 3 September 1771.
- will of Ignatius Ford, constituting Dorothy Ford executrix. Said executrix was granted administration. Sureties: Robert Wimsat, Phil. Ford. Date: 2 April 1771.
- will of Bennett Fenwick, constituting Richard Fenwick executor. Said executor was granted administration. Sureties: Samuel Bellwood, William Fenwick. Date: 5 February 1771.
- will of Peter Drury, constituting

Michael Drury executor. Said
executor was granted administration.
Sureties: Henry Spalding, Thomas
Spalding. Date: 5 February 1771.

- will of Bennett Neale, constituting
Mary Neale executrix. Said
executrix was granted
administration. Sureties: George
Slye, James Jordan. Date: 23 May
1771.
- will of Thomas Shanks, constituting
Robert Shanks executor. Said
executor was granted administration.
Sureties: Joseph Walker, Richard
James Rapier. Date: 3 June 1771.
- will of Richard Barnhouse,
constituting Jean Barnhouse
executrix. Said executrix was
granted administration. Sureties:
Henry Milburn, Adam Milburn. Date:
11 June 1771.
- will of Mark Heard, constituting
Susannah Heard & John Heard, Jr.
executors. Said executors were
granted administration. Sureties:
Samuel Belwood, Mathew Heard. Date:
10 September 1771.
- bond of Peter Carbery administrator
of John Baptist Carbery. Sureties:
William Rapour, Nicholas Manger.
Date: 9 April 1771.
44:255 • bond of Margaret Greenwell
administratrix of Justinian
Greenwell. Sureties: Justin Mills,
John Raley. Date: 11 June 1771.
- bond of John Lyon administrator of
Rachel Billingsly. Sureties: John
Cartwright, Thomas Waters. Date: 20
May 1771.
- bond of Anne Fanning administratrix
of John Fanning. Sureties: John
Gibson, Joshua Gibson. Date: 25
March 1771.
- bond of Elisabeth Teare
administratrix of Edward Tare.
Sureties: Henry Allison, James
Vaughop [!]. Date: 30 April 1771
- bond of Mary Hanworth administratrix
of Thomas Hanworth. Sureties:
William Langley, John Withrington.
Date: 5 March 1771.
- will of

Court Session: 1771

- will of Thomas Yates the elder.
- will of Ann Price.
- inventory of John Beard.
- inventory of Edward Parson.
- inventory of John Leigh.
- inventory of Robert Edward.
- inventory of John Read.
- inventory of John Ford.
- inventory of Ignatius Ford.
- inventory of John McPherson.
- inventory of Peter Drury.
- inventory of James Greenwell.
- inventory of Bennett Fenwick.
- inventory of Thomas Hansworth.
- inventory of James Thomas.
- inventory of John Bapt. Carbury.
- inventory & LoD of Bennett Neale.
- LoD on estate of Mathew Mason.
- final accounts on estate of Thomas Coode.
- final accounts on estate of Robert Chesley.
- final accounts on estate of George Aisquith.
- final accounts on estate of Richard Wimsatt.
- final accounts on estate of Richard Burroughs.
- final accounts on estate of James Manning.
- final accounts on estate of Mathew Mason.
- final accounts on estate of Elisabeth Burrough.
- final accounts on estate of Alexander Mcfarlane.
- final accounts on estate of John Thomas.
- accounts on estate of Charles Sewal.
- accounts on estate of Francis Guthrie.
- accounts on estate of Margaret Pravat.
- accounts on estate of John Stone.
- accounts on estate of William Williams.
- accounts on estate of Richard Heard. Also, accounts by trustees.
- accounts on estate of William Norriss.
- accounts on estate of Nicholas Sanner.

44:256

- bond of John Heard trustee on estate of Richard Heard, for sale of his lands. Sureties: Timothy Bower, Ignatius Abell. Date: 11 February 1771.

7 October. Elie Vallette (AA) exhibited:
- bond of Francess Brice administratrix of Robert Brice. Sureties: John Davidson, William Hutchings. Date: 12 September 1771.

44:257
- bond of Thomas Tillard administrator of Richard Llewin. Sureties: John Carty, Richard Hopkins. Date: 27 September 1771.
- bond of James Dundass administrator of Joseph Brown. Sureties: James Dick, Elie Vallette. Date: 27 July 1771.
- bond of Sarah Hollyday administratrix of James Hollyday. Sureties: William Parrit, Weymack Brashears. Date: 15 July 1771.
- bond of Joseph Davis administrator of Luke Davis. Sureties: John Dorsey (AA), John Baptist Snowden (BA). Date: 14 August 1771.
- will of John Mortan Jordan, Esq. Also, bond of Reuben Merriwether administrator. Sureties: Thomas Beal Dorsey, James Price. Date: 30 September 1771.
- will of Joseph Brewer.
- will of Lazarus Pomphrey.
- 2 inventories of Thomas Welsh.
- inventory & LoD of Henry Hall.
- inventory & LoD of William Worthington.
- LoD on estate of Alexander Campbell.
- LoD on estate of Thomas Turner.
- inventory of Paul Rauthin.
- inventory of Thomas Richardson.
- inventory of William Normand.
- inventory of Alexander Ferguson.
- inventory of Jos. Williams.
- inventory of Cornelius Howard.
- inventory of Joshua Ridgely.
- inventory of Caleb Dorsey.
- inventory of Isaac Jones.
- inventory of Edward Dorsey.
- inventory of John Cromwell.

- inventory of William Hollyday.
- inventory of Benjamin Welsh.
- inventory of Nathaniel Adams.
- inventory of Elisabeth Rutland.
- inventory of William Hall (E.R.).
- LoD on estate of William Hall (E.R.).

44:258 Thomas Wright (g, QA) exhibited:
- will of Hester Thompson, constituting Samuel Thompson, Jr. executor. Said executor was granted administration. Sureties: Henry Thompson, Robert Waters. Date: 28 September 1771.
- bond of John Deford administrator dbn of John Tomlin Deford. Sureties: John Tillotson, John Ewen. Date: 26 September 1771.
- bond of John Jadwin administrator of Solomon Jadwin. Sureties: George Temple, John Lambdin. Date: 29 August 1771.
- bond of William Wilcocks administrator of Daniel Wilcocks. Sureties: Val. Thomas Honey, James Duhamel. Date: 20 September 1771.
- will of Thomas Jones.
- final accounts on estate of Samuel Whiting.
- LoD on estate of Samuel Whiting.
- inventory of Jacob Boon.

14 October. John Goldsborough (DO) exhibited:
- will of John Oldfield, constituting Jane Oldfield executrix. Said executrix was granted administration. Sureties: Robert Dixon, Burton Loftice. Date: 13 August 1771.
- will of Zebulon Keene, constituting Richard Keene executor. Said executor was granted administration. Sureties: Edward Keene, Levin Dossey. Date: 13 August 1771.

44:259
- will of Hollyday Smith, constituting Sarah Smith executrix. Said executrix was granted administration. Sureties: John Eareckson, Olive Smith. Date: 13 August 1771.

Court Session: 1771

- bond of Nathan Bradley administrator
  of Nehemiah Boxwell. Sureties:
  William Medford, Titus Hubbert.
  Date: 14 August 1771.
- bond of Edward Woollen administrator
  of William Woollen. Sureties: Levin
  Woolford, Thomas Phillips. Date: 15
  August 1771.
- bond of Hannah Smith administratrix
  of Robert Smith. Sureties: John
  Hopkins, Isaac Jones. Date: 15
  August 1771.
- inventory of Patrick McCollister.
- inventory of Roger Hurley.
- inventory of Thomas Lane.
- inventory of William Coleson.
- inventory of Reuben Phillips.
- final accounts on estate of
  Elisabeth Hill.
- accounts on estate of James Sherwin.

19 October. Walter Hanson (g, CH)
exhibited:
- bond of Sarah Boswell administratrix
  of John Boswell. Sureties: Thomas
  Owen, Alexander Robey. Date: 17
  September 1771.
- bond of Warren Dent administrator of
  Ann Dent. Sureties: Daniel Jenifer,
  Robert Mundel. Date: <no month or
  day given> 1771.
- 44:260 • bond of Warrent Dent administrator
  dbn of William Dent. Sureties:
  Daniel Jenifer, Robert Mundel.
  Date: 16 September 1771.
- bond of Theodosia Speek
  administratrix of Hezekiah Speake.
  Sureties: Richard Speake, John
  Maddox. Date: 19 August 1771.
- bond of Benjamin Beavans
  administrator of Richard Bevans.
  Sureties: George Thompson, Samuel
  Thompson. Date: 19 August 1771.
- inventory of Posthuma Groves.
- inventory of Thomas Kersey.
- inventory of John Warder.
- inventory of Walter Warder.
- accounts on estate of Alexander
  McLeod.
- accounts on estate of Benjamin
  Reeder.
- accounts on estate of William Joy.

Court Session: 1771

26 October. Thomas Bowles (g, FR)
exhibited:
- will of Joahim Joan, constituting
  Barbara Joan & John Hergareder
  executors. Said executors were
  granted administration. Sureties:
  Jacob Young, Caspar Mantz. Date: 25
  June 1771.
- will of Mathias Pooley, constituting
  Elisabeth Pooley executrix. Said
  executrix was granted
  administration. Sureties: William
  Halsey, Hen. Slater. Date: 15 July
  1771.
- bond of Caspar Shaaf administrator
  of Leonard Moss. Surety:
  Christopher Edelin. Date: 10 July
  1771.

44:261
- bond of George Smith executor of
  John Smith. Sureties: Mathias
  Reitnauer, John Kirshner. Date: 20
  August 1771.
- bond of Simon Reeder executor of
  William Mackatee. Sureties: Thomas
  Beall, John Phelps. Date: 21 August
  1771.
- will of Balser Erbach.
- will of Richard Morry.
- inventory & LoD of Thomas Ramsey.
- inventory & LoD of Marlin Kirshner.
- additional inventory of David
  Watson.
- inventory of James McClain.
- inventory of Joseph Farriss.
- inventory of Jacob Toup.
- inventory of Samuel Skinner.
- accounts on estate of Jacob Cramer.
- accounts on estate of Catharine
  Carnhart.
- accounts on estate of Teter Tanner.
- accounts on estate of Robert Evans.
- accounts on estate of Joseph West.
- accounts on estate of William
  Gibson.
- accounts on estate of Lucy Mockbee.
- accounts on estate of Abraham
  Keller.

28 October. Exhibited from SO:
- will of William Turpin, constituting
  William Turpin executor. Said
  executor was granted administration.

Court Session: 1771

Sureties: Jarvis Ballard, William
Furnis. Date: 28 September 1771.
- inventory of Thomas Ricords.
- inventory of John Caldwell.
- accounts on estate of Rebecca
  Dashiel.

44:262 23 September. Col. William Young (BA)
exhibited:
- will of Mary St. Clair, constituting
  David Tate executor. Said executor
  was granted administration.
  Sureties: David David, William Hill.
  Date: 19 August 1771.
- will of Ralph Smith, constituting
  Buchanan Smith & Huldah Smith
  executors. Said executors were
  granted administration. Sureties:
  Garshum Slice, Samuel Bailess.
  Date: 28 August 1771.
- bond of William Aisquith
  administrator of Ann Aisquith.
  Surety: Daniel Chamier. Date: 7
  September 1771.
- bond of Sophia Talbot & John Talbot
  administrators of John Talbot.
  Sureties: Benjamin Shipley, Elisha
  Dorrey. Date: 9 September 1771.
- will of Elisabeth Arnold.
- inventory & LoD of Rebeccah Young.
- inventory of William Sikes.
- inventory of Nicholas Merryman.
- inventory of Isaac Raven.
- inventory of James Gibson.
- inventory of William Govane.
- accounts on estate of Thomas
  Wheeler.
- accounts on estate of Hance Rudolph.
- accounts on estate of David Thomas.
- accounts on estate of James Preston.
- accounts on estate of Rebeccah
  Young.
- accounts on estate of John Yerby.

44:263 9 November. John Bracco (g, TA)
exhibited:
- will of Thomas Loveday, constituting
  Anne Loveday & John Loveday
  executors. Said executors were
  granted administration. Sureties:
  James Dickinson, Jr., Jos. Turner.
  Date: 27 August 1771.

Page 43

- bond of Mary Millontong administratrix of Allenby Millington. Sureties: William Bordley, Joseph Bewley. Date: 7 August 1771.
- bond of Luke Chevers administrator ad collegium of Gabriel Sailes. Sureties: Francis Marling, Thomas Tibbalds. Date: 10 September 1771.
- will of William West.
- LoD on estate of Nicholas Goldsborough.
- inventory of John Scott.
- inventory & LoD of Thomas Beall.
- final accounts on estate of Nicholas Goldsborough.
- accounts on estate of Thomas McCleland.
- accounts on estate of Marsham Waring.

20 November. Col. William Young (BA) exhibited:
- will of Aquilla McComas, constituting Sarah McComas executrix. Said executrix was granted administration. Sureties: Abraham Whitacre, William McComas. Date: 21 October 1771.
- will of Samuel Wheeler, constituting John Wheeler executor. Said executor was granted administration. Sureties: John Stevenson, Sater Stevenson. Date: 14 October 1771.

44:264
- will of Benjamin Vanhorne, constituting Martha Vanhorne executrix. Said executrix was granted administration. Sureties: Thomas Hill, John Croesen. Date: 4 November 1771.
- bond of Elisabeth Parker executrix of John Parker. Sureties: Moses Johnson, Josias Hitchcock. Date: 10 October 1771.
- bond of James Conely administrator of James Conely. Sureties: Edward Sweeting, William Partridge. Date: 6 November 1771.
- bond of Garet Garretson administrator of Samuel Johnson. Surety: William Gallion. Date: 16 September 1771.

Court Session: 1771

- bond of Thomas Kitten administrator of Theophilus Kitten. Sureties: Thomas Cole, Jr., Richard Daughaday. Date: 4 November 1771.
- will of Benjamin Dinny.
- inventory of Daubne Buckley Partridge.
- inventory of David Morgan.
- inventory of Henry Fitch.
- inventory of Gilbert Donohoe.
- accounts on estate of Moses Morgan.
- accounts on estate of Abraham Tripolete.
- accounts on estate of William Burton.
- accounts on estate of William Bond.
- accounts on estate of William Pike.

44:265 10 October. Deputy Commissaries to examine accounts of:
- QA: Sarah Redue executrix of John Redue.
- BA: Benjamin Howard executor of Robert Dutton.

11 October.
- CH: Warren Dent administrator of William Dowie.
- CH: Theophilus Hanson executor of William Hanson.
- CH: Samuel Cooksay administrator of Cloe Gody.
- FR: Jacob Hoff executor of Christian Shoat.
- KE: Lydia Flynn administratrix of Daniel Flynn.

12 October.
- BA: Sarah Rhodes executrix of Richard Rhodes.

14 October.
- DO: Rosannah Farguson administratrix of Abraham Farguson.
- DO: James Layton & Samuel Thomas executors of Henry Thomas.
- DO: Thomas Noel & his wife Sarah executrix of Alexander Frazier.
- DO: Joseph Bright executor of James Bright.
- KE: Elisabeth Hollingsworth & Moses Alford administrators of William Hollingsworth.

16 October.
- WO: Caleb Milbourne administrator of

Court Session: 1771

Levin Dickenson.
- BA: Samuel Merryman administrator of Nicholas Merryman.

17 October.
- CH: William Warren administrator of John Gwynn.

22 October.
- CE: Hugh Mathews executor of Hugh Mathews.

28 October.
- FR: Benjamin Griffith & his wife Rachel executrix of John Gartrill.
- SO: Isaac Atkinson executor of Thomas Willen.
- SO: Ephraim King executor of John Handy.
- SO: Ephraim King administrator of John Flewellin.
- WO: Esther Spaights administrator of Palmer Spaights.

30 October.
- CH: Henrietta Brooke executrix of Basil Brooke.
- CH: Samuel Green & his wife Elisabeth executrix of John Jenkins.
- petition of Thomas Stone (CH). Administration bond on estate of Clear Sympson assigned to petitioner.

2 November.
- CE: Margaret & John Thompson administrators of Mathew Thompson.
- CE: Margaret & Edward Rumsay executors of Edward Rumsay.
- CE: Robert Whitesides & his wife Rebecca executrix of Frederick Ellsbury.
- KE: William Pearce administrator dbn of Mary Watkins.
- KE: William Pearce administrator of Beatrix Johnson.
- SM: Clement Medley & Anne Nottingham executors of Athinasius Nottingham.
- SM: Rachel Compton executrix of Mathew Compton.
- SM: Athinasius Jaboe & his wife Ann administratrix of John Lee.

44:266   4 November.
- PG: Lurana Phillips administratrix of Phillip Phillips.
- PG: Ann & Francis Bright administrators of Francis Bright.

Page 46

Court Session: 1771

8 November.
* CH: Mary & Thomas Simpson executors of Thomas Simpson.
* CH: Henry Smith Hawkins & Thomas Hawkins executors of Alexander Smith Hawkins.

9 November.
* WO: James Broadwater & his wife Betty executrix of Mary Sheldon.
* WO: James Broadwater & his wife Betty executrix of Peter Corbin.
* PG: Hezekiah Wheeler administrator of Ignatius Wheeler.

11 November.
* TA: Thomas Tibels executor of Elisabeth Exley.
* CV: Mary Heighe administratrix of Thomas Holdsworth Heighe.

12 November.
* SM: Joshua Watts executor of Thomas Watts.
* BA: Ann & William Partridge administrators of Daubne Buckly Partridge.
* QA: Ann Williams administratrix of John Williams.
* QA: Margaret Mumford administratrix of James Mumford.
* QA: James Reed & his wife Rachel executors of John Downs, Jr.

13 November.
* petition of James Seth (QA). Administration bond on estate of John Silvester assigned to petitioner.

14 November.
* KE: Cordelia Frisby administratrix of William Frisby, Jr.
* BA: Daniel Preston executor of William Grafton, Sr.

15 November.
* CH: Gerrard Fowke administrator of Ann Hutcheson.
* CH: Gerrard Fowke executor of Robert Hanson.
* CH: John Evans, Jr. & his wife Victoria executrix of Thomas Nelson.
* CH: Mary Leftwich administratrix of Elisha Leftwich.

18 November.
* FR: Sarah & William Watson executors of David Watson.

Page 47

Court Session: 1771

20 November.
- petition of Benjamin Jacobs (PG). Administration bond on estate of Thomas Williams assigned to petitioner.
- QA: William Ruth executor of Christopher Ruth.
- BA: Thomas Hatton administrator of John Hatton.

25 November.
- FR: Rebecca Thomas administratrix of Notley Thomas.
- FR: Abraham Hay & Andrew Park administrators of Jos. Park.
- FR: Thomas & John Harry administrators of Jos. Fariss.
- FR: Andrew Owler administrator dbn of Margaret Shrior administratrix of Jacob Shrior.
- FR: Andrew Owler administrator dbn of Margaret Shrior.

26 November.
- QA: John Sayer Blake administrator of Charles Blake.
- QA: John Sayer Blaker surviving executor of Mathew Bryon.
- QA: Charles Blaker administrator of Sarah Blake.
- QA: Charles Leatherbury & his wife Elisabeth executrix of James Dudly.

Court Session: July 1771

44:267 Docket (continued from f. 250):
- BA: summons to Hannah Webster administratrix of John Webster (son of Samuel) to render accounts.
- BA: John Wilmot vs. Peter Carlisle administrator of Rachel Wilmot. Summons to defendant to render accounts.
- BA: summons to William & Cordelia Hall administrators of John Hall (Swan Town) to render accounts. Accounts exhibited. To be struck off.
- BA: James Hutchison security on estate of John Hill vs. Rosannah Hill administratrix of said John Hill. Summons to defendant to render accounts. Final accounts exhibited. To be struck off.

Court Session: July 1771

- BA: summons to Sarah Johns administratrix of Aquilla Johns to render accounts.
- BA: summons to Benjamin Rogers administrator of William Rogers to render accounts.
- BA: summons to Daniel McGhee & his wife Sarah administrators of Edward Hall to render accounts.
- BA: summons to Broad Cole administrator of Ann Broad to render accounts.
- BA: summons to Sarah Dunn executrix of Robert Dunn to render accounts.

44:268
- BA: summons to Jacob Bond & Benjamin Green executors of David Thomas to render accounts.
- BA: summons to Ann McGavaran executrix of John McGavaran to render accounts.
- BA: summons to Elisabeth Bond executrix of William Bond to render accounts.
- BA: summons to James Armstrong executor of Elisabeth Chapman to render accounts.
- BA: summons to Robert Davis administrator of Mary Davis to render accounts.
- BA: summons to David Dickson administrator of James Dickson to render accounts.
- BA: summons to Samuel Purvyance, Jr. administrator of James Gibson to render accounts.
- BA: summons to William Lynch administrator of Thomas Sheridine to render accounts.
- BA: summons to Jacob Giles administrator of Gilbert Donehoe to render accounts.
- BA: summons to Isaac Webster executor of William Wood to render accounts.

44:269
- BA: summons to Hellen Gilchrist executrix of Robert Gilchrist to render accounts.
- BA: summons to Ann & William Partridge administrators of Daubne Duckler Partridge to render accounts.
- BA: summons to Sophia Clark

administratrix of John Clark to render accounts.

- BA: summons to Elisabeth Payne executrix of William Payne to render accounts.
- BA: Thomas Jones vs. Henry Riston executor of Renaldo Monk. Summons to defendant to render accounts.
- BA: summons to Henry Stevenson & William Smith administrators of William Govane to render accounts.
- AA: summons to Ann Hammond & Henry Griffith executors of John Hammond to render accounts.
- AA: summons to Susa Johns administratrix of Kinsey Johns to render accounts.
- AA: summons to Major Charles Hammond executor of Phillip Hammond to render accounts.

44:270
- AA: summons to Ann Thomas executrix of Phillip Thomas to render accounts.
- AA: summons to Elisabeth, Samuel, Thomas, & John Snowden executors of Richard Snowden to render accounts.
- AA: attachment to Robert Johnson & his wife Ann administratrix of John Golder to render accounts.
- AA: attachment to Eleanor Wright executrix of Rezin Wright to render accounts.
- AA: summons to Richard Welsh & his wife Lydia administratrix of Thomas Medcalf to render accounts.
- AA: summons to Mary Wayman administratrix of Edward Wayman to render accounts.
- AA: attachment to Nathan Dorsey administrator of James Sewell to render accounts. "Not to be taken." To be struck off.
- AA: summons to John & Charles Worthington executors of John Worthington to render accounts.
- AA: summons to Isabella Frankling administratrix of Robert Frankling to render accounts.
- AA: attachment to Ely Dorsey & Thomas Beall Dorsey administrators dbn of Edward Dorsey, Esq. to render accounts.

44:271
- AA: attachment to Edward Dorsey & Thomas Beale Dorsey administrators of Henrietta Maria Dorsey to render accounts.
- AA: summons to Samuel & John Howard executors of Samuel Howard to render accounts.
- AA: summons to James Moss executor of Richard Moss to render accounts.
- AA: summons to Benjamin Hood administrator of James Hood to render accounts.
- AA: Thomas Rutland vs. Henry Oneal Welsh administrator dbn of Thomas King. Summons to defendant to render accounts.
- AA: summons to Samuel Lane (TA) & Benjamin Lane administrators of Thomas Lane to render accounts.
- AA: Nicholas Maccubbin administrator of Robert Thilleson vs. Comfort Bounds.
- AA: summons to John Gaither (AA) & Edward Gaither (FR) administrators of Sarah Gaither to render accounts.
- AA: summons to Elisabeth Cromwell widow of John Cromwell to exhibit will. LoA granted to (N) Risteau. To be struck off.

44:272
- AA: summons to Amos Riggs administrator dbn of John Riggs to render accounts.
- AA: summons to Amos Riggs administrator of Mary Riggs to render accounts.
- AA: summons to Knighton Simmonds surviving executor of George Simmonds to render accounts.
- AA: summons to James Brown executor of Robert Brown to render accounts.
- AA: summons to Mary Simmonds administrator of James Simmonds to render accounts. Accounts exhibited. To be struck off.
- AA: summons to Alice Duvall & Fran. Sappington executors of Mark Brown to render accounts.
- AA: summons to Charles Pettibone administrator dbn of Phillip Pettibone to render accounts.
- AA: summons to Bethridge Jones administratrix of William Jones to

Court Session: July 1771

render accounts.
- AA: summons to Valentine Brown administrator of Stephen Parnall to render accounts.

44:273 • AA: summons to Mary Campbell administratrix of Alexander Campbell to render accounts.
- AA: summons to Frederick Mills & his wife Achsa administratrix of Caleb Conner to render accounts.
- AA: summons to Harrisson Lane administrator dbn of William Wells to render accounts.
- AA: summons to Samuel Jacobs administrator of John Jackson to render accounts.
- AA: Nicholas Maccubbin vs. John Iiams, Jr. & Thomas Elliot sureties to Leah Kirkland administratrix of William Kirkland. Summons to defendants to render accounts.

Court Session: 12 November 1771

44:274 Docket:
- WO: summons to James Broadway & his wife Betty executrix of Mary Sheldon to render accounts.
- WO: summons to Purnel Bowen administrator of Littleton Bowen to render accounts.
- WO: summons to Samuel Smiley administrator of Andrew Smiley to render accounts.
- WO: summons to Samuel Brittingham executor of Elijah Brittingham to render accounts.
- WO: summons to Hannah Connoway executrix of Phillip Connoway to render accounts.
- WO: summons to Levy Noble executor of James Noble to render accounts.

44:275 • WO: summons to Hannah Massey executrix of Joseph Massey to render accounts.
- WO: summons to Tabitha Tilghman administratrix of Gideon Tilghman to render accounts.
- WO: summons to Sarah Hall administratrix of Stephen Hall to render accounts.
- WO: summons to Leah Caldwell

administratrix of William Caldwell
to render accounts.

- WO: summons to Southy King
administrator of William King to
render accounts.
- WO: summons to Ezekiel Green
executor of Ezekiel Green to render
accounts.
- WO: summons to Magdalene Burn
administratrix of Solomon Burn to
render accounts.
- WO: summons to William Holland & his
wife Mary administratrix of John
Purnel to render accounts.

44:276
- SO: summons to Isabella Cox
administratrix of John Cox to render
accounts. Final accounts exhibited.
To be struck off.
- SO: summons to Mathew Kemp
administrator dbn of Richard Steph.
Bounds to render accounts. Accounts
exhibited. To be struck off.
- SO: summons to Abigal Collins
administratrix of John Collins to
render accounts. Final accounts
exhibited. To be struck off.
- SO: summons to Ellis Shores
administratrix of William Shores to
render accounts. Final accounts
exhibited. To be struck off.
- SO: summons to Sarah Harris
administratrix of James Harris to
render accounts. Final accounts
exhibited. To be struck off.
- SO: summons to Stephen Garland
administrator of John Robertson to
render accounts. Final accounts
exhibited. To be struck off.
- SO: summons to Andrew Anderson & his
wife Elisabeth administratrix of
Thomas Bond to render accounts.
- SO: summons to William Stuart
executor of Rebecca Dashiel to
render accounts. Final accounts
exhibited. To be struck off.
- SO: summons to Isaac Green executor
of Richard Green to render accounts.
- SO: summons to Job Gastineaux
executor of George Lewis Gastineaux
to render accounts. Final accounts
exhibited. To be struck off.

44:277
- DO: summons to Sarah Hicks executrix

of John Hicks to render accounts.
Final accounts exhibited. To be
struck off.

- DO: summons to Ch. Nutter & his wife
  Eleanor administratrix of William
  Nutter to render accounts. Final
  accounts exhibited. To be struck
  off.
- DO: summons to John Pagan
  administrator of William Pagan to
  render accounts. Final accounts
  exhibited. To be struck off.
- DO: summons to William & Abner
  Lecompte executors of Philemon
  Lecompte to render accounts.
  Accounts exhibited. To be struck
  off.
- DO: summons to Laurana Spedding
  executrix of Hugh Spedding to render
  accounts.
- DO: summons to John Merine
  administrator of William Merine to
  render accounts.
- DO: Patrick Moore vs. Robertson
  Stevens executor of Josias Moore.
  Summons to defendant to render
  accounts.
- DO: summons to Elisabeth Holmes
  administratrix of Nicholas Holms to
  render accounts.
- TA: summons to John Robinson
  administrator of Israel Cox to
  render accounts.
- **44:278** TA: summons to Mary Ellston
  administratrix of William Ellston to
  render accounts.
- TA: summons to John Sherwood, Jr.
  administrator of Thomas Sherwood to
  render accounts.
- TA: William Paca for Luke Chevers &
  his wife Susa, Clement Sailes, &
  Gabriel Sailes vs. S.C. for John Cox
  & his wife Jane & John Studham & his
  wife Elisabeth.
  Text of libel. Will of Gabriel
  Sailes. Legatees:
  - son Gabriel, Negro Jasper (man).
  - daughter Susannah, Negro Hannah
    (woman).
  - son Clement.
  Mentions: James Dickinson,
  44:279 Daniel Sherwood.

Several children: Gabriel, Clement,
Susannah, Jane wife of John Cox,
Elisabeth wife of John Studdon.

44:280   Mentions: Thomas Sherwood (sheriff).

44:281   Text of petition of Luke Chevers.

44:282   Text of answer.

44:283   Mentions: wife of dec'd died in
February preceding said dec'd.
Ruling: will is valid.

44:284
- TA: summons to Frances Gibson
administratrix of Francis Gibson to
render accounts.
- TA: summons to Sarah & Nicholas
Goldsborough to render accounts.
Final accounts exhibited. To be
struck off.
- TA: summons to Mary Harwood
administratrix of Peter Harwood to
render accounts.
- TA: summons to Elisabeth & Robert
Harwood administrators of William
Harwood to render accounts.
- TA: summons to Mary Smith
administratrix of Simon Steven
Miller to render accounts.
- TA: summons to William Lovell
executor of Thomas McClenan to
render accounts. To be struck off.
- TA: summons to William Harrison
administrator of John Harrison to
render accounts.
- TA: summons to Ann Feddeman
administratrix of Daniel Feddeman to
render accounts.
- TA: summons to Henrietta Maria
Carslake administratrix of John
Carslake to render accounts.
- TA: summons to Mary Brown
administratrix of Adam Brown to
render accounts.

44:285
- TA: Thomas Barrow surety on estate
of James Chapman vs. Jane Chapman
executrix of said James Chapman.
Summons to defendant to render
accounts.
- TA: summons to Jean Scott
administratrix of John Dobson to
render accounts.
- TA: summons to Hannah Turner
executrix of Edward Turner to render
accounts.
- TA: summons to John Blythe & his

wife Sophia executrix of Lawrence Porter to render accounts.

- QA: William Evans (TA) vs. Hannah & Harman Knotts administrators of Nathaniel Knotts. Summons to defendants to show cause why they conceal said estate. To be struck off.
- QA: summons to Ann & Arthur Emory executors of John Emory (surveyor) to render accounts.
- QA: summons to William Ringgold administrator of Edward Ringgold to render accounts. To be struck off.
- QA: summons to John Nabb executor of Elisabeth Nabb to render accounts.
- QA: summons to Mary Clayton executrix of Solomon Clayton to render accounts. To be struck off.

44:286
- QA: summons to Charles Blake administrator of Sarah Blake to render accounts.
- QA: summons to Giles Hicks executor of Cornelius Daily to render accounts.
- QA: James Holliday vs. John Sutton & his wife Margaret administratrix of John Mumford. Attachment to defendant to render accounts.
- QA: summons to John Brown (son of John) administrator of Joseph Meanor to render accounts.
- QA: summons to Sarah Price administratrix of William Price to render accounts.
- QA: summons to Jonathan Culbreath administrator dbn of William Culbreath to render accounts.
- QA: summons to Christopher Cox & William Price administrators of Thomas Cox to render accounts.
- QA: summons to Thomas Yewell administrator of Mary Hadley to render accounts.
- QA: summons to Samuel Brown administrator dbn of Andrew Hall to render accounts.
- QA: summons to Samuel Brown administrator of Esther Hall to render accounts.

44:287
- QA: summons to Robert Wood administrator of David Robertson to

render accounts.

- QA: summons to Absolom Sparks administrator of Sarah Reed to render accounts. "Mortus est." To be struck off.
- QA: summons to Susa Clayland executrix of Thomas Clayland to render accounts.
- QA: summons to Tabitha Bryan executrix of John Bryan to render accounts.
- QA: summons to Andrew Henesey administratrix of John Henesey (TA) to render accounts.
- QA: summons to Hannah Baley executrix of Thomas Bailey to render accounts.
- QA: William Twyford who married Lovel Warner widow of Richard Warner vs. Charles Warner surviving executor of said Richard Warner. Text of petition by plaintiff. Said Richard Warner died 4 May 1764, leaving wife & son Charles joint executors.

44:288 Said Lovel Twyford died beginning of September last. Date: 8 October 1771.

44:289 Said William Twyford to exhibit his accounts.

- KE: summons to John Gleaves administrator of John Gleaves to render accounts.
- KE: summons to Benjamin Howard administrator of Benjamin Howard to render accounts.
- KE: summons to John Osborn administrator of Henry Osborn to render accounts.
- KE: summons to William Crabbin administrator of Meredith Walton to render accounts.
- KE: summons to Joshua George executor of Hanna George to render accounts.

44:290 - KE: summons to William Freeman executor of Laurence Strainer to render accounts.

- KE: summons to Thomas Smith administrator of William Hollis to render accounts. To be struck off.
- KE: summons to William Pearce

administrator dbn of Mary Watkins to render accounts.

- KE: summons to James Chiffin executor of James Chiffin to render accounts.
- KE: summons to William Pearce administrator of Beatrise Johnson to render accounts.
- KE: Ebenezar Reyner & Jonathan Turner executors of Thomas Perkins. To be struck off.
- KE: summons to Jerutiah Barrett executrix of Jonathan Barrett to render accounts.
- KE: summons to John Crew administrator of Edward Drugan to render accounts.
- KE: summons to John Lambert Wilmer executor of Simon Wilmer to render accounts.
- KE: summons to Peter Body administrator of John Body to render accounts.
44:291 - KE: summons to William Sluby & his wife Rachel executrix of William Hynson to render accounts. Final accounts exhibited. To be struck off.
- KE: summons to James Smith executor of Thomas Sealy to render accounts.
- KE: summons to Joyce Smith administratrix of Charles Ringgold to render accounts.
- KE: summons to Dean Reed executor of John Reed to render accounts.
- KE: summons to Rachel Anderson administratrix of William Anderson to render accounts.
- KE: summons to Ann Hutchison administratrix of John Hutchison to render accounts.
- CE: summons to John Chapple administrator of Sarah Kelley to render accounts. To be struck off.
- CE: summons to Catharine & Thomas Williams executors of Robert Williams to render accounts. To be struck off.
- CE: summons to Mary Mercer administratrix of Robert Mercer, Jr. to render accounts.
- CE: summons to Samuel & Thomas

Tigart administrators of Cardiff
Tigart to render accounts.

44:292 • CE: summons to Sarah Abbot executrix
of William Abbot to render accounts.
To be struck off.

• CE: summons to Edward Dougherty
administrator of Joseph Chissel to
render accounts.

• CE: summons to Adam Vance
administrator of James Vance to
render accounts.

• CE: summons to John Ward
administrator of Henry Ward to
render accounts.

• CE: summons to Agnes & Samuel Miller
executors of Thomas Miller to show
cause why they conceal said estate.

• CE: summons to Sarah Sedgwick &
Francis Boyd executors of Richard
Sedgwick to render accounts.

• CE: Thomas, George, John, Sarah,
Esther Beatty, & John Heron & his
wife Martha vs. Sarah Sedgwick &
Francis Boyd. Libel, answer,
demurrer.

• CE: summons to Jonathan Hollings
administrator of Abigail Hollings to
render accounts.

• CE: summons to Rebeccah & Thomas
Cooper executor of John Cooper to
render accounts.

• CE: summons to Richard Oldham
executor of Ann Oldham to render
accounts.

44:293 • CE: summons to Amos & George
Alexander executors of Theophiley
Alexander to render accounts.

• CE: summons to Sarah Pennington &
William Withers administrators of
Abraham Pennington to render
accounts.

• CE: summons to Susannah Elliot
administratrix of Benjamin Elliot to
render accounts.

• CE: summons to Sarah Cunningham
administratrix of George Cunningham
to render accounts.

• CE: summons to Rebeccah Ellsbury
executrix of Frederick Ellsbury to
render accounts. To be struck off.

• CE: summons to Archibald Ankrim
executor of George Ankrim to render

accounts.
- CE: summons to Isaac Van Bebber & Pineas Chew executors of Sarah Chew to render accounts. To be struck off.
- CE: summons to James Corbit executor of James Corbit to render accounts.
- CE: summons to Andrew Welsh executor of William Callender to render accounts.

44:294
- CE: summons to Augustine Beedle executor of John Beedle, Sr. to render accounts.
- CE: Jane & John Strawbridge administrators of John Strawbridge. To be struck off.
- CE: summons to Thomas Chandler & his wife administratrix of Peter Jones to render accounts.
- CE: summons to John Anderson & William Glasgow executor of John Glasgow to render accounts.
- CE: summons to James Scott & Thomas Whitherspone executors of John Scott to render accounts.
- CE: summons to Alexander Moore & his wife Margaret executors of John Callender, Jr. to render accounts.
- CE: summons to Jonathan Humberstone administrator of George Humberstone to render accounts.
- CE: summons to John Donohoe & his wife Mary administrators of John Anderson to render accounts.
- CE: summons to Sarah Lewis administratrix of John Lewis to render accounts.
- CE: summons to Elisha Terry administrator of William Terry to render accounts.
- CE: George Milligan (KE), Michael Earle (KE), & Charles Gordon (KE) vs. administrator of John McDuff. Caveat.
- continued to f. 314.

Court Session: 1771

44:295   3 December.   Exhibited from PG:
- will of John Philpot (London) & procuration.

Court Session: 1771

Exhibited from BA:
- will of Peter Dicks (PA). Also, bond of Amos Garret (BA) administrator. Sureties: Joseph Ensor, John Paca. Date: 27 June 1771.

Exhibited from KE:
- will of Alexander Lunan & exemplification.

Exhibited from SO:
- bond of Levin Wilson administrator of William McIlvaine (Philadelphia). Sureties: Thomas Sloss, Edward Gantt. Date: 21 August 1771.

Exhibited from QA:
- accounts on estate of Richard Warner.
- final accounts on estate of Richard Warner.
- inventory & LoD of John Hall.
- final accounts on estate of John Hall.
- LoD & accounts on estate of Anthony McCulloch.
- final accounts on estate of Samuel Wright.

Exhibited from BA:
- bond of Job Garretson administrator of Samuel Groom. Sureties: William Partridge, Jos. Selby. Date: 12 November 1771.
- will of Henry Dillon.
- inventory & accounts of William Wood.
- accounts on estate of William Bond.
- accounts on estate of Rachel Wilmot.
- accounts on estate of Renaldo Monk.
- inventory of James Wells.

44:296 Exhibited from AA:
- final accounts on estate of Richard Sheckels.
- final accounts on estate of Thomas Mobberly.
- accounts on estate of Alexander Ferguson.
- accounts on estate of Thomas Richardson.

Court Session: 1771

- accounts on estate of Henry Hall.
- accounts on estate of Richard Moss.
- accounts on estate of Thomas Turner.
- accounts on estate of Thomas Welsh.
- accounts on estate of George Simmonds.
- accounts on estate of Sarah Gaither.
- accounts on estate of William Chew Brown.
- accounts on estate of Isaac Jones.

Exhibited from PG:
- will of George Scott.
- accounts on estate of Ann Allingham.
- accounts on estate of John Blandford.
- additional inventory of Francis Waring.
- accounts on estate of Francis Waring.
- accounts on estate of John Janson (?).
- accounts on estate of John Stone Hawkins.
- accounts on estate of Ann Allingham.

Exhibited from DO:
- final accounts on estate of Henry Traverse.
- LoD on estate of Henry Traverse.
- final accounts on estate of Henry Hooper.
- inventory of John Wheeler.

Exhibited from SO:
- inventory of Capt. John Dennis.

Exhibited from KE:
- additional inventory of Thomas Perkins.
- bond of Rebeccah Wheeler administratrix of Bazil Wheeler. Sureties: John Nicholson, Daniel Charles Heath. Date: 25 September 1771.

44:297 Exhibited from SM:
- bond of Benjamin Williams executor of Benjamin Williams. Sureties: Mathias Jones, James White. Date: 14 November 1771.

Court Session: 1771

Exhibited from TA:
- 2 inventories of Thomas Lane.
- final accounts on estate of John Plumer.

Exhibited from CE:
- final accounts on estate of Jacob Jones.

Thomas Bowles (g, FR) exhibited:
- will of John Reeder (alias John Retter). Also, bond of Conrod Reeder administrator. Sureties: Jacob Kersner, Peter Grosh. Date: 28 September 1771.
- will of Arthur Charlthon, constituting Eleanor Charlthon executrix. Said executrix was granted administration. Sureties: Christopher Edelin, William Murdock Beall. Date: 21 September 1771.
- will of Benjamin Perry, constituting Elisabeth Perry executrix. Said executrix was granted administration. Sureties: Alexander Offuth, Elias Harding. Date: 22 October 1771.
- bond of Peter & Ruth Mallot administrators of Catharine Mallot. Sureties: John Stull, Peter Bainbridge. Date: 5 November 1771.

44:298
- bond of Margaret Clem administratrix of George Clem. Sureties: Jacob Miller, Mathias Ringer. Date: 21 October 1771.
- LoD on estate of Christian Shoat.
- inventory of John Truerdale.
- inventory of John McKinley.
- accounts on estate of Daniel Haines.
- final accounts on estate of Christ. Shoat.

16 December. Jos. Nicholson (g, KE) exhibited:
- will of John Hynson, constituting Mary Hynson executrix. Said executrix was granted administration. Sureties: James Pearce, William Wethered. Date: 7 December 1771.
- will of Thomas Bowers, constituting Thomas Bowers executor. Said

executor was granted administration.
Sureties: Abraham Raisin, William
Cowarden. Date: 18 November 1771.

- will of Ann Blackiston, constituting
James Blackiston executor. Said
executor was granted administration.
Sureties: Hanse Hanson, Frederick
Hanson. Date: 9 December 1771.
- bond of James Pearce administrator
dbn of William Haley. Sureties:
George William Forrester, Gilbert
Falconer. Date: 20 November 1771.
- bond of Isaac Spencer administrator
of John Spencer. Sureties:
Frederick Hanson, Thomas Rasin.
Date: 24 October 1771.

44:299
- bond of James Pearce administrator
of Henrietta Haley. Sureties:
George William Forrester, Gilbert
Falconar. Date: 20 November 1771.
- bond of William Merritt
administrator of Richard Norton.
Sureties: Robert Maxwell, Amos Reed.
Date: 16 October 1771.
- bond of John Burk, Jr. administrator
of John Tharpe. Sureties: William
Copper, John Ricketts. Date: 4
October 1771.
- bond of John McGowin administrator
of Bridget Wise. Sureties: David
Falls, Absolom Duffey. Date: 2
October 1771.
- will of Mary Smith.
- will of Martha Hynson.
- will of John Reed, Sr.
- additional inventory of Robert Laws.
- inventory of John Younger.
- inventory of Thomas Bowers.
- inventory of Alexander Kelley.
- LoD & accounts on estate of Michael
Blackiston.
- LoD on estate of John Williamson.
- accounts one state of Robert Lane.
- LoD & accounts on estate of William
Hynson.
- final accounts on estate of William
Hollingsworth.
- final accounts on estate of
Alexander Kelley.

44:300 J. A. Thomas (g, SM) exhibited:
- will of Robert Cole, constituting

Robert Mattingley, Richard Melton, & Basil Haydon executors. Said executors were granted administration. Surety: William Haydon. Date: 2 December 1771.

- will of James Brown, Sr., constituting Basil Brown executor. Said executor was granted administration. Sureties: Cuthbert Abell, John Abell. Date: 22 October 1771.
- will of John Taylor. Also, bond of Christian Taylor administrator. Sureties: William Taylor, John Lynch. Date: 29 October 1771.
- will of Teresia Stratford, constituting Richard James Rapeir executor. Said executor was granted administration. Sureties: Thomas Johnson, Thomas Johnson, Jr. Date: 5 October 1771.
- bond of Anne Hill administratrix of Clement Hill. Sureties: John Smith, Ignatius Fenwick, Jr. Date: 11 November 1771.
- bond of John Mills, Jr. administrator of John Mills. Sureties: James Jordan, Charles Jordan. Date: 11 November 1771.
- bond of Ann Llewellin & James Eden administrators of Justinian Llewellin. Sureties: John Eden, John Lewellin. Date: 13 April 1771.
- bond of Leonard Seale administrator of Rebecca Swann. Sureties: John Tooir, James Scott. Date: 29 November 1771.
- will of Elisabeth Tennisson.
- will of Thomas Suite.
- inventory & LoD of George Aisquith.
- inventory of Mathew Compton.
- inventory of John Fanning.
- inventory of Bennett Timms.
- inventory of Mildred Jordan.
- inventory of Charles Hezeltine.
- LoD on estate of Margaret Pravat.
- inventory of James Heard.
- LoD & final accounts on estate of John Read.
- final accounts on estate of Mildred Jordan.
- final accounts on estate of Charles

44:301

Hezeltine.
- final accounts on estate of Joseph Manning.
- final accounts on estate of Elisabeth Holton.
- final accounts on estate of William Holton.
- final accounts on estate of Thomas Spalding.
- final accounts on estate of James Weeden.
- final accounts on estate of John Cole.
- accounts on estate of Edward Digges.
- final accounts on estate of William Harrisson.

18 December. John Bracco (g, TA) exhibited:
- will of James Akers. Also, bond of Elisabeth Akers administratrix. Sureties: Samuel Dickinson, William Akers. Date: 26 November 1771.
- bond of Robert Neale executor of Edward Neale. Sureties: Samuel Neale, Thomas Benonson. Date: 6 November 1771.
- will of John Willoughby.
- will of Henrietta Maria Goldsborough.

44:302
- bond of Mary Bromwell administratrix of Robert Bromwell. Sureties: David Robinson, Edward Bromwell. Date: 29 October 1771.
- bond of Mary Ann Garey administratrix of John Geary. Sureties: John Gordon, William Geary. Date: 5 November 1771.
- inventory of Thomas Loveday.
- inventory of James Rutherford.

21 December. William Turner Wootton (g, PG) exhibited:
- will of Winefred Lanham, constituting Edward Lanham executor. Said executor was granted administration. Sureties: Anthony Hardy, Francis Wheat, Jr. Date: 27 November 1771.
- will of Thomas Stonestreet, constituting John Stonestreet executor. Said executor was granted

administration. Sureties: Jonathan
Burk, Butler Newman. Date: 28
November 1771.
- will of Edward Stonestreet,
  constituting Eleanor Stonestreet
  executrix. Said executrix was
  granted administration. Sureties:
  Buttler Newman, Elisha Lanham.
  Date: 28 November 1771.
- will of Lancelot Wilson. Also, bond
  of Basil Wilson administrator.
  Sureties: Joseph Wilson, Sr.,
  William Ray. Date: 13 November
  1771.
- will of Edward McDaniel. Also, bond
  of John McDaniel administrator.
  Sureties: Edward Cole, James Owens.
  Date: 16 December 1771.
- accounts on estate of Ignatius
  Wheeler.
- inventory of Hugh Wilson.

44:303
- bond of Francis King administrator
  of Francis King. Sureties: Thomas
  John Clagget, Alexander H. Magruder.
  Date: 27 November 1771.
- bond of Patrick Smith administrator
  of Thomas Brooke. Sureties: John
  Perrie, Levin Covington. Date: 27
  November 1771.
- bond of Patrick Smith administrator
  of Elisabeth Brooke. Sureties: John
  Perrie, Levin Covington. Date: 27
  November 1771.

21 December. Walter Hanson (g, CH)
exhibited:
- will of George Scroggen,
  constituting Sarah Scroggen
  executrix. Said executrix was
  granted administration. Sureties:
  Henry Thompson, Gerr. Dutton. Date:
  1 November 1771.
- will of Elisabeth Clements,
  constituting George Clements
  executor. Said executor was granted
  administration. Sureties: John
  Clements, Thomas Clements. Date: 19
  November 1771.
- will of Thomas Stone, constituting
  Margery Stone & William Stone
  executors. Said executors were
  granted administration. Sureties:

Court Session: 1771

William McConchie, Samuel Stone, Jr.
Date: 4 November 1771.
- will of John Lucky, constituting
  Mary Lucky executrix. Said
  executrix was granted
  administration. Sureties: Gerrard
  Boarman, Edward Ware. Date: 21
  October 1771.

44:304
- bond of Ethelder Martin
  administratrix of John Marten.
  Sureties: Philip McGrah, Ignatius
  Hambleton. Date: 20 November 1771.
- bond of Thomas Lomax administrator
  of John Lomax. Sureties: Stephen
  Lomax, Luke Lomax. Date: 23 October
  1771.
- bond of James Anderson & James
  Vineyard administrators of John
  Morningholer. Sureties: Edward
  Miles, Daniel Nail. Date: 25
  November 1771.
- will of Samuel Farr.
- will of Marsham Queen.
- will of Edward Maddox.
- will of Francis Evans.
- inventory of William Davis.
- inventory of John Speak.
- inventory of Joseph Timm.
- inventory of Richard Bevans.
- inventory of John Boswell.
- LoD on estate of Bayne Smallwood.
- accounts on estate of Elisha
  Leftwitch.
- accounts on estate of Cloe Gody.
- accounts on estate of William
  Hanson.
- accounts on estate of Hugh Kerrick.
- accounts on estate of William Dowie.
- accounts on estate of Mary Wood.
- accounts on estate of John Wright.
- accounts on estate of Richard
  Stoddert.

44:305 23 December. John Goldsborough (g, DO)
exhibited:
- will of Joseph Allford, constituting
  Maccabeus Allford executor. Said
  executor was granted administration.
  Sureties: Luke Stevens, William
  Webster. Date: 13 November 1771.
- will of William Noble, constituting
  Mary Ann Noble executrix. Said

executrix was granted administration. Sureties: Benjamin Sherman, Levin Noble. Date: 16 December 1771.

- will of Edward Williams. Also, bond of Rachel Williams administratrix. Sureties: William Cannon, Hughlit Cannon. Date: 9 December 1771.
- will of Mary Cannon. Also, bond of Joseph Nicholson administrator. Sureties: William Cannon, Jesse Cannon. Date: 9 December 1771.
- bond of Benson Stainton administrator of David Swift. Sureties: Henry Dickinson, James Wing. Date: 11 October 1771.
- bond of Benjamin Todd administrator of Joseph Todd. Sureties: Henry Lake, William Dean. Date: 15 November 1771.
- bond of William Edmondson administrator of Josias Stamper. Sureties: Peter Edmondson, Thomas Edmondson. Date: 3 December 1771.
- will of Mary Moor.
- will of Arthur Whitely.
- will of Abraham Trice.
- will of Richard Bussic.
- inventory & accounts of Robert Polk.
- inventory & accounts of John Bright.
- inventory & LoD of Thomas Wall.
- inventory & LoD of Roger Hurley.
- additional inventory & LoD of Josias Moore.

44:306
- inventory of John Howarth.
- inventory of John Oldfield.
- inventory of Thomas McCrakin.
- inventory of James Farguson.
- inventory of John Vickars.
- inventory of William Woollen.
- inventory of Zebulon Keene.
- inventory of Alexander Morton.
- inventory of Robert Smith.
- LoD & accounts on estate of William Pagon.
- LoD & accounts on estate of Thomas Wheeler.
- LoD & accounts on estate of Benjamin Keene.
- LoD & accounts on estate of John Stewart.
- accounts on estate of Mary Jones.

- accounts on estate of Christiana Wallace.
- accounts on estate of Richard Willis.
- accounts on estate of William Green.
- accounts on estate of Richard Parish.
- accounts on estate of William Nutter.
- accounts on estate of John Hicks.
- accounts on estate of Joseph Blades.
- accounts on estate of Thomas Allcock.
- accounts on estate of Stephen Sherwin.
- accounts on estate of James Sherwin.
- accounts on estate of Abel Grace.
- accounts on estate of James Robinson.
- accounts on estate of Ambrose Aaron.
- accounts on estate of Reuben Phillips.
- accounts on estate of Richard Parish.
- accounts on estate of Mary Jarratt.
- accounts on estate of James Jarratt.
- accounts on estate of Mary Thomas.
- accounts on estate of John Thomas.
- accounts on estate of Mary Fray.
- accounts on estate of John Johnson.

44:307
- accounts on estate of Phumback Pritchet.
- accounts on estate of William Trego.
- accounts & final accounts on estate of Henry Thomas.
- accounts on estate of Thomas Farguson.
- accounts on estate of Edward Smith, Jr.

31 December. Thomas Bowles (FR) exhibited:
- will of Jacob Mullendore, constituting Jacob Stoner, Philip Engler, & Andrew Young executors. Said executors were granted administration. Sureties: Martin Gerber, Abraham Rosland. Date: 9 December 1771.
- bond of James Hale & Michel Troutman administrators of John Beard. Sureties: Charles Beatty, Peter

Copeland.   Date: 8 December 1771.
- final accounts on estate of Margaret Shroyer.
- final accounts on estate of Andrew Owler.
- final accounts on estate of David Watson.
- final accounts on estate of Joseph Parks.

44:308   24 December.   Joseph Nicholson (g, KE) exhibited:
- bond of Edward Comegys administrator of Jonathan Wales. Surety: Thomas Blake. Date: 16 December 1771.
- bond of Joseph Wicks executor of Martha Hynson. Sureties: John Bolton, Simon Wicks. Date: 13 December 1771.
- inventory of John Clark.
- inventory of John Wallis.
- inventory of Lydia Flinn.
- LoD & accounts on estate of Lydia Flinn.

31 December.   Col. William Young (BA) exhibited:
- will of George Ensor, constituting Elisabeth Ensor & George Ensor executors. Said executors were granted administration. Sureties: Humphry Chilcote, Richard Bond. Date: 21 November 1771.
- will of John Bentley, constituting Tamar Bentley executrix. Said executrix was granted administration. Sureties: Isaac Powell, James Powell. Date: 18 November 1771.
- will of Thomas Baily, constituting Thomas Bailey executor. Said executor was granted administration. Sureties: Thomas Hatton, Thomas Bond. Date: 16 December 1771.
- bond of John & Thomas Craddock executors of Benjamin Dinney. Sureties: Cornelius Howard, Mordecai Gist. Date: 5 November 1771.

44:309 • bond of Job Garretson administrator dbn of Daniel Graham. Surety: Mark Alexander. Date: 2 December 1771.
- bond of Rachel Baxter administratrix

of Benjamin Baxter. Sureties: Jacob Syndall, Thomas Gash. Date: 24 December 1771.
- bond of Job Garretson administrator of Elisabeth Graham. Surety: Mark Alexander. Date: 2 December 1771.
- bond of Catharine Hasselbach administratrix of Nicholas Hasselbach. Sureties: Frederic Meyer, John Slye. Date: 12 December 1771.
- bond of Sarah Burck administratrix of Thomas Burck. Sureties: Ulrick Burck, Thomas Burk. Date: 21 December 1771.
- bond of Rachel Jones administratrix of Jacob Jones. Sureties: Moses Collet, Daniel Collet. Date: 18 November 1771.
- inventory of John Orrick.
- inventory of James Gardiner.
- inventory of Isaijah Vansant.
- inventory of John Bentley.
- LoD & accounts on estate of Robert Dutton.
- final accounts on estate of Archibald Johnson.

44:310 Elie Vallette (AA) exhibited:
- will of Charles Griffith, constituting John Griffith & Nicholas Worthington executors. Said executors were granted administration. Sureties: B. T. B. Worthington, Baldwin Lusby. Date: 21 October 1771.
- will of Thomas Beale Dorsey, constituting Caleb Dorsey & Reuben Merrywether executors. Said executors were granted administration. Sureties: Benjamin Mackall 4th, John DeButts. Date: 28 November 1771.
- will of Ann Dorsey, constituting Joshua Dorsey executor. Said executor was granted administration. Sureties: Thomas Dorsey, B. Ridgely Warfield. Date: 11 December 1771.
- bond of John Lane executor of Nathan Lane. Sureties: Samuel Lane, Richard Lane. Date: 14 November 1771.

Court Session: 1771

- bond of Joseph Brewer & Samuel Geist executors of Joseph Brewer. Sureties: John Brewer, Sr., Nicholas Brewer. Date: 16 October 1771.
- bond of Henry Ashpaw administrator of John Ashpaw. Sureties: William Slicer, Hezekiah Cheney. Date: 8 January 1772 [!].
- bond of Samuel Dorsey administrator of William Levins. Sureties: Samuel Harvey Howard, Robert Johnson. Date: 2 December 1771.
- bond of Steven Stewart administrator of Daniel Jenners. Sureties: Jos. Cowman, Thomas Harwood, Jr. Date: 8 December 1771.
- bond of Elisabeth Maw administratrix of Edmund Maw. Sureties: Allen Quynn, William Noke. Date: 14 December 1771.

44:311
- bond of Thomas Harwood administrator of John Schneider. Surety: Thomas Hyde. Date: 28 October 1771.
- inventory of James Hollyday.
- inventory of William Black.
- inventory of Mary Hammond.
- inventory of Henry Dorsey.
- inventory of Thomas Brower.
- inventory of Charles Connant.
- inventory of Samuel Wootton.

Clement Smith (CV) exhibited:
- will of Jacob Bourne, constituting Esther Bourne executrix. Said executrix was granted administration. Sureties: Edward Swann, Daniel Rawlings. Date: 21 August 1771.
- bond of John Turner administrator dbn of Benjamin Sollers. Sureties: Joseph Wilkinson, Joseph Cambden. Date: 20 July 1771.
- bond of Edward Wood administrator dbn of William Sly. Sureties: Parker Bowen, John Denten. Date: 15 June 1771.
- bond of Sarah Kirkshaw administratrix of John Kirkshaw. Sureties: James Kirkshaw, James Byrn. Date: 21 August 1771.

44:312
- bond of James Somervell administrator of Jane Hellen.

Court Session: 1771

Sureties: Edmund Clare, Richard
Smith. Date: 27 May 1771.
- will of Stocket Sunderland.
- inventory of Elisabeth Parran.
- inventory of Roger Brookes.
- inventory of Phillip Parran.
- accounts on estate of George Bourn.
- accounts on estate of Thomas Holdsw.
  Heighe.
- accounts on estate of Benjamin
  Ellts.
- accounts on estate of Francis
  Harrison.
- accounts on estate of James
  Williamson.
- accounts on estate of James Duke.
- accounts on estate of Benjamin
  Parran.
- accounts on estate of Nicholas
  Swarmstead.
- accounts on estate of John Gray.
- accounts on estate of John Greves.
- accounts on estate of William
  Devers.
- accounts on estate of Eleanor Slye.
- accounts on estate of Elisabeth
  Parran.
- accounts on estate of Phillip
  Parran.
- accounts on estate of Benjamin
  Dixson.

44:313   Exhibited from QA:
- will of John Pratt.
- inventory of Anthony McCulloch.

Exhibited from SM:
- will of Benjamin Williams.

Exhibited from SO:
- will of Rachel Coulborn.

Exhibited from PG:
- inventory of Col. Jeremiah Belt.

Exhibited from AA:
- final accounts on estate of Nathan
  Boone.
- final accounts on estate of Humphry
  Boone.

26 November. Deputy Commissaries to examine accounts of:
* KE: Sarah Tilden administratrix of Marmaduke Tilden.

27 November.
* FR: John Evenly & George Everhart executors of Daniel Zacharias.
* FR: Elisabeth & Jacob Sprotsman administrators of William Laurence Sprotsman.

28 November.
* TA: Susannah Chamberlain, Samuel Chamberlain, & James Lloyd Chamberlain, executors of Thomas Chamberlain.

30 November.
* CH: Theodore Venables administrator of Charles Venables.
* CH: William Farr administrator of John Farr.
* SM: Catharine & Thomas Spalding executors of Thomas Spalding.

44:314 9 December.
* PG: Elisabeth & Samuel Haley executors of Thomas Haley.

14 December.
* SM: John Shanks, Jr. administrator dbn of Kenelm Cheseldine.

18 December.
* SO: Isaac Collins executor of James Quartermus.
* TA: Henrietta Maria Carslake administratrix of John Carslake.

20 December.
* SM: Robert Armstrong & his wife Martha administratrix of Samuel Caldwell.
* Robert Armstrong & his wife Martha & William Guither executors Richard Swan Edwards.

21 December.
* KE: Richard Harding & his wife Mary executrix of George Perkins.
* petition of John Cretin, et. al. (BA). Administration bond on estate of Patrick Lynch assigned to petitioners.

23 December.
* DO: John Cannon executor of Esther Ann Hodson.
* DO: Priscilla Pollock administratrix of David Pollock, Jr.

Court Session: 1771

- DO: William Lecompte surviving executor of Philemon Lecompte.
- DO: Mary Hurley administratrix of Roger Hurley, Jr.
- DO: Priscilla & Peter Colson executors of William Coleson.
- DO: Mary Lane administratrix of Thomas Lane.
- DO: Benoni Banning executor of Abraham Clark.
- DO: Isaac Jones administrator of Daniel Jones.
- DO: Sarah & Richard Coleson executors of George Coleson.
- DO: Edward Woolen administrator of William Woolen.
- DO: Alice & Daniel Polk executors of Robert Polk.

31 December.
- petition of Nicholas Maccubbin (AA). Administration bond on estate of Samuel Howard assigned to petitioner.
- BA: Sarah & Thomas Johnson executors of William Johnson.
- CV: Ann Brooke executrix of Roger Brooke.
- CV: Francis, Louther, & Hugh Hopewell executors of Ellick Parran.

Court Session: 12 November 1771

Docket (continued from f. 294):
- SM: T.J. & J.T. 3rd for James Biscoe (son of Basil) by Kellelen Harrison his next friend vs. Bennett, James, Mary Biscoe, & Thomas Crawley & his wife Ann. Libel, deposition by Robert Clark. Attachment to Ann Williams to testify; she is sick in bed.
- SM: Daniel Jenifer (taylor) or Daniel Jenifer Taylor directed to John Hammell (coroner, SM) for his contempt in not producing Thomas Clark. To be struck off.
- SM: summons to Jane Goldsborough administratrix of Ignatius Goldsborough to render accounts.

44:315
- SM: summons to Eleanor & John Johnson executors of John Johnson to render accounts.

Page 76

Court Session: 12 November 1771

- SM: summons to Leonard Briscoe one of executors of John Theobald to render accounts.
- SM: summons to Elisabeth Chesley executrix of John Chesley to render accounts.
- SM: summons to John Manning executor of Joseph Manning to render accounts. Final accounts exhibited. To be struck off.
- SM: summons to Annastatia Norris administratrix of William Norris to render accounts.
- SM: summons to Catharine William Thomas administrators of James Thomas to render accounts.
- SM: summons to Catharine Spalding & Thomas Spalding executors of Thomas Spalding (CoHo) to render accounts. To be struck off.
- SM: summons to Joshua Watts executor of Thomas Watts to render accounts.
- SM: summons to William Paltry administrator of Mildred Jordan to render accounts. Final accounts exhibited. To be struck off.
- SM: summons to John Smool administrator of Jos. Thomas Gardiner to render accounts.
- SM: summons to Elisabeth Helestine administratrix of Charles Helestine to render accounts. Accounts exhibited. To be struck off.

44:316
- SM: summons to Robert Holton administrator dbn of William Holton to render accounts. Final accounts exhibited. To be struck off.
- SM: summons to Robert Armstrong & his wife Martha & William Guyther executors of Richard Swan Edwards to render accounts.
- SM: Benjamin Williams (SM) vs. Ann Williams, Joseph Bennett & his wife Elisabeth, James Henley & his wife Henrietta, & Ann Williams, Jr. Text of petition of plaintiff. Plaintiff's father Benjamin Williams made his will, devising to:
  - wife Ann.
  - daughter Elisabeth Bennet wife of Joseph Benet.
  - daughter Henrietta Henley wife

Page 77

of James Henley.
- daughter Ann Williams.
Residue to plaintiff, unless Jacob
Williams (brother of plaintiff)
should return from across the sea.
Said will is unsigned.
Petition for such persons to testify
regarding said will.

44:317   Said Jacob Williams is presumed
dead.
Mentions: Robert Watts (sheriff,
SM).
- John Biscoe (SM), of full age,
deposed.

44:318   - Joseph Lee, of full age,
deposed. Signed: Joseph Leigh.
- Henry Gill, of full age,
deposed.

44:319   Ruling: will is valid.

- CH: summons to William Bryan
surviving executor of William Bryan
to render accounts.
- CH: summons to James Edelin & his
wife Susa executrix of Basil Hagan
to render accounts.
- CH: summons to Margaret Carrico
administratrix of Peter Carrico to
render accounts.
- CH: summons to Charles Sanders
administrator of Jane Doyne to
render accounts.
- CH: summons to Edward Boarman
executor of John Gardiner to render
accounts.
- CH: summons to William Smallwood
administrator of Lucy Herbert
Stoddert to render accounts. To be
struck off.
- CH: summons to Priscilla & William
Smallwood administrators of Bayne
Smallwood to render accounts. Libel
filed. To be struck off.
- CH: summons to Hen. Smith Hawkins &
Thomas Hawkins executors of
Alexander Smith Hawkins to render
accounts.
- CH: summons to John Wright executor
of John Wright to render accounts.
Final accounts exhibited. To be
struck off.

44:320   - CH: summons to Mary & Thomas Reeder
executors of Benjamin Reeder to

render accounts. Final accounts
exhibited. To be struck off.

- CH: summons to Elisabeth Grove
administratrix of Ebsworth Grove to
render accounts.
- CH: summons to William Smallwood &
his wife (alias Graw) administratrix
of John Hannon to render accounts.
To be struck off.
- CH: summons to Kenelm & Water
Stoddert administrators of Richard
Stoddert to render accounts. To be
struck off.
- CH: summons to Warren Dent
administrator of William Dowie to
render accounts.
- CH: summons to Hugh Hamill executor
of John Hamill to render accounts.
- CH: summons to Mary Hawkins
executrix of Rudolph Moris Hawkins
to render accounts.
- CH: summons to Walter Pye
administrator of Edward Queen to
render accounts.
- CV: summons to Edward Wood executor
of Eleanor Slye to render accounts.
Final accounts exhibited. To be
struck off.
- CV: summons to Mary Smith
administratrix of Joseph Smith to
render accounts.
- CV: summons to John Weems, Jr.
administrator of James Fleet to
render accounts.
- CV: summons to Ann & Driver Greaves
administrators of John Greaves, Jr.
to render accounts. Final accounts
exhibited. To be struck off.

44:321
- CV: summons to Elisabeth Williamson
executrix of James Williamson to
render accounts. Final accounts
exhibited. To be struck off.
- CV: summons to Ann Gray executrix of
John Gray to render accounts. Final
accounts exhibited. To be struck
off.
- CV: summons to Mary Duke
administratrix of James Duke to
render accounts. Final accounts
exhibited. To be struck off.
- CV: summons to Margaret Bourne
administratrix of George Bourne to

render accounts. Final accounts exhibited. To be struck off.

- CV: summons to John Hutchinson & his wife Elisabeth executrix of William Deaver to render accounts. Final accounts exhibited. To be struck off.
- CV: summons to following to prove will of Josias Sunderland: Thomas Reynolds, Thomas Holland, Edward Reynolds.
- PG: summons to Elisabeth Eastwood executrix of Benjamin Eastwood to render accounts.
- PG: summons to Steven West administrator of Capt. Archibald Johnson to render accounts. To be struck off.
- PG: summons to Margaret Miles administratrix of William Miles to render accounts.
- PG: summons to John Cook, Esq. administrator of Thomas Lee to render accounts.
- Samuel Selby, et. al. vs. John Dorset, et. al. Libel, answer, general replication.

44:322
- PG: summons to Marjery Lyles administratrix of Zachariah Lyles to render accounts. Final accounts exhibited. To be struck off.
- PG: summons to Christopher Lowndes administrator of William Tennally to render accounts.
- PG: summons to Elisabeth Osbourn administratrix of Robert Osbourn to render accounts.
- PG: attachment to Mary & Leonard Warring executors of Francis Warring to render accounts.
- PG: summons to Steven West one of administrators of Samuel Wells (AA) to render accounts.
- FR: summons to Catharine Mock administratrix of George Mock to render accounts.
- FR: summons to William Aldridge executor of Nicholas Aldridge to render accounts.
- FR: summons to Philipina Bonsom administratrix of Laurence Bonsom to render accounts.

Court Session: 12 November 1771

- FR: summons to Ann Williams
  administratrix of Charles Williams
  to render accounts.
- FR: summons to Andrew Williams
  administratrix of Ann Davis to
  render accounts.
- FR: summons to Andrew Owler
  administrator dbn of Jacob Screvener
  to render accounts.
  - Deputy Commissary says "wrong
    person".
  To be struck off.

44:323
- FR: summons to Catharine Norris
  administratrix of William Norris to
  render accounts.
- FR: summons to Isabella Richardson
  executrix of William Richardson to
  render accounts. To be struck off.
- FR: summons to Margaret & Jacob Ross
  administrators of Nicholas Rope to
  render accounts.
- FR: summons to Sarah Johnson
  administratrix of Thomas Johnson to
  render accounts. To be struck off.
- FR: summons to Edward Perkison
  administrator dbn of Joseph West to
  render accounts. Final accounts
  exhibited. To be struck off.
- FR: summons to Stephen William
  Watson executor of David Watson to
  render accounts. Final accounts
  exhibited. To be struck off.
- FR: summons to Amos & John McGingley
  executors of James McGingley to
  render accounts.
- FR: summons to Mary Laurence
  executrix of George Laurence to
  render accounts.
- FR: summons to David Hunter
  administrator of Anthony Hunter to
  render accounts.
- FR: summons to Abraham Hayter &
  Andrew Parker administrators of
  Joseph Parker to render accounts.
  Final accounts exhibited. To be
  struck off.
- FR: summons to Henrietta Nowland
  administratrix of Daniel Nowland to
  render accounts.
- FR: Charles Harden <nothing else>.

44:324
- BA: summons to William Harriot
  administrator of Susannah Harriot to

Page 81

render accounts.

- BA: summons to Andrew Stigar administrator of Jacob Rock to render accounts.
- BA: summons to Philip Deaver executor of Richard Miller to render accounts.
- BA: summons to John Hammond Dorsey administrator of William Gough to render accounts.
- BA: summons to Benjamin Jones administrator of Charles Jones to render accounts.
- BA: summons to Margaret Brown administratrix of Absalom Brown to render accounts.
- BA: summons to Mary Skipton administratrix of John Skipton to render accounts.
- BA: summons to Hen. Oram & Ann Statia Oram executors of Daring Haws to render accounts.
- BA: summons to Daniel Chamier administrator of Rowland Carnan to render accounts.
- BA: summons to Magdalen Tropolate administratrix of Abraham Tripolite to render accounts.
- BA: summons to John Anderson administrator of Hugh Orr to render accounts. Accounts exhibited. Estate is overpaid. To be struck off.
- BA: summons to Hannah Webster administratrix of John Webster (son of Samuel) to render accounts. Final accounts exhibited. To be struck off.
- BA: summons to Peter Carlisle executor of Rachel Wilmot to render accounts.
- 44:325 • BA: summons to Sarah Johns administratrix of Acquila Johns to render accounts.
- BA: summons to Benjamin Rogers administrator of William Rogers to render accounts.
- BA: summons to Daniel McGhee & his wife Sarah administrators of Edward Hall to render accounts.
- BA: summons to Broad Coal administrator of Ann Broad to render

accounts.

- BA: summons to Sarah Dunn executrix of Robert Dunn to render accounts.
- BA: summons to Ann McGavaran executrix of John McGavaran to render accounts. To be struck off.
- BA: summons to Elisabeth Bond executrix of William Bond to render accounts. Accounts exhibited. To be struck off.
- BA: summons to John Armstrong executor of Elisabeth Chapman to render accounts.
  - Said John Armstrong deposed that there is only 1 bond outstanding due to (N) Dorsey who refuses to deliver.

To be struck off.

- BA: summons to Robert Davis administrator of Mary Davis to render accounts.
- BA: summons to David Dickson administrator of James Dickson to render accounts. To be struck off.
- BA: summons to Samuel Purveyance, Jr. administrator of James Gibson to render accounts.
- BA: summons to William Lynch administrator of Thomas Sheredine to render accounts. To be struck off.

44:326
- BA: summons to Jacob Giles administrator of Gilbert Donohoe to render accounts.
- BA: summons to Hellen Gilchrist executrix of Robert Gilchrist to render accounts.
- BA: summons to Ann & William Partridge administrators of Daubne Buckley Partridge to render accounts.
- BA: summons to Greenbury Dorsey & his wife Sophia administratrix of John Clark to render accounts.
- BA: summons to Eleanor Payne executrix of William Payne to render accounts. To be struck off.
- BA: summons to Henry Reston executor of Renaldo Monk to render accounts.
- BA: summons to Henry Stevenson & William Smith administrators of William Govane to render accounts.
- BA: summons to Alexander Wells

administrator of James Wells to
render accounts. Final accounts
exhibited. To be struck off.

- BA: summons to Cornelia Orrick
administratrix of John Orrick to
render accounts.
- BA: summons to James Giles & his
wife Ann executrix of Edward Fell to
render accounts.
- BA: Cham. for Felix Oneal
administrator vs. T.J. for James
Kelley. Libel, answer. Summons
regarding revoking LoA.
- BA: Charles Gorsuch vs. will of
Elisha Hall. Will, caveat.

44:327
- AA: summons to Ann Hammond & Hen.
Griffith executors of John Hammond
to render accounts. To be struck
off.
- AA: summons to Susannah Johns
administratrix of Kinsey Johns to
render accounts. To be struck off.
- AA: attachment to Maj. Charles
Hammond executor of Philip Hammond
to render accounts.
- AA: summons to Ann Thomas executrix
of Philip Thomas to render accounts.
To be struck off.
- AA: summons to Elisabeth, Samuel,
Thomas, & John Snowden executors of
Richard Snowden to render accounts.
To be struck off.
- AA: summons to Robert Johnson & his
wife Ann administratrix of John
Golder to render accounts.
- AA: summons to Eleanor Wright
executrix of Rezin Wright to render
accounts. Final accounts exhibited.
To be struck off.
- AA: attachment to John Clapham
(sheriff, AA) for contempt in not
bringing in Eleanor Wright. To be
struck off.
- AA: summons to Richard Welsh & his
wife Lydia administratrix of Thomas
Medcalf to render accounts. To be
struck off.
- AA: summons to Mary Wayman
administratrix of Edward Wayman to
render accounts.
- AA: summons to John & Charles
Worthington executors of John

Worthington to render accounts.

— Said Charles Worthington deposed that Samuel & Vachel Worthington refuse to sign inventory as relations.

44:328 • AA: summons to Isabella Franklin administratrix of Robert Franklin to render accounts.

• AA: summons to Ely & Thomas Beal Dorsey administrators dbn of Edward Dorsey, Esq. to render accounts.

• AA: summons to Ely & Thomas Beal Dorsey administrators of Henrietta Maria Dorsey to render accounts.

• AA: summons to Samuel & John Howard executors of Samuel Howard to render accounts.

• AA: summons to Amos Riggs administrator dbn of John Riggs to render accounts.

• AA: summons to Amos Riggs administrator of Mary Riggs to render accounts.

• AA: summons to Benjamin Hood administrator of James Hood to render accounts.

• AA: summons to Henry Oneal Welsh administrator dbn of Thomas King to render accounts.

• AA: attachment to Samuel & Benjamin Lane administrators of Thomas Lane to render accounts.

• AA: Comfort Pounds vs. Nicholas Maccubbin administrator of Robert Kelleson. Summons to defendant to render accounts.

• AA: attachment to John Gaither (AA) & Edward Gaither (FR) administrators of Sarah Gaither to render accounts. Accounts exhibited. To be struck off.

• AA: summons to Knighton Simmons executor of George Simmons to render accounts. Final accounts exhibited. To be struck off.

• AA: attachment to James Brown executor of Robert Brown to render accounts.

44:329 • AA: attachment to Lewis Duval & his wife Alice & Francis Sappington executors of Mark Brown to render accounts.

Court Session: 12 November 1771

- AA: summons to Charles Pettibone administrator dbn of Philip Pettibone to render accounts.
- AA: summons to Bethridge Jones administratrix of William Jones to render accounts. Accounts exhibited. To be struck off.
- AA: summons to Valentine Brown administrator of Stephen Parnal to render accounts.
- AA: summons to Mary Campbell administratrix of Alexander Campbell to render accounts.
- AA: summons to Frederick Mills & his wife Acksa administratrix of Caleb Conner to render accounts. Papers in hands of Robert Norris.
- AA: attachment to Samuel Jacob administrator of John Jackson to render accounts. Final accounts exhibited. To be struck off.
- AA: summons to John Trott administrator of Jacob French to render accounts.
- AA: summons to Frances Sappington executrix of Thomas Sappington to render accounts.

Court Session: 10 January 1772

44:330 Docket:
- CH: Walter Truman Stoddert & his wife Margaret vs. William Cooke for Priscilla Smallwood & William Smallwood administrators of Bayne Smallwood. Summons to defendants to render inventory. Leter of excuse filed.
- AA: John Shaw vs. John Davis executor of William Worthing. Summons to defendant to render accounts. Summons to William Worthington to testify for plaintiff.
  - Said John Davis deposed that inventory is incomplete.
  To be struck off.
- BA: Job Garretson vs. Thomas Jones. Summons to defendant to show cause why LoA on estate of Samuel Groome should not be revoked.

44:331 10 January. Deputy Commissaries to examine accounts of:
- BA: John Wheeler executor of Samuel White.

16 January.
- QA: Gideon Emory executor of Thomas Emory.
- TA: Peter Denny & Henry Bowdle executors of Thomas Skinner.
- WO: Elisabeth Long administratrix of John Long.

17 January.
- QA: William Mumford & his wife Rachel & Thomas McCosh executors of Samuel McCosh.
- KE: John Curry & Eleanor Curry executors of William Grant.

22 January.
- SO: George Waters executor of John Waters.
- SO: George Kibble executor of William Kibble.
- SO: James Bounds executor of Jonathan Bounds.

12 February.
- BA: Ann & William Partridge administrators of Daub. B. Partridge.

18 February.
- QA: Thomas Hardcastle & John Smyth executors of Benjamin Endsworth.

21 February.
- BA: James Hutcheson administrator of John Polston.

22 February.
- TA: Mary Sluth administratrix of Simon Stephens Miller.

26 February.
- KE: Mary Garnett administratrix of Thomas Garnett.
- KE: Mary McHard administratrix of Samuel McHard.
- QA: David Davis & his wife Sophia executrix of Benjamin Roberts.
- CH: Edward Smool administrator of Posthuma Groves.
- CH: Gerrard Fowke administrator of Robert Hanson.
- CH: Gerrard Fowke administrator of Ann Hutcheson.
- CH: Ann Price administratrix of William Price.

- CH: Frances & Thomas Maddox executors of Benjamin Maddox.

27 February.
- QA: William Newman, Jr. & his wife Elisabeth administratrix of Nathaniel Comegys.
- SO: Isaac Green executor of Richard Green.
- SO: Sophia Wright executrix of Zebulon Wright.

1 March.
- petition of Charles Gordon, Esq. (KE). Administration bond on estate of Thomas Elliott assigned to petitioner.
- TA: Thomas Scott & his wife Jane administratrix of John Dobson.

44:332 2 March.
- petition of Thomas Gilpin (KE). Administration bond on estate of John Buckingham assigned to petitioner.
- petition of John Tillotson (QA). Administration bond on estate of James Williams assigned to petitioner.
- BA: William Lynch administrator of Thomas Sheridan.
- WO: Smith Frame executor of Nathan Frame.
- QA: Christopher Cox & William Price administrators of Thomas Cox.
- QA: Frances Spry administratrix of George Spry.
- SO: Joy Wolston executor of Boaz Wolston.
- BA: Thomas Constable administrator of James Kensey.
- petition of John Clements & his wife (CH). Administration bond on estate of Charles Saunders assigned to petitioners.

5 March.
- BA: Isaac Whitacre executor of John Swynard.

6 March.
- KE: William Hazel administrator of Sarah Hazel.

7 March.
- BA: Mark Alexander administrator of Benjamin Cooke.
- BA: Jos. & Thomas Burgess executors

Court Session: 1772

of Hugh Burgess.
9 March.
- WO: Howel Gladen & his wife Sarah administratrix of John Stockley.
- WO: James Broadwater & his wife Betty executors of Peter Corbin.
- WO: James Stevenson executor of Samuel Stevenson.
- WO: Daniel Hall executor of John Hall.
- WO: Levy Beachford & his wife Sara administratrix of Solomon Milbourn.
- WO: Peggy Claywell administratrix of Solomon Claywell.
- QA: Nathan Harrington executor of Barbary Richardson.
- QA: John Sutton & his wife Margaret administratrix of John Mumford.
- QA: Vaughan Jump & his wife Sarah administratrix of Richard Hammond.
10 March.
- Vaughan Jump & his wife Sarah administratrix of Robert Cade.
- petition of Thomas Bowles (FR). Administration bond on estate of Jos. Parke assigned to petitioner.
- FR: Rebecca Perry & James Owen Perry executors of James Perry.
- BA: Andrew Stigar administrator of Jacob Rock.
- BA: Elisabeth Wilkerson administratrix of John Wilkerson.
11 March.
- BA: Carolina Orrick administratrix of John Orrick.
13 March.
- KE: Sarah Browning executrix of Wrightson Browning.
- KE: John Vansant executor of Joshua Vansant.
14 March.
- SM: Barnet White Barber executor of Edward Barber.
- CH: Thomas Smith administrator of James Smith.
- SO: Joshua Hitch administrator of Joseph Hitch.
16 March.
- CH: Elisabeth Stoddert administratrix of William Truman Stoddert.
- SO: Ann Moore administratrix of

44:333

Thomas Moore.
- SO: Newton Bailey administratrix of George Bailey.

17 March.
- FR: Robert Peters administrator of Charles Watts.
- FR: Robert Peters administrator of Ignatius Simpson.

19 March.
- QA: Ann & Arthur Emory executors of John Emory.

23 March.
- KE: Rudolph Moore administrator of Henry Moore.
- KE: Hannah Smith administratrix of Jonathan Smith.
- KE: Isaac Hackett executor of James Hackett.
- KE: Ann Tuckerman administratrix of Joseph Tuckerman.
- KE: Sarah Piner administratrix of Thomas Piner.
- KE: Martha Magruder administratrix of Hezekiah Magruder.
- PG: David Marlow administrator of Samuel Middle. Marlow.
- PG: Sarah Elson administratrix of William Elson.
- PG: James Wilson administrator of William Wilson.
- PG: Ann & Rebecca Marlow executrices of Ralph Marlow.
- PG: Joseph Peach administrator of John Peach.
- CE: Elisabeth Lathom administratrix of John Manly.

24 March.
- KE: John & Samuel Wallis administrator of Hugh Wallis.

27 March.
- CV: Priscilla Hardesty executrix of Mary Lacorure.
- CV: William Sewall administrator of Edward Wilson.
- QA: Thomas Hayes administrator of James Clow.
- QA: James Miller administrator of John Clayland.
- QA: Thomas Cunningham & his wife Hannah executrix of Elbert Reed.

44:334 <u>24 January</u>. Jos. Nicholson (KE) exhibited:
- bond of Samuel West administrator of Elisabeth McDermok. Sureties: Isaac Perkins, William St. Clair. Date: 20 December 1771.
- bond of James Davis administrator of Phillip Davis. Sureties: Solomon Semons, Henry Semons. Date: 20 December 1772 [!].
- bond of Mary Hynson administratrix of Charles Hynson. Sureties: Andrew Hynson, James Hynson, Jr. Date: 20 January 1772.
- bond of John Page administrator of Alexander McLane. Sureties: Joh. Page, John Moore. Date: 20 January 1772.
- will of Jane Brown.
- inventory of Joshua Vansant.
- inventory of Thomas Kennard.
- LoD on estate of George Garnett.

Thomas Holbrook (SO) exhibited:
- will of Thomas Linzey, constituting David Linzey executor. Said executor was granted administration. Sureties: William Langford, Nehemiah Turpin. Date: 21 November 1771.

44:335
- will of Elisabeth Turpin. Also, bond of John Turpin administrator. Sureties: Nehemiah Turpin, Jesse Lister. Date: 20 November 1771.
- bond of Nelly Bozman administratrix of Nehemiah Bozman. Sureties: John Lowes, David Walker. Date: 3 December 1771.
- bond of Mary Smith administratrix of Charles Smith. Sureties: Samuel Townsend, George Dashiell. Date: 18 December 1772 [!].
- will of Thomas Covington.
- inventory of Elijah Connor.
- inventory of William Robertson.
- final accounts on estate of George Lewis Gastineau.
- final accounts on estate of Richard Stevens Bounds.
- final accounts on estate of William Bouth.
- final accounts on estate of William Kinney.

John Bracco (TA) exhibited:
- bond of Thomas Jenkins administrator of Peter Holt. Sureties: Chris. Birkhead, Peter Stevens. Date: 14 January 1772.

44:336
- bond of Lurena Jenkins administratrix of Thomas Jenkins, Jr. Sureties: William Sharp, Samuel Sharpe. Date: 16 December 1771.
- bond of Stephen Darden & Joseph Darden administrators of Mary Darden. Sureties: Lodman Elbert, Henry Martin. Date: 31 December 1771.
- will of William Harrison Brook.
- will of Thomas Martin.
- will of Elisabeth Thomas.
- will of Hugh Lynch.
- inventory of Lambert Booker.

2 March. Thomas Wright (g, QA) exhibited:
- will of Charles Bradley, constituting Nathaniel Bradley executor. Said executor was granted administration. Sureties: Ezekiel Hunter, John Casson. Date: 10 January 1772.
- bond of Gregory & Josiah Smith administrators dbn of James Dolan. Sureties: John Anderson, Daniel Ford. Date: 4 January 1771.
- bond of John Kerr administrator of Risden Smith. Sureties: Thomas Baker, Jacob Seth. Date: 2 January 1772.

44:337
- bond of Mary Ann Wright administratrix of Edward Wright (son of Nathaniel). Sureties: John Atkinson, Benjamin Elliott. Date: 12 December 1772 [!].
- bond of Elisabeth Collins administratrix of Mathew Collins. Sureties: Benjamin Earle, John Austin. Date: 4 November 1771.
- bond of Hester Heath administratrix of William Heath. Sureties: George Wharton, Andrew Graham. Date: 12 December 1772 [!].
- bond of Josiah Smith administrator of Rebecka Dolan. Sureties: John Anderson, John Smith. Date: 4

January 1772.

- bond of Turbutt Wright administrator of George Garnett. Sureties: John Crawford, Thomas Wright. Date: 6 January 1772.
- bond of Robert Smith executor of Rebecka Barnett (alias Barbara Barnett). Sureties: William Meredith, James Smith. Date: 13 January 1772.
- bond of Ruth Sparks administratrix of Absalom Sparks. Sureties: Joseph Brown, Caleb Sparks. Date: 13 January 1772.
- bond of Sophia May administratrix of Edward May. Sureties: George Elliott, John Smith. Date: 10 January 1772.
- bond of Aaron Floyd administrator of Solomon Cooper. Sureties: Thomas Hardcastle, John Casson. Date: 24 January 1772.
- bond of Edward Pinder administrator of William Pinder. Sureties: Walter Nevil, Isaac Ford. Date: 14 January 1772.

44:338
- bond of John Dames & John Chaires administrators of William Dames. Sureties: Joseph Chaires, John Kent. Date: 24 January 1772.
- bond of Elisabeth Harris administratrix of William Harris. Sureties: Samuel Keene, John Keene. Date: 16 January 1772.
- will of Rachel Chance, constituting William Boon executor. Said executor was granted administration. Sureties: Jacob Boone, Joseph Talbot. Date: 10 January 1772.
- will of Boon Chance. Also, bond of William Boon administrator. Sureties: Joseph Talbott, Jacob Boon. Date: 10 January 1771.
- will of Michael Green.
- will of Sarah Baker.
- will of John Wheatley.
- will of David Simm.
- will of George Phillips.
- will of Richard Gafford.
- will of Rebecka Cahill.
- inventory of William Hughlett.
- inventory of John Spiers.

- inventory of Solomon Jadwin.
- inventory of Daniel Wilcocks.
- inventory of William Busley.
- inventory of David Herring.
- inventory of Hawkins Downes.
- inventory of Sarah Goodman.
- inventory of John Smith.
- accounts on estate of John Redue.
- accounts on estate of John Young.
- final accounts on estate of John Spiers.
- final accounts on estate of John Massey.

44:339
- final accounts on estate of John Beall.
- final accounts on estate of John Williams.
- final accounts on estate of Nathaniel Wright.
- final accounts on estate of John Smith (Long Neck).

Thomas Bowles (g, FR) exhibited:
- will of William Coughran, constituting James Coughran & William Coughran executors. Said executors were granted administration. Sureties: Samuel Emmitt, Samuel Carrick. Date: 15 January 1772.
- bond of Samuel Swearingen administrator of Kenedy Ferrall. Sureties: Simon Nichols, Thomas Price. Date: 23 January 1772.
- bond of Anna Maria Coonce & Adam Coonce administrators of Nicholas Coonce. Sureties: Adam Link, Valentine Mokeall. Date: 18 February 1772.
- bond of Ann Cason administratrix of John Cason. Sureties: George Mundock, Christian Kemp. Date: 8 January 1772.
- inventory of Rudolp Kellar.
- inventory of William Maccatee.

44:340
- inventory of George Clem.
- inventory of Jacob Ault.
- inventory of Daniel Zacharias.
- final accounts on estate of Notley Thomas.
- final accounts on estate of Laurence Sprotsman.

Court Session: 1772

Walter Hanson (g, CH) exhibited:
- will of Frances Oden, constituting Jonathan Oden executor. Said executor was granted administration. Sureties: Thomas Hunt, Thomas Davis. Date: 24 January 1772.
- will of Humphry Berry, constituting Anne Berry executrix. Said executrix was granted administration. Sureties: James Roby (son of John), William Smallwood. Date: 21 January 1772.
- bond of Basil Payne administrator of William Payne. Sureties: James Murphy, Edward Newman. Date: 20 January 1772.
- bond of Frances Clinkscales administratrix of John Clinkscales. Sureties: William Franklin, Zephania Franklin. Date: 30 December 1771.
- will of John Lucraft.
- will of James Waters.
- will of James Neale.
- will of Ann Right.
- will of John Wedding.
- inventory of William Brooke.
- inventory of George Scrogen.
- inventory of Elisabeth Clements.
- inventory of John Lomax.
- accounts on estate of Charles Rock.
- accounts on estate of Basil Brook.
- accounts on estate of John Farris.

4 March. Thomas Holbrook (g, SO) exhibited:
- will of Solomon Long. Also, bond of David Long & Solomon Long administrators. Sureties: Zorobable King, John King. Date: 18 February 1772.
- will of George Gale, constituting Levin Gale executor. Said executor was granted administration. Sureties: Ephraim King, Henry Jackson. Date: 11 January 1772.
- will of Stephen Hopkins, constituting Richard Hopkins executor. Said executor was granted administration. Sureties: Samuel McClaster, Samuel Townshend. Date: 22 January 1772.
- will of Sarah Dowdle.

44:341

- inventory of Christopher Dowdle.
- inventory of Thomas Dowdle.

44:342 5 March. Col. William Young (BA) exhibited:
- will of Bulcher Myer, constituting Frederick Myer & John Stoler executors. Said executors were granted administration. Sureties: Jacob Sheypot, John Sligh. Date: 24 January 1772.
- will of Phillip Headshoe, constituting Catharine Headshoe & Frederick Myer executors. Said executors were granted administration. Sureties: William Clowse, Frederick Coal. Date: 24 January 1772.
- will of Phillip Hur. Also, bond of Anna Maria Hur administratrix. Sureties: Michael Henry, Henry Weartime. Date: 24 January 1772.
- bond of George Woolsey administrator of Susanna Bryan (alias Susanna Shink). Sureties: Jonathan Plowman, Benjamin Howard. Date: 24 January 1772.
- bond of Benjamin Robinson administrator of John Chew. Surety: Samuel Bungay. Date: 24 January 1772.
- bond of Alexander McIntre administrator of James Kilpatrick. Sureties: James Armstrong, Robert McDowall. Date: 23 January 1772.
- bond of Jonathan Plowman administrator of Thomas Norris. Sureties: Joseph Norris, Edward Norris (son of Jos.). Date: 11 January 1772.
- bond of Sophia Wright administratrix of Nathan Wright. Sureties: John Rutledge, John Hendrickson. Date: 2 January 1772.

44:343
- inventory of Thomas Baily.
- inventory of Samuel Hughs.
- inventory of Mary Sinklar.
- inventory of John Parker.
- additional accounts on estate of William Grafton.
- final accounts on estate of John Hatton.

- final accounts on estate of Edward Flanagan.

<u>10 March.</u> Benton Harris (g, WO) exhibited:
- bond of William Truitt executor of Mary Truitt. Sureties: Schoolfield Parker, Benjamin Purnell. Date: 25 October 1771.
- bond of Anne Windsor administratrix of John Windsor. Sureties: Thomas Jones, Phillip Windsor. Date: 11 October 1771.
- bond of William Spear administrator of John Shores. Sureties: John Spear, Henry Spear. Date: 11 November 1771.
- nuncupative will of Daniel Young. Also, bond of Ezekiel Young administrator. Sureties: James Smith, William Pitts. Date: 4 October 1771.

44:344
- will of Thomas Flint, constituting Sarah Flint executrix. Said executrix was granted administration. Sureties: Jonathan Cathell, Edmund N. Nelms. Date: 6 November 1771.
- will of James Hayman, constituting Margarett Hayman executrix. Said executrix was granted administration. Sureties: John Hayman, David Hayman. Date: 4 October 1771.
- will of Isaac Morris, constituting Luke Morris & George Hayward executors. Said executors were granted administration. Sureties: Samuel Wise, Yelverton Probart. Date: 2 November 1772 [!].
- will of Henry Spears.
- will of Priscilla Austin.
- will of Jos. Timmons.
- will of Levin Harvey.
- will of Mary Townshend.
- inventory of Stephen Hall.
- inventory of William Willett.
- inventory of Palmer Spaight.
- inventory of William Stevenson.
- inventory of Nathan Frame.
- inventory of Isaac Pain.
- inventory of Samuel Stevenson.

Court Session: 1772

- inventory of John Calloway.
- additional inventory of John Talbot.
- LoD on estate of Comfort Atkinson.
- final accounts on estate of John Thompson.
- final accounts on estate of Jephah Purnall.
- final accounts on estate of Phillip Connoway.
- final accounts on estate of Littleton Brown.
- final accounts on estate of Comfort Atkinson.
- final accounts on estate of John Talbot.

44:345
- final accounts on estate of John Smith.
- final accounts on estate of John Finissey.
- final accounts on estate of George Parson.
- final accounts on estate of Elisha Evans.
- final accounts on estate of John Henderson.

23 March. William T. Wootton (g, PG) exhibited:
- will of Christopher Edeline, constituting Jane Edeline & John Edeline executors. Said executors were granted administration. Sureties: Thomas Edeline, Edward Jenkins. Date: 20 December 1771.
- bond of Mary Wells administratrix of William Wells. Sureties: Thomas Frazier, Isaac Smith. Date: 26 February 1772.
- bond of Henry Hilleary, Jr. administrator of Thomas Hilleary, Jr. Sureties: Henry Hilleary, Sr., Thomas Williams. Date: 9 March 1772.
- will of Ann Newton.
- will of Samuel Low.
- inventory of Ralph Marlow.
- inventory of Edward McDonald.
- additional inventory of William Wilson.

44:346 Jos. Nicholson (KE) exhibited:
- bond of Hannah Reed & Samuel Reed

Court Session: 1772

executors of John Reed. Sureties:
Kinvin Wroth, Richard Willis. Date:
2 March 1772.
- will of Dorothy Hodges. Also, bond
of William Hodges administrator.
Sureties: William Ringgold, Jr.,
Daniel Farrel. Date: 3 March 1772.
- will of Robert Meeks, constituting
Mary Meeks executrix. Said
executrix was granted
administration. Sureties: Thomas
Bowers, William Cowardine. Date: 18
February 1772.
- will of John Donaldson, constituting
John Maxwell executor. Said
executor was granted administration.
Sureties: Cornelius Vansant, John
Lamb. Date: 5 March 1772.
- bond of William Hodges administrator
of Samuel Hodges. Sureties:
Lovering Merrill, Thomas Slipper.
Date: 19 February 1772.
- bond of Ann Kinnard administratrix
of John Kinnard. Sureties: Richard
Willis, Daniel Kinnard. Date: 16
January 1772.
- bond of Ann Piner administratrix of
James Piner. Sureties: William
Ringgold, William Geddes. Date: 22
February 1772.
- bond of Jonathan Roberts
administrator of Alban Roberts.
Sureties: Emory Sudler, Richard
Frisby. Date: 18 March 1772.
44:347 • bond of Nathaniel Howell
administrator of John Howell, Jr.
Sureties: Benjamin Howard, William
Howell. Date: 17 March 1772.
- bond of John Earle & Mary Earle
administrators of John Dougherty.
Sureties: Benjamin Earle, J. E.
Bruff. Date: 12 February 1772.
- will of Hance Blackiston.
- will of Frederick Hanson.
- inventory of John Sharpe.
- inventory of Ann Blackiston.
- inventory of John Ambrose.
- inventory of John Spencer.
- inventory of Martha Hynson.
- additional inventory of James
Thomas.
- inventory of William Frisby.

Page 99

- LoD on estate of Marmaduke Tilden.
- LoD on estate of William Grant.
- LoD on estate of William Frisby, Jr.
- LoD on estate of Peter Beazeley.
- accounts on estate of Marmaduke Tilden.
- accounts on estate of William Frisby, Jr.
- accounts on estate of William Grant.
- accounts on estate of Peter Beazley.

44:348 27 March. Clement Smith (g, CV) exhibited:
- will of Robert Gardner, constituting John Gardner & Kinsey Gardner executors. Said executors were granted administration. Sureties: John Gray, John Cullumber. Date: 2 January 1772.
- will of James John Mackall, constituting John Mackall executor. Said executor was granted administration. Sureties: Edward Reynolds, John Manning. Date: 21 January 1772.
- bond of Benjamin Wood administrator of Edward Wood. Sureties: Leonard Wood, John Standforth. Date: 1 January 1772.
- bond of Benjamin Skinner administrator of Thomas Woodard Taylor. Sureties: William Ireland, Jr., William Lyles. Date: 9 March 1772.
- inventory of David Slator.
- inventory of Catherine Sedwick.
- inventory of Richard Blake.
- inventory of Ann Taylor.
- inventory of John Specknoll.
- inventory of Mary Laurence.
- inventory of John Lovell.
- inventory of John Rooney.
- inventory of James Birmintine.
- inventory of William Sansbury.
- inventory of John Griffith.
- accounts on estate of Ann Brooke.

44:349 11 April. Benton Harris (g, WO) exhibited:
- bond of Luke Townsend executor of Mary Townsend. Sureties: William Lathinghouse, John Chamber Crapper.

Date: 11 December 1771.
- bond of William Spears executor of William Spears. Sureties: John Spears, Henry Spears. Date: 12 December 1771.
- bond of Mathias Austin administrator of Priscilla Austin. Sureties: Samuel Davis, David Vane. Date: 11 December 1771.
- will of Lemuel Purnell, constituting Dennis Purnell & William Purnell executors. Said executors were granted administration. Sureties: John Rosse, James Martin. Date: 23 March 1772.
- will of Graves Bashaw. Also, bond of Robert King administrator. Sureties: Joshua Sturgis, Jeremiah Morris. Date: 29 February 1772.
- will of Ebenezar Collings, constituting Mary Collings executrix. Said executrix was granted administration. Sureties: John Smith, Thomas Pointer. Date: 10 March 1772.
- will of William Beavens. Also, bond of Sarah Beavens executrix. Sureties: Rowland Beavins, William Beavins. Date: 3 January 1772.
- will of Sarah Warren, constituting Paroah Warren executor. Said executor was granted administration. Sureties: John Postly, Solomon Long. Date: 10 March 1772.

44:350
- will of John Schoolfield, constituting Thomas Schoolfield executor. Said executor was granted administration. Sureties: John Richardson, Levi Richardson. Date: 4 March 1772.
- will of Purnel Fletcher Smith, constituting Sarah Smith executrix. Said executrix was granted administration. Sureties: William Fassitt, John Smith. Date: 13 December 1771.
- will of Levi Hopkins, constituting Margaret Hopkins executrix. Said executrix was granted administration. Sureties: Levin Hopkins, Leonard Johnson. Date: 3 January 1772.

- will of Isaac Brittingham, constituting Peggy Brittingham executrix. Said executrix was granted administration. Sureties: Levin Davis, Isaac Brittingham. Date: 28 February 1772.
- will of John Nairn, constituting John Drummond Marshall executor. Said executor was granted administration. Sureties: Littleton Davis, Joseph Schoolfeild. Date: 11 December 1771.
- will of Jane Irons, constituting Aaron Irons executor. Said executor was granted administration. Sureties: Samuel Powell, Thomas Godwin. Date: 3 January 1772.
- will of James Houston, constituting Mary Houston executrix. Said executrix was granted administration. Sureties: Littleton Dennis, Littleton Long. Date: 3 March 1772.
- will of Daniel Godwin, constituting Mary Godwin executrix. Said executrix was granted administration. Sureties: Samuel Hill, Joshua Hill. Date: 11 December 1771.
- will of John Handy, constituting Benjamin Handy executor. Said executor was granted administration. Sureties: Thomas Martin, Patrick Glasgow. Date: 7 March 1772.

44:351
- will of William Smock, constituting Mary Smock executrix. Said executrix was granted administration. Sureties: Hammond Reynolds, Ezekiel Porter. Date: 21 February 1772.
- will of George Parker, constituting Jacob Parker executor. Said executor was granted administration. Sureties: Elisha Parker, James Purdue. Date: 21 March 1772.
- bond of Caleb Whyatt administrator of William Wyatt. Sureties: John Postly, John Hudson. Date: 17 March 1772.
- bond of John Postly administrator of William Warren. Sureties: David Hudson, Caleb Wyat. Date: 17 March

1772.

- bond of Mary Nicholson administratrix of Josep Nicholson. Sureties: William Lane, Solomon Brittingham. Date: 17 January 1772.
- bond of Catharine Harper administratrix of John Harper. Sureties: Samuel Adams, Levin Hopkins. Date: 27 December 1771.
- bond of Turvill Gladstone administrator of Obediah Gladstone. Sureties: John Rackcliff, John Selby. Date: 3 January 1772.
- bond of Elisabeth Ennis administratrix of Charles Ennis. Sureties: Elijah Laws, Thomas Cottingham. Date: 3 March 1772.

44:352

- bond of Sarah Polk administratrix of James Polk. Sureties: Nehemiah Staton, Obediah Smith. Date: 4 March 1772.
- inventory of John Windsor.
- inventory of John Shore.
- inventory of Henry Spears.
- inventory of Jane Irons.
- inventory of Martin Kennett.
- inventory of John Long.
- inventory of Cornelius Kollock.
- inventory of Isaac Morris.
- inventory of Thomas Milbourne.
- inventory of John Timmons.
- inventory of Samuel Nicholson.
- inventory of Levin Fassitt.
- inventory of Joseph Nicholson.
- inventory of Samuel Richardson.
- final accounts on estate of Thomas Milbourne.
- final accounts on estate of Henry Sheldon.
- final accounts on estate of William Hayman.
- final accounts on estate of Levin Dickeson.
- final accounts on estate of Solomon Walton.
- final accounts on estate of Charles Cottingham.
- final accounts on estate of Samuel Richardson.
- final accounts on estate of Gideon Tilghman.

Court Session: 1772

44:353 27 March. Deputy Commissaries to examine accounts of:
- QA: William Harrington executor of William Harrington.
- PG: Elisabeth Osbourne administratrix of Robert Osbourne.
- PG: Cloe Walker administratrix of Robert Walker.
- PG: Eleanor Tree administratrix of John Tree.

31 March.
- QA: Samuel Brown administrator dbn of Andrew Hall.
- QA: Thomas Smith & his wife Mary administratrix of James Ruth.
- QA: Benjamin Toalson administrator of James Toalson.
- QA: William Elliot executor of William Elliot.

1 April.
- DO: Robertson Stevens executor of Josias Mace.
- FR: Eve BomGardner, Daniel Steiniffer, & John Mostane executors of Everhart BomGardner.
- FR: Charles Engell & Michael Kibles administrators of George Haun.

2 April.
- CE: Jane Corbit administratrix of James Corbit.

4 April.
- CH: Josias Hawkins administrator of Henry Hawkins.
- SM: John Goldsmith & his wife Mary administratrix of John Fanning.
- SM: Jane Barnhouse executrix of Richard Barnhouse.
- CV: Edward Hall administrator of John Hoverton.
- CV: John & Dorcas Spicknall executors of John Spicknall.

7 April.
- QA: John Young executor of John Young.

8 April.
- FR: Joseph Cheyney & his wife Ann executrix of Ezekiel Cheyney.
- QA: Ann & Francis Bright administrators of Francis Bright.
- BA: Cassandra Wyle administratrix of Luke Wyle.

11 April.

Page 104

Court Session: 1772

- WO: Tabitha Townsend executrix of John Townsend.
- WO: Milby Atkinson & William Drummond & his wife Sarah executors of Samuel Atkinson.
- WO: Mary Nicholson administratrix of Joseph Nicholson.
- WO: Milby Atkinson administrator of Levy Atkinson.
- WO: Sarah Atkinson administratrix of Angelo Atkinson.
- WO: William Holland & his wife Mary administratrix of John Purnell.

44:354
- WO: Jos. Richards administrator of John Richards.
- FR: Henry Cock executor of Susannah Beatty.

14 April.
- SO: George Hardy administrator of Ann Hardy.
- SO: Joshua Hayman & Liddy Hayman executors of Isaac Hayman.
- SO: Ephraim King administrator of John Flewelling.
- SO: Sarah Will administratrix of Benjamin Wills.

15 April.
- CE: Mary Abbott executrix of William Abbott.
- CE: Sarah Cunningham administratrix of George Cunningham.

16 April.
- CE: John Hendrickson executor of Richard Jones.
- BA: Jane & John Strawbridge administrators of John Strawbridge.
- CE: William Withers & Sarah Pennington administrators of Abraham Pennington.
- CE: William Withers & his wife Rosannah executrix of Walter Divin.
- CE: Barbus Piner & his wife Susannah executrix of John Day.
- SM: Leonard Briscoe & Prior Theobald executors of John Theobald.
- PG: Elisabeth Pagett administratrix of John Padgett.

17 April.
- FR: Matthew Clarke administrator of Jos. Clark.
- BA: Elisabeth Gover executrix of Ephraim Gover.

Page 105

Court Session: 1772

- CE: Mary Cookrah administratrix of Moses Cookrah.
- BA: Samuel Lowry administrator of John Lowry.
- BA: Samuel Lowry administrator of Robert Lowry.

20 April.
- KE: Mary Smith executrix of John Smith.
- TA: Jane Chapman executrix of James Chapman.
- TA: Hannah Turner executrix of Edward Turner.
- KE: Samuel West administrator of Elisabeth McDermott.

21 April.
- TA: Ann Bowman executrix of Samuel Bowman.

44:355 22 April.
- SO: Joseph Humphreys executor of Thomas Humphreys.

23 April.
- SO: William Fountain executor of Mary Fountain.
- BA: Gerrard Hopkins executor of Jos. Wilson.

24 April.
- QA: John Sayer Blake executor of Matthew Bryon.
- KE: Richard Harding & his wife Mary executrix of George Perkins.
- FR: Henry Snebely administrator of James Grubb.
- FR: George Smith administrator of James Smith.
- FR: Lurana Stallings executrix of Richard Stallings.

25 April.
- KE: Ann Smith executrix of William Smith.
- KE: Andrew Hickman & his wife Elisabeth administrators of Isaac Wilson.

26 April.
- KE: John Bavington & Augustine Beedle administrators of William Bavington.

27 April.
- WO: Mathias Austin & his wife Sarah executrix of John Maglamore.
- WO: John Elzey administrator of Arnold Elzey.

- BA: William Lux executor of Nicholas Ruxton Gay.
- CE: Adam Vance administrator of James Vance.
- SM: Henrietta Ford executrix of John Ford.

28 April.
- CH: Sarah Cole executrix of James Cole.
- SM: George Slye surviving executor of John Whitenhall.

30 April.
- CH: Henry Smith Hawkins & Thomas Hawkins executors of Alexander Smith Hawkins.

1 May.
- KE: Michael Jobson executor of Dennis Shehawer.

2 May.
- SM: Thomas Fowler & his wife Elisabeth administratrix of Charles Hazelfine.
- CH: William Manbury Smallwood & his wife Grace administratrix of John Harman.
- CH: Marjory Stone executrix of Thomas Stone.

7 May.
- BA: Joseph Burgess administrator of Paul Penington.

8 May.
- FR: Jacob Young administrator of Jacob Ault.

11 May.
- SO: John Paden administrator of John Paden.
44:356
- DO: Daniel Polk executor of Robert Polk.
- DO: Ezekiel King executor of William Phillips.
- DO: James Brown administrator of John Brown.
- DO: John Brumagen administrator of John Warren.
- DO: John Fisher administrator of Alexander Morton.
- DO: Mary Ann Noble executrix of William Noble.
- DO: Rachel Williams administratrix of Edward Williams.
- DO: Moses Broadus administrator dbn of Richard Cole.

- DO: Mary Shehawn administratrix of David Shehawn.
- DO: Emanuel Manlove & his wife Betty administratrix of Robert Polk.
- DO: John Lecompt administrator of Nehemiah Lecompt.
- DO: Mathew Driver, Jr. administrator of Ramour Land.

12 May.
- DO: Nany Webb administratrix of Edgar Webb.
- QA: William Smith, James Ringgold Blunt, & James Thompson executors of John Smith.
- WO: Samuel Brittingham executor of Elijah Brittingham.

18 May.
- BA: Mary Carlisle administratrix of David Carlisle.
- petition of Thomas Kitten, Jr. (AA). Administration bond on estate of James Williams assigned to petitioner.
- KE: John Crew administrator of Edward Drugan.
- KE: Joseph Younger executor of John Younger.
- KE: Thomas Wilkins executor of Joseph Garnett.
- KE: James Edelin & his wife Susa executrix of Basil Hagan.

25 May.
- CV: George Gray administrator dbn of John Gray.
- CV: Edward Wood administrator dbn of John Sly.
- CV: John Leaveille administrator of John Leaveille.
- BA: Ann & William Partridge administrators of Daubne Buckley Partridge.

27 May.
- KE: Walter Miffling administrator of Southey Miffling.

29 May.
- TA: Elisabeth Smallwood & Hugh Rice administrators of Daniel Sherwood.
- WO: Joshua Hall & his wife Sophia & John Cord administrators of Joseph Cord.

44:357 2 April. Thomas Holbrook (g, SO) exhibited:
- will of Elias Taylor, constituting Sarah Taylor executrix. Said executrix was granted administration. Sureties: Isaac Addams, Levi Wood. Date: 10 March 1772.
- will of James Phillips, constituting Sarah Phillips executrix. Said executrix was granted administration. Sureties: John Roberson, Levin Huffington. Date: 5 March 1772.
- will of Solomon Wright, constituting Levin Wright executor. Said executor was granted administration. Sureties: William Darby, Jonathan Cordery. Date: 5 March 1772.
- bond of John Huffington administrator of John Huffington, Jr. Sureties: William Darby, John Robinson. Date: 5 March 1772.
- bond of Peter Waters administrator of Edward Waters. Sureties: Josiah Dashiell, George Hayward. Date: 20 February 1772.
- inventory of Young Magdalin [!].
- inventory of Coventon Messick.

44:358 17 April. William T. Wooton (g, PG) exhibited:
- bond of Frank Luke & George Digges administrators of Charles Digges, agreeable to Act of Assembly for sale of lands. Sureties: John Read Magruder, Richard B. Hall. Date: 25 March 1772.
- will of James Plummer, constituting Mary Plummer executrix. Said executrix was granted administration. Sureties: Daniel Clark, Thomas Ramsay Hodges. Date: 13 April 1772.
- bond of Elisabeth Green executrix of Francis Green. Sureties: William Foard, John Wynn. Date: 25 March 1772.
- bond of Sarah Cox administratrix of John Cox. Sureties: Henry Brooke, James Wilson. Date: 25 March 1772.
- bond of Nathaniel Newton

administrator of Ann Newton.
Sureties: C. Wheeler, Joseph
Nicholson. Date: 25 March 1772.
- inventory of Winefred Lanham.
- inventory of Lansolot Wilson.
- inventory of Thomas Stonestreet.
- inventory of Edward Stonestreet.
- accounts on estate of Hezekiah Magruder.
- accounts on estate of Thomas Holly.
- accounts on estate of Henry Gear.

44:359 Thomas Wright (g, QA) exhibited:
- will of Timothy Tool, constituting William Phillips executor. Said executor was granted administration. Sureties: Robert Noble, James Burk. Date: 5 March 1772.
- will of Edward Clayton, constituting Hannah Clayton executrix. Said executrix was granted administration. Sureties: Edward Chetham, James Chetham. Date: 30 March 1772.
- bond of John Walker administrator of Sarah Baker. Sureties: William Yoe, Thomas Price. Date: 27 February 1772.
- bond of Bazil Warfield administrator of George Phillips. Sureties: John Atkinson, William Hackett. Date: 27 February 1772.
- bond of Sarah Green executrix of Michael Green. Sureties: John Green, John Downing. Date: <no day given> March 1772.
- bond of John Dwiggens executor of William Webb. Sureties: Joshua Clark, Andrew Silvester. Date: 27 March 1772.
- bond of Frances Artlett administratrix of William Artlett. Sureties: James Burkett, William Rooke. Date: 13 April 1772.
- bond of Lydia Scotton administratrix of Richard Scotton. Sureties: Richard Smith, Joseph Furlaid. Date: 9 April 1772.

44:360 - bond of Elisabeth Leatherbury administratrix of Charles Leatherbury. Sureties: Thomas Vine, Abraham Roberts. Date: 9 April

1772.
- bond of James Moore administrator of Sarah Moore. Sureties: James Sparks, John Downey. Date: 6 April 1772.
- bond of William Evans administrator of William Haley. Sureties: William Cannon, John Davis, Jr. Date: 26 March 1772.
- bond of Robert Walters administrator of Ann Walters. Sureties: Ely Bishop, John Hawkins. Date: 26 March 1772.
- bond of Hannah Turner administratrix of Isaac Turner. Sureties: William Mason, Thomas Hardcastle. Date: 26 March 1772.
- bond of John Wilson administrator of Andrew Phoenix. Sureties: John Hamond, William Carradine. Date: 26 March 1772.
- bond of Robert Casson administrator of William Nutrell. Sureties: Joshua Clark, Robert Hardcastle. Date: 25 March 1772.
- bond of William Mooth administrator of Charles Warner. Sureties: George Wharton, William Young. Date: 20 February 1772.
- bond of Samuel Ridgaway administrators of William Ridgaway. Sureties: Charles Murphy, William Willcocks. Date: 24 February 1772.

44:361
- bond of William Young administrator of William Young, Jr. Sureties: William Mooth, David Preston. Date: 20 February 1772.
- will of Thomas Bruff.
- inventory of John Smith.
- inventory of Absalom Sparks.
- inventory of Rebecka Dolan.
- inventory of James Dolan.
- additional inventory of Elisabeth Elliott.
- LoD on estate of Christopher Brown.
- final accounts on estate of Thomas Edge.
- final accounts on estate of Christopher Brown.

Col. William Young (BA) exhibited:
- will of Gilbert Crocket,

constituting William Webb executor. Said executor was granted administration. Sureties: Ignatius Wheeler, Robert Bryarly. Date: 4 April 1772.

- will of William Debruller, constituting William Debruller executor. Said executor was granted administration. Sureties: William Presbury, Will. Rob. Presbury. Date: 10 March 1772.

44:362
- will of Benjamin Norris, constituting Jos. Norris executor. Said executor was granted administration. Sureties: Benjamin Burgess Cheyney, Jacob Bond, Jr. Date: 25 February 1772.

- will of Charles Robinson, constituting William Robinson executor. Said executor was granted administration. Sureties: William Robinson, Jr., Richard Robinson. Date: 23 March 1772.

- bond of William Robinson administrator of Richard Robinson. Sureties: William Robinson, Jr., Richard Robinson. Date: 23 March 1772.

- bond of Mary Jacquery Desales administratrix of Samuel Jacquery Desales. Sureties: John Willmott, John Thompson. Date: 6 March 1772.

- bond of Alexander McMechen administrator of Thomas Williamson. Surety: Gerrard Hopkins. Date: 5 March 1772.

- bond of John Sheilds administrator of James Kelley. Sureties: Nathan Johnson, John Stevenson. Date: 8 April 1772.

- bond of William Hitchcock administrator of William Hitchcock. Sureties: Alexander Rigdon, Robert Kennedy. Date: 30 March 1772.

- bond of Margret Lowry administratrix of Hugh McKenney. Surety: Robert Long. Date: 4 March 1772.

44:363
- bond of Mary Norris administratrix of Benjamin Norris. Sureties: Jacob Brown, John Taylor, Jos. Norris. Date: 24 March 1772.

- bond of Susanna Norris & Benjamin B.

Norris administrators of John
Norris. Sureties: William Smithson,
Isaac Whitaker. Date: 8 April 1772.
- bond of James Gordon administrator
of John Crook. Sureties: William
Montgomery, William Whiteford.
Date: 30 March 1772.
- nuncupative will of William
Copeland.
- will of Joseph Gates.
- inventory of James Wilson.
- inventory of James Cambley.
- inventory of Samuel Wheeler.
- inventory of Samuel Johnson.
- inventory of Benjamin Denney.
- accounts on estate of James Kinsey.
- accounts on estate of Samuel
Wheeler.
- accounts on estate of John Robson.

44:364 22 April. Thomas Holbrook (g, SO)
exhibited:
- bond of John Pullett administrator
of Sarah Dowdle. Sureties: George
Pollitt, Mathias Miles. Date: 31
March 1772.
- bond of Sarah Gray administratrix of
William Gray. Sureties: George
Pollitt, Charles Vaughan. Date: 31
March 1772.
- bond of Mary Beachamp administratrix
of Handy Beachamp. Sureties: Levin
Beauchamp, B. Davis. Date: 18 March
1772.
- bond of Isaac White administrator of
Abigal White. Sureties: David
Langford, Jesse Adams. Date: 18
March 1772.
- will of Mary Ackworth.
- inventory of Stephen Hopkins.
- inventory of James Neairn.
- inventory of John Benston.
- inventory of Thomas Linsey.
- inventory of Nehemiah Harris.
- inventory of George Balley.
- final accounts on estate of Jonathan
Bounds.

44:365 Andrew Pearce (g, CE) exhibited:
- bond of Stephen Porter executor of
Richard Porter. Sureties: James
Porter, Samuel Gillespy. Date: 17

Court Session: 1772

April 1772.

- bond of Thomas Savin administrator dbn of William Boyer Penington. Surety: William Bristow. Date: 18 March 1772.
- will of John Buckhannon. Also, bond of Samuel Shepard administrator. Sureties: Alexander Scott, Eli Alexander. Date: 21 March 1771.
- will of Robert Walmsly, constituting Allethea Walmsly & Nicholas Walmsly executors. Said executors were granted administration. Sureties: James Cosden, Alphonso Cosden. Date: 21 March 1772.
- will of John Davidge, constituting Rachel Davidge executrix. Said executrix was granted administration. Sureties: John Davidge, Nathaniel Ward. Date: 3 March 1772.
- will of Francis Fulton. Also, bond of Ann Fulton administratrix. Sureties: James Porter, William Ewing. Date: 15 March 1772.
- will of Elias Eliason, constituting Elias Eliason & Abraham Eliason executors. Said executors were granted administration. Sureties: John Eliason, Cornelius Eliason. Date: 8 August 1771.

44:366

- will of Henry Henrickson, constituting Augustine Hendrickson & John Hendrickson executors. Said executors were granted administration. Sureties: Bartholomew Etherington, John Bateman. Date: 9 April 1772.
- bond of Thomas Moore administrator of Ann Flynn. Sureties: Peter Rider, Alexander Kirk. Date: 8 May 1772 [!].
- bond of Edward Ware administrator of Jane Fryer. Sureties: Hugh Long, Hezekiah Smith. Date: 27 March 1771.
- bond of Mary Chick administratrix of Joseph Chuck. Sureties: Thomas Henderson, Jeremiah Taylor. Date: <no day or month given> 1771.
- bond of James Porter administrator of Charles Regan. Sureties: Stephen

Page 114

Court Session: 1772

Porter, Samuel Gillispy. Date: 17 April 1771.

- bond of James Hughs administrator of John McDuff. Sureties: Hugh Matthew, John Stoops. Date: 21 January 1771.
- bond of Thomas Carson administrator of Dennis Nowland. Sureties: Isaac Gibbs, Aug. Beedle. Date: 3 March 1772.
- bond of Edward Furroner & Elisabeth Furroner administrators of Edward Furroner. Sureties: James Heath, Cornelius Vansant. Date: 26 February 1772.

44:367

- bond of Elisabeth Cunning administratrix of William Cunning. Sureties: Zebulon Beaston, William Taylor. Date: 10 April 1772.
- bond of Lydia Eliason administratrix of John Eliason. Sureties: Joshua Donoho, Abraham Eliason. Date: 27 March 1772.
- bond of Mary Beard & Lewis Beard administrators of Thomas Beard, Jr. Sureties: Benjamin Nowland, James Beard. Date: 3 April 1772.
- bond of John Hodgson administrator of Phenias Hodgson. Sureties: John Macky, Hugh Gay. Date: 15 May 1771.
- bond of Gavin Hamilton administrator of Robert Ramsay. Surety: J. Hughes. Date: 9 October 1771.
- bond of Rosanna Scott & Adam Vance administrators of James Scott. Sureties: William Clark, Robert Whitesides. Date: 14 August 1771.
- bond of Elisabeth Latham & Joseph Ensor administrators of John Latham. Sureties: Peter Rider, Hyland Prig. Date: 6 October 1771.
- bond of William West administrator of William Makin. Sureties: G. Milligan, George Ffrisby. Date: 30 September 1771.

44:368

- will of Thomas Savin.
- will of Jacob Jacobs.
- will of Dorothy Roberts.
- inventory of Matthew Thompson.
- inventory of James Corbit.
- inventory of Ann Flynn.
- inventory of John Eliason.

- inventory of D. McDermott.
- inventory of Thomas Beard, Jr.
- inventory of James Ashton Bayard.
- inventory of Sarah Chew.
- inventory of Gaving Hutcheson.
- inventory of William Cunning.
- inventory of Jane Fryer.
- inventory of Richard Whelch.
- inventory of Joseph Chisel.
- inventory of Amos Evans.
- inventory of William Calender.
- inventory of William Bavington.
- inventory of Francis Rock.
- inventory of Isaac Benson.
- inventory of Robert Ramsey.
- inventory of John Lewis.
- inventory of Charles Rigan.
- inventory of William Makin.
- inventory of Phenias Hodgkin.

44:369
- LoD on estate of William Bavington.
- LoD on estate of William Makin.
- LoD on estate of Isaac Benson.
- LoD on estate of James Ashton Bayard.
- LoD on estate of John Glasgow.
- final accounts on estate of Ann Oldham.
- final accounts on estate of Amos Evans.
- final accounts on estate of Michael Manycousins.
- final accounts on estate of Michael Manycousins, Jr.
- final accounts on estate of Edward Oldham.
- final accounts on estate of John Hyland.
- final accounts on estate of John Beedle.
- final accounts on estate of Fra. Rock.
- final accounts on estate of Benjamin Elliott.
- final accounts on estate of Hannah Ward.
- final accounts on estate of Thomas Crouch.
- final accounts on estate of Hugh Matthews.
- final accounts on estate of Moses Jones.
- final accounts on estate of John

Barnaby.
- final accounts on estate of Elisabeth Miller.
- final accounts on estate of William Bateman.
- final accounts on estate of Fra. Maulding.
- final accounts on estate of Henry Ward.
- final accounts on estate of Richard Armstrong.
- final accounts on estate of Mathew Hyland.
- accounts on estate of James Bayard.
- accounts on estate of Richard Sedgwick.
- accounts on estate of William Tury.

44:370 21 April. John Bracco (g, TA) exhibited:
- will of Francis Register, constituting William Nicols executor. Said executor was granted administration. Sureties: William Thomas, Samuel Dickinson. Date: 17 March 1772.
- will of William Jones, constituting Thomas Jones executor. Said executor was granted administration. Sureties: Henry Troth, John Burkham. Date: 18 February 1772.
- will of Thomas Powell, constituting Elisabeth Powell executrix. Said executrix was granted administration. Sureties: Benjamin Parratt, Aaron Parratt. Date: 17 March 1772.
- bond of Joseph Bruff executor of Thomas Bruff. Sureties: John Hall, Richard Parrott. Date: 19 February 1772.
- bond of John Willoughby administrator of Rachel Willoughby. Sureties: Moses Rigby, Levin Spadding. Date: 4 March 1772.
- bond of Thomas Harrison administrator of William Dawson. Sureties: J. Harrington, J. Hopkins. Date: 31 March 1772.
- bond of Elisabeth Laurence administratrix of George Laurence. Sureties: Thomas Martin, Thomas

Court Session: 1772

Stevens. Date: 4 March 1772.
- bond of John Gibson administrator of Edward Watts. Sureties: Benedict Hutchings, R. Hall. Date: 5 March 1772.

44:371
- will of Anthony Booth.
- inventory of Alenbye Millington.
- inventory of Daniel Kellum.
- inventory of James Rutherford.
- LoD on estate of James Rutherford.
- LoD on estate of James Rutherford [!].

13 May. Jos. Nicholson (KE) exhibited:
- will of Dorcas Hollis, constituting John Page executor. Said executor was granted administration. Sureties: Thomas Slipper, Thomas Jerrum. Date: 23 April 1772.
- will of Javis James, constituting Sarah James executrix. Said executrix was granted administration. Sureties: William Slubey, Simon Wilmer. Date: 9 May 1772.
- bond of John Page administrator of Henry Russell. Sureties: Thomas Slipper, Thomas Jerrum. Date: 23 April 1772.
- bond of William Reed administrator of Michael Reed. Sureties: William Wilson, Samuel Reed. Date: 25 April 1772.

44:372
- bond of Tapenah Chandler administratrix of Michael Chandler. Sureties: John Crew, Nathaniel Chandler. Date: 4 May 1772.
- will of Jonathan Latherbury
- inventory of Charles Hynson.

2 March. John Bracco (g, TA) exhibited:
- will of Edward Neall.
- inventory of John Hynasy.
- inventory of Jonathan Neall.
- LoD on estate of Adam Brown.
- LoD on estate of Feddeman Rolle.
- LoD on estate of George Dobson.
- final accounts on estate of Feddeman Rolle.
- final accounts on estate of John Hynasy.
- final accounts on estate of George

Court Session: 1772

Dobson.
- final accounts on estate of Daniel Fiddeman.
- final accounts on estate of Phillip McManus.
- final accounts on estate of Adam Brown.

44:373 Clement Smith (g, CV) exhibited:
- will of Barbara Brook. Also, bond of Ann Brook administratrix. Sureties: John Bond, Benjamin Bond. Date: 7 April 1772.
- will of Roger Brook, constituting Elisabeth Brook, Roger Brook, Boz Brook, & John Brook executors. Said executors were granted administration. Sureties: Ignatius Fenwick, Jr., Joshua Watts. Date: 10 April 1772.
- will of Young Parran, constituting Richard Parran executor. Said executor was granted administration. Sureties: John Bond, J. Taylor. Date: 8 April 1772.
- bond of Lydia Sunderland administratrix of Stockit Sunderland. Sureties: Thomas Sunderland, John Stevens. Date: 24 April 1772.
- inventory of Jane Hellen.
- accounts on estate of James Shirmentine.
- accounts on estate of John Howerton.

44:374 2 May. Jos. Nicholson (KE) exhibited:
- will of Thomas Ringgold, constituting Thomas Ringgold executor. Said executor was granted administration. Sureties: James Hollyday, Upton Scott. Date: 25 April 1772.
- will of Ebenezar Blackiston, constituting Henrietta Blackiston executrix. Said executrix was granted administration. Sureties: James Blake, Abraham Milton. Date: 6 April 1772.
- bond of Mary Hanson, John Page, & Richard Miller executors of Frederick Hanson. Sureties: Micha Miller, Nathaniel Miller. Date: 1

April 1772.
- bond of Hester Stevens administratrix of Hester Stevens. Sureties: John Clark, John Clark, Jr., Abraham Milton. Date: 6 April 1772.
- bond of Christopher Hall administrator of Elisabeth Hall. Sureties: Thomas Boyer, Benjamin Palmer. Date: 30 March 1772.
- bond of Isaac Perkins administrator of Thomas Spencer. Sureties: Frederick Perkins, Moses Alford. Date: 13 April 1772.
- bond of Abraham Milton administrator of Abraham Miller. Sureties: Charles Baker, Joseph Milton. Date: 13 April 1772.
- bond of Martha Whichcote administratrix of Paul Whichcote. Sureties: Samuel Griffith, Nathaniel Comegys. Date: 15 April 1772.

44:375
- will of Catharine Massey.
- inventory of Elisabeth McDermott.
- inventory of Archibald Boyd.
- LoD on estate of Elisabeth McDermott.

Walter Hanson (g, CH) exhibited:
- will of Timothy Flanagan, constituting Gerrard Fowke executor. Said executor was granted administration. Sureties: John Muschett, Ignatius Ryan. Date: 25 February 1771.
- will of Benjamin Douglass, constituting Ann Douglass & George Smoot executors. Said executors were granted administration. Sureties: Charles Ford, Richard Smith. Date: 28 February 1772.
- will of Benjamin Craycroft. Also, bond of William Matthew & William Leigh administrators. Sureties: John Sanders, John Brooke. Date: 13 March 1772.
- will of Jacob Forrey, constituting Rachel Leman (alias Rachel Forrey) executrix. Said executrix was granted administration. Sureties: Daniel Jenifer, James Key. Date: 24 March 1772.

44:376 • will of Boles Tyer Bolthrop, constituting Ann Bolthrop & Edward Smoot executors. Said executors were granted administration. Sureties: Theop. Yates, Stephen Chandler. Date: 10 April 1772.

• bond of Phoebe Evans executrix of Francis Evans. Sureties: Ignatius Maddock, Samuel Hudson. Date: 20 April 1772.

• bond of Ann Farr administratrix of Samuel Farr. Sureties: Richard Ratcliff, George Steel. Date: 18 March 1772.

• bond of Thomas Jenkins administrator of Jane Jenkins. Sureties: David Phillpot, Thomas Rigg. Date: 17 April 1772.

• bond of John Ferdinand Smith administrator of George Carter. Sureties: John Craig, Walter Hanson. Date: 9 August 1772 [!].

• bond of Elisabeth Nelson administratrix of William Nellson. Sureties: Edward Maddock, James Davis. Date: 18 March 1772.

• bond of John Derrick executor of Edward Derrick. Sureties: William Thomas, James Kerrick. Date: 14 March 1772.

• bond of Mary Grove administratrix of Matthew Grove. Sureties: Jeremiah Skinner, Patrick McDaniel. Date: 27 February 1772.

44:377 • bond of Margret McCoy administratrix of Benjamin McCoy. Sureties: John Alley Robey, Peter Harriot Roby. Date: 28 February 1772.

• will of Benjamin Ward.
• will of Richard Harrison.
• inventory of Thomas Stone.
• inventory of Benjamin Garner.
• inventory of John Lucky.
• inventory of Bassil Hamilton.
• inventory of Hezekiah Speake.
• accounts on estate of Robert Hanson.
• accounts on estate of George Thomas Farr.
• accounts on estate of Posthuma Groves.
• accounts on estate of Lodwick Adams.
• accounts on estate of Benjamin

Maddox.
- accounts on estate of Ann Hutcheson.
- additional accounts on estate of William Price.

44:378 John Goldsborough (g, DO) exhibited:
- will of William Lecompt, constituting William Lecompt executor. Said executor was granted administration. Sureties: Benjamin Woodard, Charles Lecompt. Date: 17 January 1772.
- will of Henry Keene, constituting John Keene & Benjamin Keene executors. Said executors were granted administration. Sureties: Edward Stevens, Benjamin Keene. Date: <none given>.
- will of Mary Boxall, constituting Jeremiah McCollister executor. Said executor was granted administration. Sureties: Luke Stevens, Ezekiel McCollister. Date: 13 March 1772.
- will of Thomas Taylor, constituting Sarah Taylor & William Taylor executors. Said executors were granted administration. Sureties: William Jones, Charles Lecompt. Date: 7 March 1772.
- will of Joseph Bowdle, constituting Elisabeth Bowdle executrix. Said executrix was granted administration. Sureties: John Cheezum, Daniel Edgele. Date: 1 April 1772.
- will of George North, constituting Reb. North executrix. Said executrix was granted administration. Sureties: Ezekiel Keen, Nicholas Mace. Date: 6 February 1772.
- will of James Wallace, constituting Arthur Whitely executor. Said executor was granted administration. Sureties: William Byus, John Darby. Date: 4 April 1772.

44:379
- will of Andrew Lord, constituting David Harper executor. Said executor was granted administration. Sureties: Oliver Hacket, John Wallace. Date: 6 January 1772.
- will of William Hitch, constituting

Mary Hitch executrix. Said executrix was granted administration. Sureties: Spencer Hitch, Whittenton Hitch. Date: 26 March 1772.

- will of Thomas Faulconer, constituting Nathan Faulconer executor. Said executor was granted administration. Sureties: Salathiel Falconer, John Faulconer. Date: 16 March 1772.
- will of Mary Ennalls, constituting Thomas Ennalls, Jr. executor. Said executor was granted administration. Sureties: Thomas Ennalls, Joseph Ennalls. Date: 22 January 1772.
- bond of Moses Broadus, Jr. administrator dbn of Richard Cole. Sureties: J. Travilion Stewart, Edward Brodess. Date: 18 February 1772.
- bond of Massey Whitely administrator dbn of John Webster. Sureties: Jesse Grayless, Robert Bishop. Date: 20 January 1772.
- bond of Elijah Hatfield administrator of William Hatfield. Surety: Francis Wright. Date: 27 March 1772.
- bond of Bridget Simmons administratrix of Thomas Simmons. Sureties: James Read, Andrew Simmons. Date: 24 March 1772.

44:380
- bond of Elisabeth Green administratrix of William Green, Jr. Sureties: Henry Bradley, Kinneth McKenny. Date: 24 March 1772.
- bond of Jane Pritchet administratrix of Zebulon Pritchet. Sureties: John Trevilion Stewart, Levin McNamarra. Date: 11 March 1772.
- bond of Ann White Brown administratrix of John Brown (son of John). Sureties: Joseph Dawson, James Brown, Jr. Date: 23 January 1772.
- bond of Mary Hayward administratrix of Francis Hayward, Jr. Sureties: James Cannon, Abraham Reed. Date: 9 March 1772.
- will of Benjamin Granger.
- will of Joseph Mills.

Court Session: 1772

- will of Sarah Falconer.
- inventory of William Noble.
- inventory of Edward Williams.
- inventory of Joseph Allford.
- inventory of Mary Cannon.
- inventory of Nehemiah Boxwell.
- inventory of William Byus, Jr.
- inventory of Lucretia Warren.
- LoD on estate of Thomas Lane.
- LoD on estate of William Woolen.
- LoD on estate of David Pollock.
- accounts on estate of David Pollock.
- accounts on estate of Thomas Lane.

44:381
- accounts on estate of Patrick McCollister.
- final accounts on estate of Philemon Lecompt.
- final accounts on estate of Lucretia Warren.

Thomas Wright (g, QA) exhibited:
- will of Thomas Meredith, constituting Margaret Meredith & Thomas Meredith executors. Said executors were granted administration. Sureties: Edward Pickering, John Meredith. Date: 17 April 1772.
- will of John Tillotson, constituting Sarah Tillotson executrix. Said executrix was granted administration. Sureties: Edward Chetham, John Tillotson. Date: 18 April 1772.
- bond of Sarah Garford executrix od Richard Garford. Sureties: Thomas Chaires, John Ponder. Date: 25 April 1772.
- bond of John Dwigan administrator dbn of James White. Sureties: Thomas Hall, Henry Downes. Date: 3 April 1772.
- will of William Webb.

44:382
9 May. J. A. Thomas (g, SM) exhibited:
- will of Clement Medley, constituting Mary Medley executrix. Said executrix was granted administration. Sureties: Nicholas Mills, James Pike. Date: 12 December 1772 [!].
- will of Andrew Mills, constituting

Charles Mills executor. Said executor was granted administration. Surety: John Mills. Date: 3 January 1772.

- will of Richard Watts, constituting Sarah Watts & Richard Watts executors. Said executors were granted administration. Sureties: John Black, John Lynch. Date: 24 February 1772.
- will of William Mattingly, constituting Leonard Wathen executor. Said executor was granted administration. Surety: Edward Mattingly. Date: 30 December 1772 [!].
- will of Ignatius French, constituting James French executor. Said executor was granted administration. Sureties: John French, John Baptist Pain. Date: 18 February 1772.
- will of George Fenwick, constituting Jane Fenwick executrix. Said executrix was granted administration. Sureties: Igna. Fenwick, Cuthbert Fenwick. Date: 27 April 1772.
- will of John Morgan. Also, bond of William Watts administrator. Surety: George McCaul Clark. Date: 18 February 1772.
- bond of Elisabeth Baxter administratrix of John Baxter. Sureties: John Downie, John Hendly. Date: 7 April 1772.

44:383
- bond of Margaret Askom administratrix of Charles Askom. Sureties: John Cartwright, William Cartwright. Date: 30 March 1772.
- bond of Susannah Wright administratrix of Samuel Wright. Sureties: John Hoskins, Clement Gardiner. Date: 21 February 1772.
- bond of Grace Guyther administratrix of William Guyther. Sureties: Vernon Webb, John Richard Jenifer. Date: 23 February 1772.
- bond of Elisabeth Frasier administratrix of William Frasier. Sureties: James Thompson, George Mills. Date: 23 April 1772.

- bond of Zachariah Bond administrator of John Tuill. Surety: John Abell, Jr. Date: 5 March 1772.
- bond of Sabina Pain administratrix of Peter Pain. Sureties: William Hayward, Francis Hamersly. Date: 12 January 1772.
- will of James Smith.
- will of Mary Smith.
- inventory of Clement Medley.
- inventory of Mark Heard.
- inventory of Nicholas Griffin.
- inventory of Edward Teare.
- inventory of William Locker.
- inventory of John Wheatley.
- inventory of Justinian Lluwellin.
- inventory of John Taylor.
- inventory of Justinian Greenwell.
- inventory of Benjamin Williams.
- final accounts on estate of James Thomas.
- final accounts on estate of Thomas Watts.
- final accounts on estate of Peter Drury.
- final accounts on estate of Stephen Milburn.
- final accounts on estate of Samuel Caldwell.
- final accounts on estate of Kenelm Cheseldine.
- final accounts on estate of Richard Swan Edwards.

44:384

26 May. William T. Wootton (g, PG) exhibited:
- will of James Leiper. Also, bond of Thomas Leiper administrator dbn. Sureties: John Hamilton, John Brown. Date: 28 April 1772.
- bond of John Read Magruder executor of Thomas Willett. Sureties: Jeremiah Magruder, Singleton Wootton. Date: 16 May 1772.
- inventory of Christopher Eddeline.
- LoD on estate of William Elson.
- accounts on estate of John True.
- accounts on estate of Samuel McMarlow.
- final accounts on estate of William Elson.
- final accounts on estate of Ralph

44:385

Court Session: 1772

Marlow.
* final accounts on estate of John Peach.

4 June. Exhibited from DO:
* accounts on estate of John Wheeler.

Exhibited from TA:
* final accounts on estate of James Hindman.

Exhibited from SM:
* bond of Normand Bruce administrator dbn of Phillip Key, Esq. Sureties: U. Scott, William Beall. Date: 22 April 1772.
* bond of Normand Bruce administrator of Theodosia Key. Sureties: U. Scott, William Beall. Date: 22 April 1772.

Exhibited from KE:
* accounts on estate of Cornelius Vantsaveran.
* will of John Gresham.

Exhibited from CE:
* inventory & accounts of Abraham Pennington.
* inventory of William Dovin.

44:386 Exhibited from QA:
* inventory & accounts of Barbarah Richardson.
* final accounts on estate of Thomas Addison.
* will of John Cooper.

Exhibited from PG:
* bond of William Turner Wootton as Deputy Commissary (PG). Sureties: Benjamin Brooks, William Berry. Date: 26 November 1772.
* inventory & final accounts of Mordecai Jacobs.
* final accounts on estate of Hilleary Lyles.
* inventory of Thomas Snowden.
* additional inventory of Col. Jeremiah Belt.
* will of Thomas Lancaster, constituting Isaac Lansdale

executor. Said executor was granted administration. Sureties: Joseph Sprigg, Edward Hall (son of Henry). Date: 7 April 1772.

Exhibited from FR:
- will of Rebecca Perry, constituting James Perry executor. Said executor was granted administration. Sureties: Alexander Williamson, Simon Nicholls. Date: 9 May 1772.
- accounts on estate of Cornelius Davis.
- final accounts on estate of John Trundel.
- accounts on estate of Edward Owen.
- accounts on estate of James Perry.
- inventory of Benjamin Perry.
- LoD on estate of Cornelius Davis.

Exhibited from CV:
- LoD & final accounts on estate of Joseph Smith.
- additional inventory & final accounts of Joseph Isaack, Sr.
- final accounts on estate of Joseph Isaack, Jr.

44:387 Exhibited from BA:
- will of Edward Norwood, constituting Edward Norwood executor. Said executor was granted administration. Sureties: Nicholas Norwood, Joshua Griffith. Date: 21 January 1772.
- additional inventory & 2nd accounts of George Sater.
- will of Roger Boyce.
- inventory of Nicholas Ruxton Gay.

Exhibited from AA:
- final accounts on estate of Rezin Wright.
- accounts on estate of Nathan Adams.
- accounts on estate of James Simmonds.
- final accounts on estate of Thomas Hutchcraft.
- final accounts on estate of John Jackson.
- final accounts on estate of Daniel Stansbury.

Court Session: 1772

6 June. Elie Vallette (g, AA)
exhibited:

- will of Philemon Dorsey, constituting Philemon Dorsey executor. Said executor was granted administration. Sureties: John Dorsey, Caleb Dorsey. Date: 23 March 1772.
- will of Joseph Penn, constituting Joseph Penn executor. Said executor was granted administration. Sureties: Gerrard Warfeild, John Elder. Date: 7 January 1772.

44:388

- bond of James Williams administrator of Capt. James Ruth. Sureties: Robert Couden, Thomas Williams. Date: 27 May 1772.
- bond of John Linthicumb administrator dbn of Hezekiah Linthicumb. Sureties: Jeremiah Ducker, John Ducker. Date: 23 March 1772.
- bond of Elie Vallette administrator of Ralph Dobinson. Surety: Thomas Brook Hodkin. Date: 7 March 1772.
- bond of Elisabeth Snowden administratrix of Richard Snowden. Sureties: Thomas Rutland, Thomas Snowden. Date: 20 May 1772.
- bond of Edward Dorsey administrator of John Heason. Sureties: Robert Pinkney, Joseph Dorsey. Date: 21 April 1772.
- bond of Charles Oneal administrator of Frances Oneal. Sureties: Allen Quynn, Jonathan Pickering. Date: 23 May 1772.
- bond of Rezin Pumphrey administrator of Walter Pumphrey. Sureties: William Pumphrey, William Ridgely, Jr. Date: 24 February 1772.
- bond of Samuel Watkins & Richard Watkins administrators of Daniel Brooks. Surety: Thomas Harwood, Jr. Date: 18 March 1772.
- bond of Milcah Snowden administratrix of Edward Snowden. Sureties: Joseph Gardiner, Richard Gardiner. Date: 11 January 1772.

44:389

- bond of Comfort Williams administratrix of Benjamin Williams. Sureties: Gideon Gary, Jos.

Williams. Date: 25 April 1772.
- bond of William Smyth administrator of Dr. James Thompson. Sureties: Jos. Cowman, Thomas Harwood, Jr. Date: 12 February 1772.
- bond of Cornelius Garretson & William Slivers administrators of James Cannon. Sureties: Jere. To. Chase, H. George Peale. Date: 24 January 1772.
- bond of James French administrator of Isaac Hall, Sr. Sureties: William Gambril, Richard Dorsey. Date: 24 April 1772.
- bond of Nathan Hammond administrator of Caroline Hammond. Sureties: John Campbell, Joseph Selby. Date: 17 January 1772.
- bond of Nathan Hammond administrator of Hamutal Hammond. Sureties: John Campbell, Joseph Selby. Date: 17 January 1772.
- will of Cornelius Howard.
- will of Elisabeth Stockett.
- will of John Cromwell.
- inventory of Caroline Hammond.
- inventory of Hamutal Hammond.
- inventory of Joseph Norman.
- inventory of Dr. Joseph Thompson.
- inventory of Joseph Penn.
- inventory of John Hawkins.
- inventory of Luke Davis.
- inventory of Joseph Brewer.
- inventory of John Waters.
- inventory of Edward Snowden.
- final accounts on estate of Caroline Hammond.
- final accounts on estate of Hamutal Hammon.

44:390

5 June. Col. William Young (BA) exhibited:
- bond of Robert Lendrum & John Lee Webster administrators of Rev. Andrew Lendrum. Sureties: Amos Garrett, Isaac Whitister. Date: 16 April 1772.
- bond of Abraham Jarrett administrator of William Standifor, Jr. Surety: James Barton. Date: 25 May 1772.
- bond of Sarah Thompson

Court Session: 1772

administratrix of William Ramsay.
Sureties: James Thompson, Samuel
Thompson. Date: 25 May 1772.

- bond of Garret Cruson administrator
  of Garret Crusone. Sureties: Samuel
  Lockhart, Richard James. Date: 11
  May 1772.
- bond of Mary Stansbury
  administratrix of Catherine North.
  Sureties: Aquila Paca, Mordecai
  Grist. Date: 10 February 1771.

44:391
- bond of Nathaniel Smith
  administrator of Armstrong Buckanan.
  Sureties: Samuel Purviance, Jr.,
  Robert Purviance. Date: 15 April
  1772.
- bond of Sarah Beck administratrix of
  Mary Beck. Sureties: Benjamin
  Debruler, John Wilson. Date: 20
  April 1772.
- will of John Bosley.
- inventory of Robert Robinson.
- inventory of John Crooke.
- inventory of Ann Howard.
- inventory of Thomas Sheredine.
- inventory of Charles Robinson.
- inventory of Rezin Moore.
- inventory of Acquilla McComas.
- accounts on estate of Ephraim Jones.
- final accounts on estate of Luke
  Wyle.
- final accounts on estate of Richard
  Rhode.
- final accounts on estate of John
  Wilkinson.
- final accounts on estate of John
  Swynard.
- final accounts on estate of David
  Morgan.
- final accounts on estates of Robert
  Lowry & John Lowry.

44:392 11 June. Thomas Holbrook (g, SO)
exhibited:
- will of Samuel Haynie, constituting
  Judith Haynie executrix. Said
  executrix was granted
  administration. Sureties: Jonathan
  Hearn, Ed. Nelms. Date: 2 May 1772.
- bond of Thomas Pallitt, Jr.
  administrator of William Pallitt.
  Sureties: Josiah Polk, Josiah

Page 131

Dashiell. Date: 14 April 1772.
- bond of Isaac Moore administrator of James Moore. Sureties: John Moor, Samuel Hearn. Date: 25 April 1772.
- bond of Elisabeth Kibble administratrix of William Kibble. Sureties: Thomas Collins, George Kibble. Date: 21 April 1772.
- will of Thomas Rencher.
- inventory of James Moore.
- inventory of Thomas Simms.
- inventory of John Done.
- inventory of Thomas Humphris.
- final accounts on estate of Richard Green.
- final accounts on estate of Boz Wolston.
- final accounts on estate of Mary Fountaine.
- final accounts on estate of Zebulon Wright.
- final accounts on estate of Joseph Hitch.
- final accounts on estate of William Kibble.
- final accounts on estate of Ann Hardy.

44:393 26 June. Walter Hanson (g, CH) exhibited:
- will of Henrietta Thompson, constituting Raphel Brooke executor. Said executor was granted administration. Sureties: Joseph Thompson, William Tyers. Date: 2 May 1772.
- will of Benjamin Douglass, constituting Joseph Douglass executor. Said executor was granted administration. Sureties: James Cottrell, Thomas Jenkins. Date: 25 April 1772.
- bond of Sarah Ward & Henry Ward executors of Benjamin Ward. Sureties: Peter Dent, Thomas Smallwood. Date: 27 May 1772.
- bond of Ann McDaniel administratrix of Miles McDaniel. Sureties: William McPherson, Alexander McDonald. Date: 18 May 1772.
- bond of Leonard Brooke administrator of Ann Brook. Sureties: Thomas

Contee, George Lee.   Date: 27 May
1772.

- bond of Charles Allison Ford
administrator of Edward Ford.
Sureties: George Smoot, John Ford.
Date: 29 May 1772.
- bond of Charles Allison Ford
administrator of Elisabeth Ford.
Sureties: Stephen Chandler, Charles
Brandt.   Date: 1 June 1772.
- will of Thomas Cotterell.
- inventory of Benjamin Cracroft.
- inventory of Matthew Grove.
- inventory of Samuel Farr.
- accounts on estate of Alexander
Smith Hawkins.
- accounts on estate of Henry Hawkins.
- accounts on estate of William
Trueman Stoddert.
- additional accounts on estate of
James Smith.
- accounts on estate of Benjamin
Garner.
- accounts on estate of John Hannan.
- additional accounts on estate of
John Theobald.

44:394

Col.   William Nicholson (KE) exhibited:
- bond of Peregrine Leatherbury
executor of Jonathan Leatherbury.
Sureties: William St. Clair, Gilbert
Falconer.   Date: 11 June 1772.
- bond of Richard Gresham, Jr.
executor of John Gresham.   Sureties:
Thomas Smyth, Th. B. Hands.   Date:
13 May <no year given>.
- bond of Rebecca Boots administratrix
of Isaac Boots.   Sureties: George
Tillon, William Hazel.   Date: 11 May
1772.
- bond of Susannah Rezin & William
Resin administrators of Thomas
Resin.   Sureties: James Pearce,
Robert Buchanan.   Date: 29 May 1772.
- bond of John Wales administrator of
Edward Coley.   Surety: Robert
Gresham.   Date: 13 June 1772.
- will of Richard Bruce.
- will of George Little.
- inventory of John Kinnard.
- inventory of George Perkins.
- inventory of Joseph Tuckerman.

44:395

- inventory of James Hacket.
- inventory of John Smith.
- inventory of Dorothy Hodges.
- inventory of Joseph Tuckerman.
- inventory of Thomas Crow.
- inventory of John Buckhanan.
- inventory of Richard Norton.
- inventory of Andrew Toalson.
- inventory of Writson Browning.
- inventory of Jonathan Smith.
- LoD on estate of Hugh Wallis.
- LoD on estate of Writson Browning.
- LoD on estate of Thomas Piner.
- LoD on estate of George Perkins.
- LoD on estate of John Smith.
- LoD on estate of James Hacket.
- LoD on estate of Nicholas Smith.

44:396
- accounts on estate of Hugh Wallis.
- final accounts on estate of Henry Moore.
- final accounts on estate of James Hacket.
- final accounts on estate of John Smith.
- final accounts on estate of Joseph Tuckerman.
- final accounts on estate of Wilson Browning.
- final accounts on estate of Nicholas Smith.
- final accounts on estate of Thomas Piner.
- final accounts on estate of John Day.
- final accounts on estate of George Perkins.

27 June. Thomas Bowles (g, FR)
exhibited:
- will of John Adamson, constituting Richard Beall & Andrew Hugh executors. Said executors were granted administration. Sureties: En. Campbell, Basil Beall. Date: 19 March 1772.
- will of Smith Carnall, constituting William Cornall & Richard Cornall executors. Said executors were granted administration. Sureties: Jos. Sparks, Rus. Philips. Date: 22 May 1772.
- will of Catharine Hardman,

constituting Abraham Miller executor. Said executor was granted administration. Sureties: Christian Shuter, James Miller. Date: 4 March 1772.

44:397
- will of Edward Willett, constituting Michael Litton executor. Said executor was granted administration. Sureties: Lawrence Oneal, Robert Owen. Date: 8 April 1772.
- will of John Boyd, constituting Susannah Boyd executrix. Said executrix was granted administration. Sureties: William Dent, Samuel Swearingen. Date: 18 May 1772.
- bond of William Lease administrator of Jacob Fout. Sureties: Jacob Lease, C. Beatty. Date: 4 April 1772.
- bond of Milcor Tablor administrator of Michael Hardman. Sureties: Frederick Whitman, P. Grindle. Date: 24 March 1772.
- bond of Catharine Chany administratrix of Richard Chany. Sureties: James Smith, John Kinnesbrick. Date: 24 March 1772.
- bond of Nathaniel Harris administrator of Thomas Harris. Sureties: Carlton Camehill, Samuel Perry. Date: 13 April 1772.
- bond of John Hopkins administrator of Thomas Jones. Sureties: Jacob Schley, Peter Grosh. Date: 29 February 1772.
- bond of Robert Peter administrator of John Allison. Sureties: John Cary, Jacob Young. Date: 25 May 1772.
- bond of Adam Steuart administrator of Kensey Sparrow. Surety: John Cary. Date: 28 May 1772.

44:398
- will of Lorando Travey.
- will of William Downy.
- will of John Dowden.
- inventory of Charles Watts.
- inventory of Jacob Grub.
- inventory of Michael Hardman.
- inventory of John Smith.
- inventory of Nicholas Coome.
- inventory of Catharine Hardman.

- inventory of William Cockran.
- inventory of John Wason.
- inventory of Yocham John.
- inventory of John Beard.
- LoD on estate of William Cochran.
- final accounts on estate of Charles Watts.
- final accounts on estate of Everhart Bomgarner.
- final accounts on estate of Ezekiel Cheyny.
- final accounts on estate of George Haun.
- final accounts on estate of William Burgess.
- final accounts on estate of Peter Light.

<u>29 June</u>. Thomas Wright (g, QA) exhibited:
- will of Abraham Oldson, constituting Thomas Oldson executor. Said executor was granted administration. Sureties: Nathaniel Wright, John Railey. Date: 6 June 1772.
- will of John Atkinson, constituting William Carpenter executor. Said executor was granted administration. Sureties: Benjamin Elliott, Richard Costin. Date: 21 May 1772.
- will of William Kirkman, constituting James Towers & Charles Manship executors. Said executors were granted administration. Sureties: Thomas Meeds, Jeremiah Colston. Date: 30 April 1772.
- will of William Hopper, constituting William Hopper & James Bordley executors. Said executors were granted administration. Sureties: Chris. Cross Routh, Joshua Clark. Date: 15 May 1772.
- nuncupative will of John Brown. Also, bond of Nathan Brown administrator. Sureties: John Kent, Thomas Lindsay. Date: 6 May 1772.
- bond of Thomas Cooper executor of John Cooper. Sureties: James Wilson, Solomon Eagle. Date: 14 May 1772.
- bond of Henry Downes, Jr. administrator of John Pickering.

44:399

Sureties: Charles Nabb, Robert Tate.
Date: 4 June 1772.
- bond of Alice Garner administratrix
  of James Garner. Sureties: Thomas
  Pennington, Thomas Hardcastle.
  Date: 21 May 1772.
- bond of Emory Sudler administrator
  of Charles Basnett. Sureties:
  Thomas Carradine, William Carradine.
  Date: 30 April 1772.
- bond of Frances Downes & James
  Downes, Jr. administrators of Henry
  Downes. Sureties: Henry Downes,
  Jr., Richard Small. Date: 7 May
  1772.

44:400
- will of Eleanor Anthony.
- will of Elisabeth Price.
- will of Benjamin Sparks.
- inventory of Edward Slay.
- inventory of William Heath.
- inventory of Charles Warner.
- inventory of John Clayland.
- inventory of John Mumford.
- inventory of William Young, Jr.
- inventory of Sarah Moore.
- inventory of Thomas Cox.
- inventory of John Meredith.
- accounts on estate of Elisabeth
  Elliott.
- final accounts on estate of William
  Harrington.
- final accounts on estate of John
  Clayland.
- final accounts on estate of John
  Mumford.
- final accounts on estate of Thomas
  Cox.
- final accounts on estate of Robert
  Cade.
- final accounts on estate of George
  Spry.
- final accounts on estate of Richard
  Hammond.
- final accounts on estate of Benjamin
  Endsworth.
- final accounts on estate of Francis
  Bright.

44:401 1 July. Col. William Young (BA)
exhibited:
- will of Daniel Preston, constituting
  Ann Preston executrix. Said

Court Session: 1772

executrix was granted
administration. Sureties: Jacob
Bond, Thomas Johnson. Date: 22 June
1772.
- bond of Ann Preston administratrix
of William Grafton. Sureties: Jacob
Bond, John Lowe. Date: 22 June
1772.
- bond of Hugh Scott administrator of
Abraham Scott. Sureties: William
Spear, James Stevett. Date: 28 May
1772.
- bond of Catharine Hatton
administratrix of Thomas Hatton.
Sureties: China Hatton, Thomas
Bailey. Date: 22 June 1772.
- bond of John Cannon administrator of
John Skees. Surety: Owen Allen.
Date: 19 June 1772.
- bond of William Raven administrator
of Lettuce Raven. Sureties:
Richardson Stansbury, Luke Raven.
Date: 1 June 1772.
- bond of Hannah Rutter administratrix
of Thomas Rutter. Sureties: Richard
Carter, William Carter. Date: 8
June 1772.
- will of Charles Ridgely.

44:402
- inventory of Philip Hars.
- inventory of Benjamin Cook.
- inventory of John Chew.
- inventory of Benjamin Vanhornel.
- inventory of David Carlile.
- accounts on estate of David Carlile.
- accounts on estate of Benjamin
Cooke.
- accounts on estate of Phillip Har.
- accounts on estate of James Wilson.

11 July. Clement Smith (g, CV)
exhibited:
- bond of George Gray administrator
dbn of John Gray. Sureties: James
Gray, Edward Wood, Jr. Date: 2 May
1772.
- bond of Mordecai Smith administrator
of Richard Crosbey. Sureties:
Daniel Smith, John Tanyhill. Date:
20 June 1772.
- bond of Margaret Dalton & James
Stone administrator of Thomas
Dalton. Sureties: James Ennis,

Court Session: 1772

William Crandall. Date: 11 June 1772.

44:403
- bond of Martin Norriss & Rachel Allen administrators of Thomas Allen. Sureties: Henry Cambden, Joseph Smith. Date: 1 July 1772.
- bond of Aaron Williams, Jr. administrator of Chris. Hance. Sureties: Michael Catterton, Hezekiah Bussey. Date: 11 May 1772.

15 July. Thomas Holbrook (g, SO) exhibited:
- will of Phillip Addams, constituting William Adams executor. Said executor was granted administration. Sureties: Jacob Adams, Sr., Jesse Addams. Date: 30 June 1772.
- bond of John Evans, Jr. administrator of Thomas Evans. Sureties: William Allen, Jr., John Crockett. Date: 16 June 1772.
- inventory of Isaac Hayman.
- final accounts on estate of Isaac Hayman.
- final accounts on estate of Arnold Elzey.

44:404 6 June. Deputy Commissaries to examine accounts of:
- KE: Thomas Smith administrator of George Greenwood.
- CH: Bennet Dyson & Henry Clarkson & his wife Dorcas executors of Joseph Dyson.
- CH: Joseph Townslin executor of Frances Semmes.
- CH: John Evans, Jr. & his wife Victoria executrix of Thomas Nellson.
9 June.
- KE: Hannah Tolson & Nathaniel Tolson administrators of Andrew Tolson.
- KE: Mary McHard administratrix of Samuel McHard.
10 June.
- KE: Sarah Record administratrix of Thomas Record.
- BA: Ann Maria Har administratrix of Phillip Har.
- SO: Hope Adams executor of Hope Adams.

Court Session: 1772

- WO: Isaac Layfield administrator of George Layfield.
- SO: Isaac Atkinson executor of Thomas Willin.

12 June.
- SO: Nicholas Smith administrator of Nicholas Smith.

14 June.
- QA: Henry Elliott administrator of William Elliott.

16 June.
- QA: William Ruth executor of Christopher Brown.
- PG: Sarah Ryan administratrix of James Ryan, Jr.
- QA: Catharine Sherwood executrix of John Sherwood.

17 June.
- BA: Helen Ogg executrix of George Ogg.
- BA: Robert Watson executor of Charles Watson.

19 June.
- TA: William Harrison administrator of John Harrison.

23 June.
- KE: Abraham Milton administrator dbn of William Crew.

24 June.
- BA: John Scoolfield administrator of John Purnal.

25 June.
- CE: Elias Eliason & Abraham Eliason executors of Elias Eliason.
- CE: John Hodgson administrator of Phineas Hodgson.
- CE: Edward Mitchel executor of Elisabeth Mitchell.
- QA: Hannah Bayly executrix of Thomas Baily.
- KE: John Lambert Wilmer executor of Thomas Wilmer.

26 June.
- KE: John Williamson executor of George Williams.
- KE: Hannah Kelly administratrix of Joshua Kelly.

29 June.
- QA: Sarah Meredith administratrix of John Meredith.
- QA: Rebecka Glass administratrix of Thomas Glass.

Court Session: 1772

- FR: Ann Dickson administratrix of James Dickson.

2 July.
- WO: Thomas Jones executor of Hannah Jones.
- WO: Ann Winsor administratrix of John Winsor.

44:405
- FR: Margaret Rope & Jacob Rope administrators of Nicholas Rope.

6 July.
- QA: William Newman, Jr. & Elisabeth Comegys administrators of Nathaniel Comegys.
- BA: Buchanan Smith & Huldah Smith executors of Mr. Ralph Smith.

11 July.
- BA: Dennis Garret Cole administrator of Dennis Cole.
- BA: Mary Cole executrix of William Cole.
- CV: Hannah Smith executrix of William Smith.
- CV: Francis Lowther & Hugh Hopewell administrators of Elleck Parran.

13 July.
- SM: Sabra Corsair administratrix of John Corsair.
- BA: James Moore administrator of James Moore.
- BA: James Moore administrator of Rezin Moore.
- BA: Thomas Baily executor of Thomas Baily.
- BA: Henry Stevenson & William Smith administrators of William Govane.

14 July.
- QA: Rachel Imbert administratrix of Thomas Imbert.
- QA: John Corse administrator of Samuel Corse.

16 July.
- SO: Thomas Irving & his wife Mary executrix of Samuel Handy.
- SO: Alexander Adams, John Adams, & William Adams administrators of Alexander Adams.

21 July.
- SO: Isabella Connor executrix of Elijah Connor.
- SO: William Moore administrator of Thomas Moore.

25 July.

Page 141

Court Session: 1772

- SO: Ann Moore administratrix of Thomas Moore.
- SO: Elverton Caldwell administrator of John Caldwell.

27 July.
- SO: Benjamin Howard administrator of Ann Howard.

29 July.
- WO: Robert Melson executor of Robert Melson.
- BA: Greenbury Dorsey & his wife Sophia administrators of John Clark.
- QA: Ann & Arthur Emory executors of John Emory.

Court Session: 10 Mar, 12 May, 14 Jul 1772

44:406-7 Docket:
- WO: James Broadway & his wife Betty executrix of Mary Sheldon to render accounts.
  - March: summons.
  - May: summons. Accounts exhibited. To be struck off.
- WO: Purnel Bowen administrator of Littleton Bowen to render accounts.
  - March: summons. Final accounts exhibited.
- WO: Samuel Smiley administrator of Andrew Smiley to render accounts.
  - March: summons. Petition filed.
  - May: summons.
  - July: summons.
- WO: Tabitha Tilghman administratrix of Gideon Tilghman to render accounts.
  - March: summons.
  - May: summons. Final accounts exhibited. To be struck off.
- WO: Hannah Connaway executrix of Phillip Connaway to render accounts.
  - March: summons. Final accounts exhibited. To be struck off.
- WO: Samuel Brittingham executor of Elijah Brittingham to render accounts.
  - March: summons.
  - May: summons.
  - July: summons.
- WO: Levy Noble executor of James Noble to render accounts.
  - March: summons.

- May: summons.
- July: summons.

44:408-9 • WO: Avery Morgan & his wife Hannah executrix of Joseph Massey to render accounts.
- March: summons:
- May: summons.
- July: summons.

• WO: Sarah Hall administratrix of Stephen Hall to render accounts.
- March: summons.
- May: summons.
- July: summons.

• WO: Leah Caldwell administratrix of William Caldwell to render accounts.
- March: summons.
- May: summons.
- July: summons.

• WO: Southy King administrator of William King to render accounts.
- March: summons.
- May: summons.
- July: summons.

• WO: Ezekiel Green executor of Ezekiel Green to render accounts.
- March: summons.
- May: summons.
- July: summons.

• WO: Magdalen Burer administratrix of Solomon Burer to render accounts.
- March: summons.
- May: summons.
- July: summons. Final accounts exhibited. To be struck off.

• WO: William Holland & his wife Ann administratrix of John Purnall to render accounts.
- March: summons.
- May: summons.
- July: summons.

• WO: Solomon Long & his wife Comfort executrix of Stephen White to render accounts.
- March: summons.
- May: summons.
- July: summons.

• WO: Tabitha Townshend executrix of John Townshend to render accounts.
- March: summons.
- May: summons.
- July: summons. Final accounts exhibited. To be struck off.

Court Session: 10 Mar, 12 May, 14 Jul 1772

44:410 \<does not exist.\>
44:411-2 • WO: Mary King Whittington executrix
of William Whittington to render
accounts.
- March: summons.
- May: summons.
- July: summons. To be struck
off.
• WO: Tabitha Stevenson executrix of
William Stevens to render accounts.
- March: summons.
- May: summons.
- July: summons.
• WO: Elisha Hall executor of Robert
Hall to render accounts.
- March: summons.
- May: summons.
- July: summons.
• WO: Daniel Hall executor of John
Hall to render accounts.
- March: summons.
- May: summons.
- July: summons.
• WO: Presgrave Kennett executor of
Martin Kennett to render accounts.
- March: summons.
- May: summons.
- July: summons.
• WO: Ann Smith executrix of John
Smith to render accounts.
- March: summons. Final accounts
exhibited. To be struck off.
• WO: William Richardson executor of
Samuel Richardson to render
accounts.
- March: summons.
- May: summons.
- July: summons. Final accounts
exhibited. To be struck off.
• WO: John Purnel Robins administrator
of Ann Milbourne to render accounts.
- March: summons.
- May: summons.
- July: summons.
• WO: Kinal Kennett administrator of
Ann Milbourne to render accounts.
- March: summons.
- May: summons.
- July: summons.
44:413-4 • WO: Elisabeth Long administratrix
of John Long to render accounts.
- March: summons.

- May: summons.
- July: summons.
- WO: James Stevenson executor of Samuel Stevenson to render accounts.
  - March: summons.
  - May: summons.
  - July: summons.
- WO: Smith Frame executor of Nathan Frame to render accounts.
  - March: summons.
  - May: summons.
  - July: summons.
- WO: Jeremiah Townshend executor of Brickus Townshend to render accounts.
  - March: summons.
  - May: summons.
  - July: summons.
- WO: David Vance administrator of Joshua Langford to render accounts.
  - March: summons.
  - May: summons.
  - July: summons.
- WO: James Houston administrator of Sophia Stokely to render accounts.
  - March: summons.
  - May: summons.
  - July: summons. Final accounts exhibited. To be struck off.
- WO: Siner Calloway administratrix of John Calloway to render accounts.
  - March: summons.
  - May: summons.
  - July: summons.
- WO: Thomas Willett administrator of William Willett to render accounts.
  - March: summons.
  - May: summons.
  - July: summons.

44:415-6
- SO: Mathew Kemp administrator dbn of Richard Steven Bounds to render accounts.
  - March: summons. Final accounts exhibited. To be struck off.
- SO: Adam Adamson & his wife Elisabeth administratrix of Thomas Bond to render accounts.
  - March: summons.
  - May: summons.
  - July: summons.
- SO: Isaac Green executor of Richard Green to render accounts.

- March: summons.
- May: summons.
- July: summons. Final accounts exhibited. To be struck off.
- SO: John Paden administrator of John Paden to render accounts.
  - March: summons.
  - May: summons.
  - July: summons.
- SO: Ann Moor administratrix of Thomas Moore to render accounts.
  - March: summons.
  - May: summons.
  - July: summons.
- SO: Sophia Wright executrix of Zebulon Wright to render accounts.
  - March: summons.
  - May: summons.
  - July: summons. Final accounts exhibited. To be struck off.
- SO: Joshua & Lydia Hayman executors of Isaac Hayman to render accounts.
  - March: summons.
  - May: summons.
  - July: summons. Final accounts exhibited. To be struck off.
- SO: Newton Bayly administratrix of George Bayly to render accounts.
  - March: summons.
  - May: summons. Final accounts exhibited. To be struck off.
- SO: John Nelms administrator of Charles Brown to render accounts.
  - March: summons. No effects.
- 44:417-8 • SO: Sarah Wills administratrix of Benjamin Wills to render accounts.
  - March: summons.
  - May: summons.
  - July: summons.
- SO: Joy Walston executor of Boax Walston to render accounts.
  - March: summons.
  - May: summons.
  - July: summons. Final accounts exhibited. To be struck off.
- DO: Lurana Spedding executrix of Hugh Spedding to render accounts.
  - March: summons.
  - May: summons.
  - July: summons.
- DO: John Merine administrator of William Merine to render accounts.

Court Session: 10 Mar, 12 May, 14 Jul 1772

- March: summons.
- May: summons.
- July: summons.
- DO: Patrick Moore vs. Robertson Stevens executor of Josias Moore. Summons to render accounts.
  - March: summons.
  - May: summons.
  - July: summons.
- DO: Elisabeth Holmes administratrix of Nicholas Holmes to render accounts.
  - March: summons.
  - May: summons.
  - July: summons.
- DO: James Shaw & his wife Mary executrix of John Lecompt to render accounts.
  - July: summons.
- DO: David Harper executor of Andrew Lord vs. Ann Lord.
  - May: summons to show cause why she conceals said estate. Also, summons to Henry Lord & his wife Susanna, Cratcher Lord, Sally Thompson, Elisabeth Hubbert.
  - Said Ann Lord (widow of dec'd), age 70 & in bad state of health, deposed on 21 April 1772. Mentions: Mr. Sullivane, Attested by: Daniel Sullivane, Henry Ennalls.
  - Elisabeth Hubbert, of full age, deposed on 13 May 1772 that she lived with David Harper & attended the dec'd. Signed: Elisabeth Hubbard.
  - Sally Thompson deposed on 13 May 1772.

44:419-20

44:421-2

- TA: John Robinson administrator of Isaac Cox to render accounts.
  - March: summons
  - May: summons. Letter of excuse filed by Nicholas Thomas.
  - July: summons.
- TA: Mary Ellston administratrix of Israel Cox to render accounts.
  - March: summons.
  - May: summons.
  - July: summons.
- TA: John Sherwood, Jr. administrator

Page 147

    of Thomas Sherwood to render accounts.
- March: summons.
- May: summons.
- July: summons.

- TA: Frances Gibson administratrix of Peter Gibson to render accounts.
  - March: summons.
  - May: summons.
  - July: summons.

44:423-4
- TA: Mary Harwood administratrix of Peter Harwood to render accounts.
  - March: summons.
  - May: summons.
  - July: summons.

- TA: Elisabeth & Robert Harwood administrators of William Harwood to render accounts.
  - March: summons.
  - May: summons.
  - July: summons.

- TA: Mary Smith (alias Mary Sleith) administratrix of Simon Steven Miller to render accounts.
  - March: summons.
  - May: summons. To be struck off.

- TA: William Harrison administrator of John Harrison to render accounts.
  - March: summons.
  - May: summons.
  - July: summons.

- TA: Henrietta Maria Carslake administratrix of John Carslake to render accounts.
  - March: summons.
  - May: summons.
  - July: summons.

- TA: Ann Feddeman administratrix of Daniel Feddeman to render accounts.
  - March: summons. Final accounts exhibited. To be struck off.

- TA: John Blyth & his wife Sophia executrix of Laurence Porter to render accounts.
  - March: summons.
  - May: summons.
  - July: summons.

- TA: Jane Chapman executrix of James Chapman to render accounts.
  - March: summons.
  - May: summons.
  - July: summons.

Court Session: 10 Mar, 12 May, 14 Jul 1772

44:425-6 • TA: Jean Scott executrix of John
Dobson to render accounts.
   - March: summons.
   - May: summons.
   - July: summons.
• Hannah Turner executrix of Edward
Turner to render accounts.
   - March: summons.
   - May: summons.
   - July: summons.
• TA: Jonathan Dorsey & his wife Mary
administratrix of Macklin Elbert to
render accounts.
   - March: summons.
   - May: summons.
   - July: summons.
• TA: Rebecca & John Roberts executors
of Thomas Roberts to render
accounts.
   - March: summons.
   - May: summons.
   - July: summons.
• TA: Perry Parrott administrator of
Joseph Parrott to render accounts.
   - March: summons.
   - May: summons.
   - July: summons.
• TA: Richard Pritchard administrator
of John Pritchard to render
accounts.
   - March: summons.
   - May: summons.
   - July: summons.
• TA: James Sparks administrator of
Samuel Whiting to render accounts.
   - March: summons.
   - May: summons.
   - July: summons.
• TA: William Nicholas & James Lloyd
Chamberlain administrators of
William Coburn to render accounts.
   - March: summons.
   - May: summons.
   - July: summons.
• TA: Daniel Merrick administrator dbn
of Thomas Porter to render accounts.
   - March: summons. James Tilghman
3rd alleges suits in Provincial
Court.
   - May: summons.
   - July: summons.
44:427-8 • TA: Thomas Young & his wife Rebecca

administratrix of John Price to
render accounts.
- March: summons.
- May: summons.
- July: summons.
- TA: Thomas Henney administrator of
William Henney to render accounts.
  - March: summons.
  - May: summons.
  - July: summons.
- TA: Henry Boidel administrator of
Jonathan Woods to render accounts.
  - March: summons.
  - May: summons.
  - July: summons.
- TA: John Beall administrator of
Thomas Beall vs. Elisabeth Jump &
Robert Ault. To show cause why they
conceal said estate.
  - May: summons. To be struck off.
- QA: Ann & Arthur Emory executors of
John Emory (surveyor) to render
accounts.
  - March: summons.
  - May: summons.
  - July: summons.
- QA: Charles Blake administrator of
Sarah Blake to render accounts.
  - March: summons.
  - May: summons.
  - July: summons.
- QA: James Hollyday vs. John Sutton
& his wife Margaret administratrix
of John Mumford. To render
accounts.
  - March: summons.
  - May: summons.
  - July: summons.
- QA: Samuel Brown administrator dbn
of Andrew Hall to render accounts.
  - March: summons.
  - May: summons.
  - July: summons.

44:429-30 • QA: John Nabb executor of
Elisabeth Nabb to render accounts.
- March: summons.
- May: summons.
- July: summons.
- QA: Giles Hicks executor of
Cornelius Daily to render accounts.
  - March: summons.
  - May: summons.

- July: summons.
- QA: John Brown (son of John) administrator of Joseph Meanor to render accounts.
  - March: summons.
  - May: summons. "Mortus est". To be struck off.
- QA: Sarah Price administratrix of William Price to render accounts.
  - March: summons.
  - May: summons.
  - July: summons.
- QA: Jonathan Culbreath administrator dbn of William Culbreath to render accounts.
  - March: summons.
  - May: summons.
  - July: summons.
- QA: Christopher Cox & William Price administrators of Thomas Cox to render accounts.
  - March: summons. To be struck off.
- QA: Robert Wood administrator of David Robertson to render accounts.
  - March: summons.
  - May: summons.
  - July: summons.
- QA: Tabitha Bryan executrix of John Bryan to render accounts.
  - March: summons.
  - May: summons.
  - July: summons. Runaway. To be struck off.
- QA: Andrew Hennesey administrator of John Hennesey to render accounts.
  - March: summons.
  - May: summons.
  - July: summons.
44:431-2 • QA: William Ruth vs. Hannah Baily executrix of Thomas Baily. To render accounts.
  - March: summons.
  - May: summons.
  - July: summons.
- QA: Susannah Clayland executrix of Thomas Clayland to render accounts.
  - March: summons.
  - May: summons.
  - July: summons. To be struck off.
- QA: John Comegys vs. Ann Comegys

surviving executrix of John Comegys.
To render accounts.
- March: summons. "Mortus est."
  To be struck off.
- QA: James Kent administrator dbn of
  Robert Hawkins to render accounts.
  - March: summons. No estate. To
    be struck off.
- QA: Elisabeth Smith executrix of
  Nathan Smith to render accounts.
  - March: summons.
  - May: summons.
  - July: summons.
- QA: Nathan Harrington executor of
  Barbarah Richardson to render
  accounts.
  - March: summons.
  - May: summons.
  - July: summons. Accounts
    exhibited. To be struck off.
- QA: Margaret Farrow administratrix
  of Nathan Farrow to render accounts.
  - March: summons.
  - May: summons.
  - July: summons. Runaway. To be
    struck off.
- QA: Ann & Francis Bright
  administrators of Francis Bright to
  render accounts.
  - March: summons.
  - May: summons.
  - July: summons. Final accounts
    exhibited. To be struck off.
- QA: Catharine Sherwood executrix of
  John Sherwood to render accounts.
  - March: summons.
- 44:433-4 • QA: John Whaley administrator of
  Benjamin Whaley to render accounts.
  - March: summons.
  - May: summons.
  - July: summons. Runaway. To be
    struck off.
- QA: Andrew Cox administrator of
  William Thomas to render accounts.
  - March: summons.
  - May: summons.
  - July: summons.
- QA: Vaughan Jump & his wife Sarah
  administratrix of Richard Hammond to
  render accounts.
  - March: summons.
  - May: summons.

- July: summons. Final accounts exhibited. To be struck off.
- QA: Mary Eagle administratrix of James Carradine to render accounts.
  - March: summons.
  - May: summons.
  - July: summons. "Mortus est." To be struck off.
- QA: Ris Hutchings & his wife Dorothy administratrix of Dr. Jos. Haslet to render accounts.
  - March: summons. Letter of excuse.
  - May: summons.
  - July: summons.
- QA: William Elliot executor of Elisabeth Elliot to render accounts.
  - March: summons.
  - May: summons.
  - July: summons. Final accounts exhibited. To be struck off.
- QA: John Kerr administrator of Zachariah Martin to render accounts.
  - March: summons.
  - May: summons.
  - July: summons.
- QA: Thomas Smith & his wife Mary administratrix of James Ruth to render accounts.
  - March: summons.
  - May: summons.
  - July: summons.

44:435-6 • QA: William Smith & James Ringgold Blunt executors of James Smith to render accounts.
  - March: summons. James Thompson is "mortus est".
  - May: summons.
  - July: summons.
- QA: William Yoe administrator of Thomas Yoe to render accounts.
  - March: summons.
  - May: summons.
  - July: summons.
- QA: Nathan Harrington executor of Barbarah Richardson to render accounts.
  - March: summons.
  - May: summons.
  - July: summons.
- QA: James Wilson, James Kenton, & Nathaniel King (3 witnesses to will

of John Cooper) to prove said will.
- March: summons. Will proved.
  To be struck off.
- QA: Arthur Emory 3rd vs. Charles
  Emory & Caleb Clements & his wife
  Rebecca.
  - March: summons to show cause why
    accounts of John Emory should be
    exhibited.
- QA: William Ringgold surviving
  administrator of Edward Brown, Jr.
  to render accounts.
  - May: summons.
  - July: attachment.
- KE: John Gleaves administrator of
  John Gleaves to render accounts.
  - March: summons.
  - May: summons.
  - July: summons.
- KE: John Osborn administrator of
  Henry Osborn to render accounts.
  - March: summons.
  - May: summons.
  - July: summons.
- KE: William Crabbin administrator of
  Meredith Wilson to render accounts.
  - March: summons.
  - May: summons.
  - July: summons.

44:437-8
- KE: Joshua George executor of Hannah
  George to render accounts.
  - March: summons.
  - May: summons.
  - July: summons.
- KE: William Freeman executor of
  Laurence Stainer to render accounts.
  - March: summons.
  - May: summons.
  - July: summons.
- KE: James Chiffin executor of James
  Chiffin to render accounts.
  - March: summons.
  - May: summons.
  - July: summons.
- KE: Jeruliah Barret executrix of
  Jonathan Barret to render accounts.
  - March: summons.
  - May: summons.
  - July: summons.
- KE: Thomas Drugan vs. John Crew
  administrator of Edward Drugan. To
  render accounts.

- March: summons.
- May: summons.
- July: summons.

- KE: John Lambert Wilmer executor of Simon Wilmer to render accounts.
  - May: summons.
  - July: summons.

- KE: Benjamin Howard administrator of Benjamin Howard to render accounts.
  - March: summons.
  - May: summons.
  - July: summons.

- KE: William Pearce administrator dbn of Mary Watkins to render accounts.
  - March: summons.
  - May: summons.
  - July: summons.

- KE: William Pearce administrator of Beatrix Johnson to render accounts.
  - March: summons.
  - May: summons.
  - July: summons.

44:439-40 • KE: Peter Body administrator of John Body to render accounts.
  - March: summons.
  - May: summons.
  - July: summons.

- KE: James Smith executor of Thomas Sealy to render accounts.
  - March: summons.
  - May: summons.
  - July: summons.

- KE: Joyce Ringgold administratrix of Charles Ringgold to render accounts.
  - March: summons.
  - May: summons.
  - July: summons.

- KE: Dean Read executor of John Read to render accounts.
  - March: summons.
  - May: summons. Settled. To be struck off.

- KE: Rachel Anderson administratrix of William Anderson to render accounts.
  - March: summons.
  - May: summons. To be struck off.
  - July: summons. [!]

- KE: Ann Hutchison administratrix of John Hutchison to render accounts.
  - March: summons.
  - May: summons.

- July: summons.
- KE: Martha Newcomb administratrix of Thomas Newcomb to render accounts.
  - March: summons.
  - May: summons.
  - July: summons.
- KE: John Gresham administrator of John Ralph to render accounts.
  - March: summons.
  - May: summons. "Mortus est." To be struck off.
- KE: Sarah Ringgold executrix of Josias Ringgold to render accounts.
  - March: summons.
  - May: summons.
  - July: summons.

44:441-2
- KE: Philemon & Robert Pratt administrators of Benjamin Pratt to render accounts.
  - March: summons.
  - May: summons.
  - July: summons.
- KE: Ann Cleaver administratrix of William Cleaver to render accounts.
  - March: summons.
  - May: summons.
  - July: summons.
- KE: Elisabeth Crew administratrix of William Crew to render accounts.
  - March: summons.
  - May: summons. "Mortus est." To be struck off.
- KE: John Corse administrator of Samuel Corse to render accounts.
  - March: summons.
  - May: summons.
  - July: summons.
- KE: Rudolph Moore administrator of Henry Moore to render accounts.
  - March: summons.
  - May: summons.
  - July: summons. Final accounts exhibited. To be struck off.
- KE: Eleanor Vansant administratrix of George Vansant to render accounts.
  - March: summons.
  - May: summons. "Mortus est." To be struck off.
- KE: William Hazel administrator of Sarah Hazel to render accounts.
  - March: summons.

- May: summons.
- July: summons.
- KE: Eleanor Grant administratrix of William Grant to render accounts.
  - March: summons. Married John Cary. Final accounts exhibited. To be struck off.
- KE: John Watson executor of Esther Watson to render accounts.
  - March: summons.
  - May: summons.
  - July: summons.

44:443-4 • KE: John Vansant executor of Joshua Vansant vs. Jacob Comegys. To show cause why conceals said estate.
  - July: summons.
- KE: John Vansant executor of Joshua Vansant vs. Joshua Vansant. To show cause why conceals said estate.
  - July: summons.
- CE: Mary Marcer administratrix of Robert Marcer, Jr. to render accounts.
  - March: summons.
  - May: summons.
- CE: Samuel & Thomas Tigart administrators of Cardiff Tigart to render accounts.
  - March: summons.
  - May: summons.
- CE: Edward Dougherty administrator of Jos. Chissel to render accounts.
  - March: summons.
  - May: summons.
- CE: Adam Vance administrator of James Vance to render accounts.
  - March: summons.
  - May: summons.
- CE: John Ward administrator of Henry Ward to render accounts.
  - March: summons.
  - May: summons. Final accounts exhibited. To be struck off.
- CE: Thomas Allison legatee of Thomas Miller vs. Agness & Samuel Miller executors of said Thomas Miller. To show cause why they conceal said estate.
  - March: attachment.
  - May: attachment. To be struck off.
- CE: Mathew Sedgwick vs. Sarah

Sedgwick & Fran. Boyd executors of Richard Sedgwick. Summons to render accounts.
- March: libel, answer, demurrer.
- May: additional accounts exhibited.
- July: final accounts exhibited.

44:445-6 • CE: Thomas, George, John, Sarah, Esther Beatty, & John Herron & his wife Martha vs. Sarah Sedgwick & Francis Boyd. To render accounts.
- March: libel, answer, demurrer.
- May: summons.
- July: summons.

• CE: Jonathan Holling administrator of Abigail Holling to render accounts.
- March: summons.
- May: summons.
- July: summons.

• CE: Richard Oldham executor of Ann Oldham to render accounts.
- March: summons.
- May: summons. Final accounts exhibited. To be struck off.

• CE: Amos & George Alexander executors of Theophilus Alexander to render accounts.
- March: summons.
- May: summons.
- July: summons.

• CE: Sarah Pennington & William Withers administrators of Abraham Pennington to render accounts.
- March: summons.
- May: summons. Accounts exhibited. To be struck off.

• CE: Susannah Elliott administratrix of Benjamin Elliott to render accounts.
- March: summons.
- May: summons. Final accounts exhibited. To be struck off.

• CE: Jos. Earle vs. Sarah Cunningham administratrix of George Cunningham. To render accounts.
- March: summons.
- May: summons. Final accounts exhibited. To be struck off.
- July: summons. [!]

• CE: Archibald Ankim executor of George Ankrim to render accounts.

Court Session: 10 Mar, 12 May, 14 Jul 1772

- – March: summons.
- – May: summons.
- – July: summons.
- • CE: Andrew Welsh executor of William Callender to render accounts.
  - – March: summons.
  - – May: summons.
  - – July: summons.

44:447-8 • CE: James Corbit executor of James Corbit to render accounts.
- – March: summons.
- – May: summons.
- – July: summons.
- • CE: Agustine Beedle executor of John Beedle, Sr. to render accounts.
  - – March: summons.
  - – May: summons. Final accounts exhibited. To be struck off.
- • CE: William Chandler & his wife administratrix of Peter Jones to render accounts.
  - – March: summons.
  - – May: summons.
  - – July: summons.
- • CE: John Anderson & William Glasgow executors of John Glasgow to render accounts.
  - – March: summons.
  - – May: summons.
  - – July: summons.
- • CE: James Scott & Thomas Whetherspoon executors of John Scott to render accounts.
  - – March: summons.
  - – May: summons.
  - – July: summons.
- • CE: Alexander Moore & his wife Margaret executrix of John Callender to render accounts.
  - – March: summons.
  - – May: summons.
  - – July: summons.
- • CE: Jonathan Humberstone administrator of George Humberstone to render accounts.
  - – March: summons.
  - – May: summons.
  - – July: summons.
- • CE: John Donohoe & his wife Mary administratrix of John Anderson to render accounts.
  - – March: summons.

Court Session: 10 Mar, 12 May, 14 Jul 1772

- — May: summons.
- — July: summons.
- CE: Sarah Lewis administratrix of John Lewis to render accounts.
  - — March: summons.
  - — May: summons.
  - — July: summons.

44:449-50 • CE: Elisha Ferry administrator of William Ferry to render accounts.
  - — March: summons.
  - — May: summons.
  - — July: summons.

- CE: George Milligan, Michael Earl, & Charles Gordon vs. administration on estate of John McDuff. Caveat to take LoA.
  - — March: summons. LaC granted.
  - — May: summons.
  - — July: summons.

- CE: Nathaniel Martin vs. William Baxter executor of Francis Baxter. To take LoA.
  - — May: summons.
  - — July: summons.

- CE: Jos. Earl for children of Phineas Hodgson vs. John Hodgson administrator of said Phineas Hodgson. To render accounts.
  - — July: summons.

- CE: John Hodgson administrator of Phineas Hodgson vs. Abel Hodgson. To show cause why he conceals said estate.
  - — July: summons.

- SM: James Biscoe (son of Bazil) by his next friend Kenelm Harrison vs. Bennett, James, Mary Biscoe, & Thomas Crowley & his wife Ann.
  - — March: libel, answer, several depositions.
  - — May: summons to Ann Williams.
  - — July: summons to Ann Williams.

- SM: Jane Goldsborough administratrix of Ignatius Goldsborough to render accounts.
  - — March: summons.
  - — May: summons.
  - — July: summons.

- SM: Eleanor & John Johnson executors of John Johnson to render accounts.
  - — March: summons.
  - — May: summons.

- July: summons.

44:451-2 • SM: Leonard Biscoe one of executors of John Johnson to render accounts.
- March: attachment.
- May: attachment.
- July: attachment. To be struck off.

• SM: John Smoot administrator of John Thomas Gardiner to render accounts.
- March: summons.
- May: summons.
- July: summons.

• SM: Joshua Watts executor of Thomas Watts to render accounts.
- March: attachment.
- May: attachment.
- July: attachment. Final accounts exhibited. To be struck off.

• SM: Anastatius Norris administratrix of William Norris to render accounts.
- March: summons.
- May: summons.
- July: summons.

• SM: Catharine & Wilson Thomas administrators of James Thomas to render accounts.
- March: summons.
- May: summons.
- July: summons. Final accounts exhibited. To be struck off.

• SM: Elisabeth Chesley executrix of John Chesley to render accounts.
- March: summons. Suit in Court of Appeals. To be struck off.
- May: summons. To be struck off.

• SM: Robert Armstrong & his wife Mary & William Guyther executors of Richard Swan Edwar to render accounts.
- March: summons.
- May: summons.
- July: summons.

• SM: Barnet Barber executor of Edward Barber to render accounts.
- March: summons.
- May: summons.
- July: summons.

• SM: Ann Tarlton executrix of John Tarlton to render accounts.
- March: summons.

- May: summons.
- July: summons.

44:453-4 • SM: Jemima Lynch & William Taylor executors of Francis Lynch to render accounts.
- March: summons.
- May: summons.
- July: summons.

• SM: Mary Lee executrix of Charles Lee to render accounts.
- March: summons.
- May: summons.
- July: summons.

• SM: Mary Tare executrix of John Tare to render accounts.
- March: summons.
- May: summons.
- July: summons.

• SM: Ignatius French executor of John French to render accounts.
- March: summons.
- May: summons.
- July: summons.

• SM: Robert Watts administrator of Thomas Fortes to render accounts.
- March: summons. No effects.

• SM: Robert Watts administrator of John Feild to render accounts.
- March: summons. No effects. To be struck off.

• SM: Sabra Corsair administratrix of John Corsair to render accounts.
- March: summons.
- May: summons.
- July: summons.

• SM: William Guyther administrator of Thomas Guyther to render accounts.
- March: summons. Dead. To be struck off.

• SM: William Guyther administrator of David Rice to render accounts.
- March: summons. Dead. To be struck off.

44:455-6 • SM: Enoch Fenwick administrator of Edward Cole to render accounts.
- March: summons.
- May: summons. No effects. To be struck off.

• SM: Jesse Tennison administrator of Thomas Tennison to render accounts.
- March: summons.
- May: summons.

- July: summons. To be struck off.
- SM: Elisabeth Wheatly administratrix of John Wheatly to render accounts.
  - March: summons. To be struck off.
- SM: Benedict Fenwick executor of William Fenwick to render accounts.
  - March: summons.
  - May: summons.
  - July: summons.
- SM: Ann Thompson & Basil Brook executors of Mary Earle to render accounts.
  - March: summons.
  - May: summons.
  - July: summons.
- SM: Bennet Heard executor of John Heard to render accounts.
  - March: summons.
  - May: summons.
- SM: Normand Bruce vs. George Watts & his wife Rebecca, Daniel & Charles Heath & Mary Heath, & Susannah Key. To render accounts.
  - March: summons.
  - May: libel, answer, replication. Summons to: James Jordan, John Reeder, Jr., William Thomas.
  - July: summons.
- SM: John Able, Jr. & his wife Ann vs. Richard Stanfield administrator of John Stanfield. To show cause to show lease to J. Atta Clark.
  - July: summons. Letter filed. To be struck off.

44:457-8
- CH: William Bryan surviving executor of William Bryan to render accounts.
  - March: summons.
  - May: summons.
  - July: summons.
- CH: Charles Sanders administrator of Jane Doyne to render accounts.
  - March: summons.
  - May: summons.
  - July: summons.
- CH: Elisabeth Grove administratrix of Ebsworth Grove to render accounts.
  - March: summons.
  - May: summons.
  - July: summons.

- CH: Hugh Hamill executor of John Hamill to render accounts.
  - March: summons.
  - May: summons.
  - July: summons.
- CH: Mary Hawkins executrix of Rudolph Morris Hawkins to render accounts.
  - March: summons.
  - May: summons. In PG. To be struck off.
- CH: Henry Jameson vs. Walter Pye administrator of Edward Queen. To render accounts.
  - March: summons.
  - May: summons.
  - July: summons.
- CH: John Eddelin & his wife Susa executrix of Bazil Hagan to render accounts.
  - March: summons.
  - May: summons.
  - July: summons.
- CH: Margaret Carrico administratrix of Peter Carrico to render accounts.
  - March: summons.
  - May: summons. In PG. To be struck off.
- CH: Edward Boarman executor of John Gardiner to render accounts.
  - March: summons.
  - May: summons.
  - July: summons.

44:459-60
- CH: Henry Smith Hawkins & Thomas Hawkins executors of Alexander Smith Hawkins to render accounts.
  - March: summons.
  - May: summons.
  - July: summons. Final accounts exhibited. To be struck off.
- CH: Virlinda Adams executrix of Lodwick Adams to render accounts.
  - March: summons.
  - May: summons. Final accounts exhibited. To be struck off.
- CH: Dorcas & Bennett Dyson executors of Joseph Dyson to render accounts.
  - March: summons.
  - May: summons.
  - July: summons.
- CH: Elisabeth Mathews administratrix of William Mathews to render

    accounts.
- March: summons.
- May: summons.
- July: summons.
- CH: Smith Middleton executor of Cornelius Davis (FR) to render accounts.
  - March: summons.
  - May: summons.
  - July: summons.
- CH: Richard Hudson administrator of Johannah Stromat to render accounts.
  - March: summons.
  - May: summons.
  - July: summons.
- CH: Elisabeth Stoddert administratrix of William Truman Stoddert to render accounts.
  - March: summons.
  - May: summons.
  - July: summons.
- CH: Edward Smoot administrator of Posthuma Smoot to render accounts.
  - March: summons. Accounts exhibited. To be struck off.
- CH: William Franklin administrator of Benjamin Garner to render accounts.
  - March: summons.
  - May: summons.
  - July: summons. Final accounts exhibited. To be struck off.

44:461-2 • CH: Edward Candle administrator of Robert Candle to render accounts.
- March: summons.
- May: summons.
- July: summons.
- CH: Francis & Thomas Maddox executors of Benjamin Maddox to render accounts.
  - March: summons. Accounts exhibited. To be struck off.
- CH: Richard Harrison administrator of Joseph Harrison to render accounts.
  - March: summons.
  - May: summons.
  - July: summons.
- CH: Thomas Smith administrator of James Smith to render accounts.
  - March: summons.
  - May: summons.

Court Session: 10 Mar, 12 May, 14 Jul 1772

- July: summons. Final accounts exhibited. To be struck off.
- CH: Josias Hawkins administrator of Henry Hawkins to render accounts.
  - March: summons.
  - May: summons.
  - July: summons. Accounts exhibited. To be struck off.
- CH: Priscilla & William Smallwood administrators of Bayne Smallwood to render accounts.
  - March: libel.
  - May: attachment to render answer.
  - July: attachment to render answer.
- CV: Mary Smith administratrix of Joseph Smith to render accounts.
  - March: summons.
  - May: summons. Final accounts exhibited. To be struck off.
- CV: John Weems, Jr. administrator of James Fleet to render accounts.
  - March: summons.
  - May: summons.
  - July: summons.
- CV: Thomas Reynolds & Edward Reynolds (2 of witnesses to will of Josias Sunderland) to prove said will.
  - March: summons. Thomas Holland (3rd witness) filed deposition.
  - May: summons.
  - July: summons. Will proved. LoA granted. To be struck off.
- CV: Hileary & Thomas Wilson executors of Joseph Wilson, Sr. to render accounts.
  - March: summons.
  - May: summons. Mentions: accounts expected from ENG.
  - July: summons. Accounts exhibited. To be struck off.
- CV: Dorcas & John Spicknall executors of John Spicknall to render accounts.
  - March: summons.
  - May: summons.
  - July: summons. To be struck off.
- CV: John Peasalle administrator of John Peasalle to render accounts.

Page 166

44:463-4

Court Session: 10 Mar, 12 May, 14 Jul 1772

- March: summons.
- May: summons.
- July: summons.
- CV: Barbara Brooke executrix of John Brooke to render accounts.
  - March: summons. Dead. To be struck off.
- CV: Priscilla Hardesty executrix of Mary Laurence to render accounts.
  - March: summons.
  - May: summons.
  - July: summons.
- CV: George & Elisabeth Grant executors of John Beckett to render accounts.
  - March: summons.
  - May: summons.
  - July: summons.
- PG: Elisabeth Eastwood executrix of Benjamin Eastwood to render accounts.
  - March: attachment.
  - May: attachment.
  - July: attachment.
- 44:465-6 • PG: Marjory Lyles administratrix of Zachariah Lyles to render accounts.
  - March: attachment.
  - May: attachment.
  - July: attachment.
- PG: Mary & Leonard Waring executors of Francis Waring to render accounts.
  - March: attachment.
  - May: attachment.
  - July: attachment. To be struck off.
- PG: Margaret Miles administratrix of William Miles to render accounts.
  - March: summons.
  - May: summons.
  - July: summons.
- PG: John Cook, Esq. administrator of Thomas Lee to render accounts.
  - March: summons.
  - May: summons.
  - July: summons.
- PG: Jen for Samuel Selby, et. al. vs. S.C. for John Dorset, et. al.
  - March: libel, answer, general replication.
  - May: libel, answer, general replication.

Page 167

Court Session: 10 Mar, 12 May, 14 Jul 1772

- July: libel, answer, general
  replication.
- PG: Phil. Tennally vs. Christopher
  Lowndes administrator of William
  Tennally. To render accounts.
  - March: summons.
  - May: summons.
  - July: summons.
- PG: Harrison Lane joint
  administration of Samuel Wells vs.
  Stephen West administrator of said
  Samuel Wells. To render accounts.
  - March: summons.
  - May: summons.
  - July: summons. Accounts
    exhibited.
- PG: Elisabeth Osbourne
  administratrix of Robert Osbourne to
  render accounts.
  - March: summons.
  - May: summons.
  - July: summons.
- PG: William Weedon executor of Henry
  Gear to render accounts.
  - March: summons.
  - May: summons. Accounts
    exhibited.
- 44:467-8 PG: Walter Evans administrator dbn
  of Elisabeth Evans to render
  accounts.
  - March: summons.
  - May: summons.
  - July: summons.
- PG: Mary, Henry, Richard, & Thomas
  Snowden executors of Thomas Snowden
  to render accounts.
  - March: summons. In AA.
- PG: James Wilson administrator of
  William Willson to render accounts.
  - March: summons.
  - May: summons.
  - July: summons.
- PG: Joseph Peach administrator of
  Joseph Peach, Jr. to render
  accounts.
  - March: summons.
  - May: summons. Final accounts
    exhibited. To be struck off.
- PG: Ann & Rebecca Marloe executrices
  of Ralph Marloe to render accounts.
  - March: summons.
  - May: summons. Final accounts

- exhibited. To be struck off.
- PG: Richard Brooke executor of Lucy Brooke to render accounts.
  - March: summons. No estate. To be struck off.
- PG: Charity Mitchell administratrix of James Mitchell to render accounts.
  - March: summons.
  - May: summons.
  - July: summons.
- PG: Robert Kissick & his wife Jane administratrix of Richard Bowes to render accounts.
  - March: summons.
  - May: summons.
  - July: summons.
- PG: Sarah Elson administratrix of William Elson to render accounts.
  - March: summons.
  - May: summons. Final accounts exhibited. To be struck off.
44:469-70 • FR: Catharine Mock administratrix of George Mock to render accounts.
  - March: summons.
  - May: summons.
  - July: summons.
- FR: William Aldridge executor of Nicholas Aldridge to render accounts.
  - March: summons.
  - May: summons.
  - July: summons.
- FR: Philipina Bonsom administratrix of Laurence Bonsom to render accounts.
  - March: summons.
  - May: summons.
  - July: summons.
- FR: Ann Williams administratrix of Charles Williams to render accounts.
  - March: summons.
  - May: summons.
  - July: summons.
- FR: Andrew Williams administrator of Ann Davis to render accounts.
  - March: summons.
  - May: summons.
  - July: summons.
- FR: Catharine Morris administratrix of William Morris to render accounts.

- March: summons.
- May: summons.
- July: summons.
- FR: Margaret & Jacob Ross administrators of Nicholas Rope to render accounts.
  - March: summons.
  - May: summons.
  - July: summons.
- FR: Amos & John McGingley executors of James McGingley to render accounts.
  - March: summons.
  - May: summons.
  - July: summons.
- FR: Mary Laurence executrix of George Laurence to render accounts.
  - March: summons.
  - May: summons.
  - July: summons.

44:471-2
- FR: David Hunter administrator of Anthony Hunter to render accounts.
  - March: summons.
  - May: summons.
  - July: summons.
- FR: Henrietta Nowland administratrix of Daniel Nowland to render accounts.
  - March: summons.
  - May: summons.
  - July: summons.
- FR: Elias Harden administrator of Elisabeth Harden vs. Charles Harden. To show cause why he conceals Negro Sam & Negro George. [N.B. Entry x'ed out, as being erroneous.]
  - Said Elias Harden deposed.
  - Said Charles Harden deposed.
  - Mary Davis deposed.
  Withdrawn. To be struck off.
- FR: Judah Burck & James Galt administrators of Patrick Burck to render accounts.
  - March: summons.
  - May: summons.
  - July: summons.
- FR: Eve Cover executrix of Daniel Cover to render accounts.
  - March: summons.
  - May: summons.
  - July: summons.

Court Session: 10 Mar, 12 May, 14 Jul 1772

- FR: Sarah Mathews executrix of Samuel Mathews to render accounts.
  - March: summons.
  - May: summons.
  - July: summons.
- FR: Lurana Stallings executrix of Richard Stallings to render accounts.
  - March: summons.
  - May: summons.
  - July: summons.
- FR: Loline Kimbol executrix of John Kimbol to render accounts.
  - March: summons.
  - May: summons.
  - July: summons. To be struck off.
- FR: Mary & Henry Brown executors of George Brown to render accounts.
  - March: summons.
  - May: summons.
  - July: summons.
- **44:473-4** FR: John Cary & Christopher Edelen executors of James Carrick to render accounts.
  - March: summons.
  - May: summons.
  - July: summons.
- FR: Phillip Crouss administrator of Vendel Crouss to render accounts.
  - March: summons.
  - May: summons. Accounts exhibited. To be struck off.
- FR: Henry Snebely administrator of James Grub to render accounts.
  - March: summons.
  - May: summons. Accounts exhibited. To be struck off.
- FR: Mary Davis administratrix of Clement Davis to render accounts.
  - March: summons.
  - May: summons.
  - July: summons.
- FR: James Thompson administrator of Edward Smith to render accounts.
  - March: summons.
  - May: summons.
  - July: summons.
- FR: Susannah Powles & George Stricker executors of Jacob Powles to render accounts.
  - March: summons.

Page 171

- May: summons.
- July: summons.
- FR: Jacob Siner executor of Henry Siner to render accounts.
  - March: summons.
  - May: summons.
  - July: summons.
- FR: Rebecka Smith executrix of Andrew Smith to render accounts.
  - March: summons.
  - May: summons.
  - July: summons.
- FR: Jacob & Joshua Swagler executors of George Swagler to render accounts.
  - March: summons.
  - May: summons.
  - July: summons.

44:475-6
- FR: Sarah Henry executrix of Adam Henry to render accounts.
  - March: summons.
  - May: summons.
  - July: summons.
- FR: Nathaniel Harriss administrator of Thomas Harris.
  - July: summons to Aaron Harris to show cause why he conceals said estate Summons to Ninian Tanehill.
- FR: John Stull & James Vardel executors of David Fourney to render accounts.
  - May: summons.
- BA: William Harriot administrator of Susannah Harriot to render accounts.
  - March: summons.
  - May: summons.
  - July: summons. To be struck off.
- BA: Andrew Stigar administrator of Jacob Rock to render accounts.
  - March: summons.
  - May: summons.
  - July: summons. To be struck off.
- BA: Philemon Deaver executor of Richard Miller Cole to render accounts.
  - March: summons.
  - May: summons.
  - July: summons.
- BA: John Hammond Dorsey

Court Session: 10 Mar, 12 May, 14 Jul 1772

administrator of William Gough to
render accounts.
- March: summons.
- May: summons.
- July: summons.

44:477-8 • BA: Benjamin Jones administrator of
Charles Jones to render accounts.
- March: summons.
- May: summons.
- July: summons.

• BA: Margaret Brown administratrix of
Absalom Brown to render accounts.
- March: summons.
- May: summons.
- July: summons.

• BA: Dennis McSwain & his wife Mary
administratrix of John Skipton to
render accounts.
- March: summons.
- May: summons.
- July: summons.

• BA: Henry Oram & Ann Statia Oram
executors of Ann Statia Haws to
render accounts.
- March: summons.
- May: summons.
- July: summons. "N. sunt." To
be struck off.

• BA: John Anderson administrator of
Hugh Orrs to render accounts.
- March: summons.
- May: summons.
- July: summons. Runaway. To be
struck off.

• BA: Daniel Chamier administrator of
Rowland Carnan to render accounts.
- March: attachment. Voucher
expected from ENG.
- May: attachment.
- July: attachment.

• BA: Peter Carlisle executor of
Rachel Wilmott to render accounts.
- March: summons.
- May: summons.
- July: summons.

• BA: Sarah Johns administratrix of
Aquila Johns to render accounts.
- March: summons. No such person.
To CV. To be struck off.

• BA: Benjamin Rogers administrator of
William Rogers to render accounts.
- March: summons.

Court Session: 10 Mar, 12 May, 14 Jul 1772

- May: summons.
- July: summons.

44:479-80 • BA: Daniel McGhee & his wife Sarah administrators of Edward Hall to render accounts.
- March: summons.
- May: summons.
- July: summons.

• BA: Broad Cole administrator of Ann Broad to render accounts.
- March: summons.
- May: summons.
- July: summons.

• BA: Sarah Dunn executrix of Robert Dunn to render accounts.
- March: summons.
- May: summons.
- July: summons.

• BA: Robert Davis administrator of Mary Davis to render accounts.
- March: summons.
- May: summons.
- July: summons.

• BA: Samuel Purveyance, Jr. administrator of James Gibson to render accounts.
- March: summons. Settled. To be struck off.

• BA: Jacob Giles administrator of Gilbert Donohoe to render accounts.
- March: summons.
- May: summons.
- July: summons.

• BA: Helen Gilchrist executrix of Robert Gilchrist to render accounts.
- March: summons. To be struck off.

• BA: Greenbury Dorsey & his wife Sophia administratrix of John Clark to render accounts.
- March: summons.
- May: summons.
- July: summons.

• BA: Ann & William Partridge administrators of Daubin Buckley Partridge to render accounts.
- March: summons.
- May: summons.
- July: summons.

44:481-2 • BA: Henry Stevenson & William Smith administrators of William Govane to render accounts.

Court Session: 10 Mar, 12 May, 14 Jul 1772

- March: summons.
- May: summons.
- July: summons.
- BA: Carolina Orrick administratrix of John Orrick to render accounts.
  - March: summons.
  - May: summons.
  - July: summons.
- BA: Thomas Johnson, Jr. for Mary Kelly vs. G. Chalmers for Felix Oneal (merchant, Baltimore Town). March Term.
  - Text of libel. Plaintiff is widow of James Kelly, who died 8 September last, without children or other relations. Defendant was granted LoA. Mentions: Robert Hollyday (sheriff).

44:483-4
  Text of answer. Mentions: Andrew Buchanan (JoP).
  - Nathan Johnson, of full age, deposed that he has been married 18 years & that Thomas Beemsly (former husband of plaintiff) is gone from these parts for many years.
44:485-6
  - Arthur Lookery, of full age, deposed that he has been a resident of BA for 8 years & that the plaintiff was married to (N) Beazly who has runaway. Signed: Arthur Coskery.
  - Miles Love, of full age, deposed that he has been a resident of BA for 26 years & that the plaintiff's husband (N) Beezly was still alive in southern part of VA towards Carolina.
44:487-8
  Ruling: LoA to defendant revoked & LoA granted to plaintiff.
- BA: G. Chalmers for Charles Gossage vs. Thomas Jennings for estate of Elisha Hall. Caveat.

  Text of libel. Plaintiff married Sarah only sister of Elisha Hall who died 28 September 1771 without children or other relations other than plaintiff except for Mary Hall (supposed widow).
44:489-90
  Summons to said Mary Hall (widow).

Page 175

Text of will of said Elisha Hall
(Baltimore Town), dated 25 September
1771. Legatees: wife Mary.
Witnesses: Elisabeth Aisquith, Sarah
Pamer, Ann Lloyd.

44:491-2

- Elisabeth Aisquith, of full age,
  deposed. Mentions: Dr. John
  Boyd, MM Alexander Chamier
  (Annapolis) & Thomas Aisquith
  (Annapolis), Mr. Mordecai Gist
  (Annapolis) & Thomas Townshend
  (Annapolis), Mr. McCubbins,
  dec'd's sister Mrs. Gossage &
  her children, Mrs. Ann Lloyd,
  Mrs. Sarah Palmer.
- Sarah Palmer, of full age,
  deposed.

44:493-4

- Ann Lloyd, of full age,
  deposed.
- Dr. John Boyd, of full age,
  deposed.

44:495-6

- Barbarah Wilkinson, of full age,
  deposed.
- William Maccubbing, of full age,
  deposed.

44:497-8   Mentions: Robert Holliday (sheriff).

Text of will of Mary Hall (widow).
44:499-500 Before: Jonathan Plowman (JoP, BA).
44:501-2   Ruling: will is valid.
44:503-4 • BA: Henry Reston executor of Renaldo
Monk to render accounts.
- March: attachment.
- May: attachment.
- July: attachment. Runaway, say
  Mary Monk. To be struck off.
• BA: John Giles & his wife Ann
executrix of Edward Fell to render
accounts.
- March: attachment.
- May: attachment.
- July: attachment.
• BA: Elisabeth Gover executrix of
Ephraim Gover to render accounts.
- March: attachment.
- May: summons.
- July: summons.
• BA: Elisabeth Carnan executrix of
Christopher Carnan to render
accounts.
- March: summons.

- May: summons.
- July: summons.
- BA: Clement Lewis administrator of Joseph Lewis to render accounts.
  - March: summons.
  - May: summons.
  - July: summons.
- BA: Kerenhapuch Hamilton executor of William Hamilton to render accounts.
  - March: summons. No such man. To be struck off.
- BA: Michael Gladman executor of Thomas Gladman to render accounts.
  - March: summons.
  - May: summons.
  - July: summons. Dec'd was son of executor. All debts are paid. To be struck off.
- BA: Joseph & Thomas Burgess executors of Hugh Burgess to render accounts.
  - March: summons.
  - May: summons.
  - July: summons.
- BA: Mary Cole executrix of William Cole to render accounts.
  - March: summons.
  - May: summons.
  - July: summons.
- 44:505-6 • BA: John Hendrickson executor of Richard Jones to render accounts.
  - March: summons.
  - May: summons.
  - July: summons.
- BA: William Lux executor of Nicholas Ruxton Gay to render accounts.
  - March: summons.
  - May: summons.
  - July: summons.
- BA: Hellen Ogg executrix of George Ogg to render accounts.
  - March: summons.
  - May: summons.
  - July: summons.
- BA: Christiana Kirchner (alias Christiana Craswick) executrix of Caspar Kirchner (alias Caspar Craswick) to render accounts.
  - March: summons.
  - May: summons.
  - July: summons.
- BA: Gerrard Hopkins executor of

James Wilson to render accounts.
- March: summons.
- May: summons.
- July: summons. Final accounts exhibited. To be struck off.

- BA: Mary Bowen executrix of Benjamin Bowen to render accounts.
  - March: summons.
  - May: summons.
  - July: summons.

- BA: Mary Bowen executrix of Nathan Bowen to render accounts.
  - March: summons.
  - May: summons.
  - July: summons.

- BA: Arena French executrix of Hannah Hughs to render accounts.
  - March: summons.
  - May: summons.
  - July: summons.

- BA: Mark Alexander administrator of Benjamin Cook to render accounts.
  - March: summons.
  - May: summons.
  - July: summons.

44:507-8 • BA: Joseph & William Bearman executors of William Bearman to render accounts.
  - March: summons.
  - May: summons.
  - July: summons. "N. Sunt." To be struck off.

- BA: Mary Carlisle administratrix of David Carlisle to render accounts.
  - March: summons.
  - May: summons.
  - July: summons.

- BA: Elisabeth Wilkinson administratrix of John Wilkinson to render accounts.
  - March: summons.
  - May: summons.
  - July: summons. Final accounts exhibited. To be struck off.

- BA: James Moore administrator of James Moore to render accounts.
  - March: summons.
  - May: summons.
  - July: summons.

- BA: Thomas Presbury administrator of Richard Crawley to render accounts.
  - March: summons.

Court Session: 10 Mar, 12 May, 14 Jul 1772

- May: summons.
- July: summons.
- BA: Francis Davis administrator of
  David Davis to render accounts.
  - March: summons.
  - May: summons.
  - July: summons.
- BA: William Westbay administrator of
  James Postlewaith to render
  accounts.
  - March: summons.
  - May: summons.
  - July: summons. To be struck
    off.
- BA: William Westbay administrator of
  David Fulton to render accounts.
  - March: summons.
  - May: summons.
  - July: summons. To be struck
    off.
- BA: Sarah & John Chilcote
  administrators of James Chilcote to
  render accounts.
  - March: summons.
  - May: summons.
  - July: summons. To be struck
    off.

44:509-10 • BA: Thomas Jennings for Thomas
Jones vs. Samuel Chase for Job
Garretson. LoA was granted on 12
November 1771 on estate of Samuel
Groome (BA) to defendant.

Text of petition. On 2 November
1771, petitioner (BA) applied for
LoA on estate of Samuel Groom who
died in KE some 80 years ago.
Another person of the same name died
in BA on 12 November 1771.

Mentions: Robert Hollyday (sheriff).
44:511-2   Text of answer. On 1 July 1712,
Seaborn Tucker (AA) executed a deed
of indenture to Samuel Groom
(merchant, London) & patented "Chevy
Chase" to said Thomas Groom [!].
Said Samuel Groom afterwards came to
the Province & died about 4/5 years
ago. On 22 October 1771, defendant
bought land from John Tucker
(grandson & heir-at-law of said
Seaborn Tucker). Before: Elisha

Court Session: 10 Mar, 12 May, 14 Jul 1772

Harrison.

Ruling: defendant.

44:513-4 • BA: Alexander Lawson vs. will of Walter Smith. Caveat against will.
- May: summons.
- July: summons.

• BA: John Lynch & his wife Mary executrix of John Webster to show cause why they conceal said estate.
- July: summons.

• BA: Capt. Clark vs. W.R. for Rachel Sharpe administratrix of Edward Sharpe. To show cause why she conceals said estate.
- July: summons. Final accounts exhibited. To be struck off. Mentions: John Wilmot brother of said Rachel.

• BA: William Presbury administrator of Constant Irwin to show cause why LoA should not be revoked & LoA granted to Thomas Chambers (executor).
- July: summons.

• AA: Maj. Charles Hammond executor of Phillip Hammond to render accounts.
- March: Duces Tecum.
- May: Duces Tecum.
- July: summons.

• AA: Robert Johnson & his wife Ann administratrix of Phillip Golder to render accounts.
- March: attachment.
- May: attachment.
- July: attachment. Suit in chancery.

• AA: Mary Wayman administratrix of Edward Wayman to render accounts.
- March: summons. Vouchers in hands of John Hammond.
- May: summons.
- July: summons. To be struck off.

• AA: Isabella Franklin administratrix of Robert Franklin to render accounts.
- March: summons.
- May: summons.
- July: summons.

44:515-6 • AA: John & Charles Worthington

Page 180

executors of John Worthington to render accounts.
- March: summons.
- May: summons.
- July: summons.

- AA: John & Charles Worthington vs. Samuel & Vachel Worthington. To show cause why they refuse to sign inventory as next of kin.
  - March: summons.
  - May: summons. In BA.
  - July: summons. Inventory returned signed by 2 kindred. To be struck off.

- AA: Ely Dorsey surviving administrator dbn of Edward Dorsey, Esq. to render accounts.
  - March: summons.
  - May: summons.
  - July: summons.

- AA: Ely Dorsey administrator of Henrietta Maria Dorsey to render accounts.
  - March: summons.
  - May: summons.
  - July: summons.

- AA: Samuel & John Howard executors of Samuel Howard to render accounts.
  - March: summons.
  - May: summons.
  - July: summons.

- AA: Amos Riggs administrator dbn of John Riggs to render accounts.
  - March: attachment.
  - May: attachment.
  - July: attachment.

- AA: Amos Riggs administrator of Mary Riggs to render accounts.
  - March: attachment.
  - May: attachment.
  - July: attachment.

- AA: John Clayton vs. Samuel & Benjamin Lane administrators of Thomas Lane. To render accounts.
  - March: attachment.
  - May: attachment.
  - July: attachment.

- AA: Henry Oneal Welsh administrator dbn of Thomas King to render accounts.
  - March: attachment.
  - May: attachment.

- July: attachment. Suit in chancery. To be struck off.

44:517-8 • AA: Benjamin Hood administrator of James Hood to render accounts.
- March: summons.
- May: summons.
- July: attachment.

• AA: Lewis Duvall & his wife Alice & Francis Sappington executors of Mark Brown to render accounts.
- March: summons.
- May: summons.
- July: attachment. To be struck off.

• AA: Charles Pettibone administrator dbn of Phillip Pettibone to render accounts.
- March: summons.
- May: summons.
- July: summons.

• AA: Mary Campbell administratrix of Alexander Campbell to render accounts.
- March: summons.
- May: summons.
- July: summons.

• AA: Valentine Brown administrator of Stephen Purnall to render accounts.
- March: summons.
- May: summons.
- July: summons.

• AA: John Scott administrator of Jacob French to render accounts.
- March: summons. Papers left with Mr. Ridout. To be struck off.

• AA: Frederick Mills & his wife Achsa administratrix of Caleb Conner to render accounts.
- March: summons. Papers left with Robert Norris.
- May: summons.
- July: summons. To be struck off.

• AA: Francis Sappington executrix of Thomas Sappington to render accounts.
- March: summons.
- May: summons.
- July: attachment.

44:519-20 • AA: Ann Pindel executrix of Phillip Pindel to render accounts.

- March: summons.
- May: attachment.
- July: attachment. To be struck off.
* AA: Nicholas & John Normand executors of Nicholas Normand to render accounts.
  - March: summons.
  - May: summons.
  - July: summons. To be struck off.
* AA: Benjamin Stevens executor of Benjamin Stevens to render accounts.
  - March: summons.
  - May: summons.
  - July: summons.
* AA: Thomas Hawkins administrator of John Hawkins to render accounts.
  - March: summons.
  - May: summons.
  - July: summons.
* AA: George Watts administrator of Darky Hill to render accounts.
  - March: summons.
  - May: summons.
  - July: summons.
* AA: John Davis executor of William Worthington to render accounts.
  - March: summons.
  - May: summons.
  - July: summons. Mentions: Dr. John Shaw to show cause why he conceals said estate. To be struck off.
* AA: Elisabeth Hopkins administratrix of Phillip Hopkins to render accounts.
  - May: summons.
  - July: attachment.
* AA: Mary, Henry, Richard, & Thomas Snowden executors of Thomas Snowden to render accounts.
  - May: summons. "Mortus est."
  - July: summons. To be struck off.
* AA: Priscilla Plummer executrix of Yate Plummer to render accounts.
  - July: summons.
44:521-2 * AA: Charles Harding vs. Elias Harding administrator of Elias Harding.
  - March: summons to Charles

Harding (FR) to show cause why
he refuses to deliver estate of
Elisabeth Harding (dec'd).
- John Garrott, of full age,
deposed on 13 February 1769 that
said Charles Harding desired him
to witness the delivery of some
Negroes his mother wished to
give him: Negro Sam, Negro
George.
- William Condon, of full age,
deposed on 20 November 1769.
Mentions: Negro Sam (man), Negro
George (boy), John Garrett & 2
of his sons.
- Benjamin Perry, of full age,
deposed on 20 November 1769.
44:523-4   - Mary Daviss (FR), age 69,
deposed on 11 January 1772.
Mentions: Eleanor Harding wife
of Charles Harding. Signed:
Mary Davis. In presence of:
Charles Harding, Elias Harding.
Signed: David Lynn.
- Lucy Swearingen, age 30, deposed
on 10 January 1772. Mentions:
her sister Eleanor wife of
Charles Harding, Elias Harding
(brother of said Charles).
Before: David Lynn.
44:525-6 <blank>
44:527-8 • AA: William Paca for Stephen Beard
by John Beard his next friend vs.
Thomas Jennings for Nathan Watkins &
Bennett Chew. July court.
Plaintiff is a legatee of Thomas
Watkins (AA).

Text of libel. Plaintiff is under
age 21, by his father John Beard.
Plaintiff's grandfather Thomas
Watkins had land "Lydia's Rest".
Legatee in codicil to will: Mr.
Bennett Chew (AA) "Lydia's Rest"
until testator's grandson Stephen
Beard becomes of age. If said
grandson dies before he comes of
age, then to Joseph Beard.
44:529-30   Nathaniel Watkins is heir at law.

Summons to following witnesses to
testify: John Geary, Mark Geary,

Court Session: 10 Mar, 12 May, 14 Jul 1772

Jr., John Lusby, William Phelps.
Summons to following to testify for
plaintiff: Nathaniel Watkins,
Elisabeth Downes, Lydia Johnson,
Bennett Chew, Richard Beard, Jr.

44:531-2   -   John Geary & Mark Geary deposed.
      -   John Lusby deposed on 14 July
         1772.

44:533-4   -   William Phelps deposed.
         Mentions: Mr. Chew, Mr. Paca,
         Mr. Heselius, Mr. Jennings,

44:535-6   children of dec'd.
      -   Elisabeth Downs deposed.
         Mentions: Lydia Johnson
         (daughter of said dec'd).

44:537-8   -   Richard Beard deposed.
      -   Jacob Lusby deposed for
         Nathaniel Watkins.
      -   Hellen Yates, of full age,
         deposed. Mentions: Mr. Condon.

44:539   ...

Court Session: 1772

44:540   21 July. William T. Wootton (g, PG)
exhibited:
- will of Peter Moore, constituting
  James Moore & Zadock Moore
  executors. Said executors were
  granted administration. Sureties:
  Benjamin Moore, James Moore (son of
  Benjamin). Date: 15 June 1772.
- bond of Thomas Duckett administrator
  of Daniel Pearce. Sureties: Richard
  Duckett, R. B. Hall. Date: 6 June
  1772.
- inventory of Ann Newton.
- LoD on estate of Robert Osborn.
- accounts on estate of Robert Osborn.
- accounts on estate of John Padgett.
- final accounts on estate of James
  Ryon, Jr.

6 August. Thomas Holbrook (g, SO)
exhibited:
- will of George Irving, constituting
  Thomas Irving executor. Said
  executor was granted administration.
  Sureties: Levin Dashiell, Thomas
  Sloss. Date: 14 July 1772.
- will of Henry Graham, constituting
  Ann Graham executrix. Said

executrix was granted
administration. Sureties: Ezekiel
Graham, William Kennely. Date: 29
July 1772.

44:541 • will of Thomas Todvine, constituting
Stephen Todvine & Arnold Todvine
executors. Said executors were
granted administration. Sureties:
Jonathan Stanford, Thomas Cannon.
Date: 24 July 1772.

• will of David Wilson, constituting
Elenor Wilson executrix. Said
executrix was granted
administration. Sureties: James
Wilson, William Gravenor. Date: 29
July 1772.

• will of Charles Wolford,
constituting Mary Mary Ann Woolford
executrix. Said executrix was
granted administration. Sureties:
Peter Waters, William Gilliss.
Date: 21 July 1772.

• bond of Benjamin Gilliss
administrator of Benjamin Gilliss
(alias Ezekiel Gilliss). Sureties:
William Gravenor, William Kennely.
Date: 29 July 1772.

• bond of Esther Handy administratrix
of Isaac Handy. Sureties: David
Wilson, John Winder. Date: 29 July
1772.

• bond of Mary Waggaman administratrix
of Edward Stevenson. Sureties:
Henry Jackson, Job Elsey. Date: 21
July 1772.

• bond of Thomas Pullit administrator
of Christopher Dowdle. Sureties: C.
Dashiell, David Lumford. Date: 14
July 1772.

• will of John Hopkins.
• inventory of William Kibble.
• inventory of Nehemiah Bozman.
• inventory of James Phillips.
44:542 • inventory of Mary Fountain.
• inventory of Abigail Wright.
• inventory of Edward Waters.
• inventory of Elisabeth Turpin.
• inventory of Solomon Wright.
• inventory of Michael Dorman.
• inventory of John Killiam.
• final accounts on estate of Joseph
Humphris.

Court Session: 1772

- final accounts on estate of John Flewellin.
- final accounts on estate of Thomas Richards.
- final accounts on estate of Thomas Simms.

7 August. Col. William Young (BA) exhibited:
- will of William Towson, constituting Thomas Baily executor. Said executor was granted administration. Sureties: John Buck, Benjamin Mead. Date: 1 August 1772.
- bond of Benjamin Debrular administrator of John Jordan. Sureties: John Day (son of Edward), B. Roberts. Date: 3 August 1772.
- bond of Jane Cole & James Coal executors of James Coal. Sureties: William Arnold, Benjamin Hubert. Date: 9 July 1772.

44:543
- will of Josephus Murray.
- will of James Cole.
- inventory of Hugh Burgess.
- LoD on estate of Hugh Burgess.
- inventory of Paul Penington.
- inventory of Thomas Burk.
- inventory of Jacob Jones.
- LoD on estate of Paul Penington.
- LoD on estate of H. Jacob Jones.
- accounts on estate of Hugh Burgess.
- accounts on estate of Paul Penington.

21 August. William T. Wootton (g, PG) exhibited:
- will of Benjamin Hodges, constituting Deborah Hodges executrix. Said executrix was granted administration. Sureties: Charles Hodges, Thomas Ramsay. Date: 3 August 1772.
- will of George Hardey, constituting Thomas Dent & Lucy Hardy executors. Said executors were granted administration. Sureties: Thomas Clagett, Barton Phillips. Date: 25 July 1772.

44:544
- bond of Saphanah Lowe executrix of Samuel Lowe. Sureties: Mareen Duvall, Isaac Parnall. Date: 18

Court Session: 1772

August 1772.
- bond of James Fry administrator of James Fry. Sureties: Henry Boteler, Kenelmn Selby. Date: 4 August 1772.
- inventory of James Leiper.
- inventory of Thomas Hilleary.
- inventory of Peter Moore.
- LoD on estate of James Leiper.

Walter Hanson (g, CH) exhibited:
- will of Walter Truman Stoddert, constituting Margaret Stoddert executrix. Said executrix was granted administration. Sureties: J. H. Harrison, William Smallwood. Date: 12 August 1772.
- will of John Gray, constituting Stephen Gray & Jeremiah Gray executors. Said executors were granted administration. Sureties: John Milstead, William H. Gray. Date: 17 June 1772.
- will of John Pye, constituting Henrietta Pye & Walter Pye executors. Said executors were granted administration. Sureties: Thomas Semmes, Raphaele Neal. Date: 17 July 1772.

44:545
- inventory of Benjamin Douglass.
- inventory of Henrietta Thompson.
- inventory of Francis Evans.
- inventory of Jane Jenkins.
- inventory of Benjamin Douglass, Jr.
- inventory of William Nellson.
- inventory of Benjamin Ward.
- accounts on estate of James Cole.
- accounts on estate of Matthew Groves.
- accounts on estate of Francis Semmes.
- accounts on estate of Thomas Nellson.
- accounts on estate of Thomas Stone.

29 August. John Bracco (g, TA) exhibited:
- will of Edward Needles, constituting Ann Needles executrix. Said executrix was granted administration. Sureties: George Dudley, Aaron Parratt. Date: 12 May 1772.

Page 188

Court Session: 1772

- bond of Nathaniel Cox administrator of Clement Sailes. Sureties: John Stevens, Heny Martin. Date: 26 May 1772.

44:546
- bond of John Dougherty administrator of Barnaby Dougherty. Sureties: James Gibson, John Young. Date: 6 July 1772.
- bond of Henry Elbert administrator of Lodman Elbert. Sureties: Jacob Gibson, James Gibson, William Geary. Date: 6 August 1772.
- bond of Sarah Stevens administratrix of William Stephens. Sureties: Peter Stevens, Samuel Stevens. Date: 6 August 1772.
- bond of Sarah Patterson administratrix of Wilson Paterson. Sureties: Richard Garbin Robinson, Edward Harrison. Date: 12 May 1772.
- bond of Henry Hollyday administrator of Henrietta Maria Goldsborough. Sureties: William Hayward, William Perry. Date: 10 December 1771.
- bond of Mary Perkins administratrix of Solomon Perkins. Sureties: William Ratcliff, Philip Perkins. Date: 26 May 1772.
- bond of Richard Mansfield administrator of Richard Mansfield. Sureties: John Hall, Thomas Manfield. Date: 22 August 1772.
- bond of Hannah Falconaner administratrix of John Falconer. Sureties: James Lloyd Chamberlain, James Evans. Date: 19 May 1772.

44:547
- bond of Sarah Loveday administratrix of John Loveday. Sureties: Richard Johns, Samuel Thomas. Date: 22 May 1772.
- bond of Rebeccah Eubank administratrix of George Eubankes. Sureties: Robert Haner, James Ratcliff. Date: 2 May 1772.
- bond of Thomas Goldsborough administrator of Robert Tuking. Sureties: Foster Goldsborough, Thomas Stevens, Jr. Date: 6 May 1772.
- bond of Pollard Edmonson executor of William Priestly. Sureties: Joseph Bruff, Thomas Barrow. Date: 8 May

1772.

- bond of Sarah Turbutt administratrix of Richard Turbut. Sureties: Thomas Goldsborough, Foster Goldsborough. Date: 6 May 1772.
- bond of Elisabeth Fairbrother & Phillip Mackey administrators of Richard Fairbrother. Sureties: James Chaplin, Henry Carey. Date: 19 May 1772.
- bond of William Stephens administrator of William Stephens. Sureties: John Stephens, Richard Pritchard. Date: 28 July 1772.
- will of Sarah Register.
- inventory of William White.
- inventory of Edward Turner.

44:548
- LoD on estate of Samuel Bowman.
- LoD on estate of James Chapman.
- final accounts on estate of John Dobson.
- accounts on estate of Simon Stephens Miller.
- accounts on estate of James Chapman.
- accounts on estate of Samuel Bowman.

Thomas Wright (QA) exhibited:
- will of Robert Brody, constituting Margaret Brody executrix. Said executrix was granted administration. Sureties: John Swift, William Harrington, Jr. Date: 21 June 1772.
- will of James Hicks, constituting Rebecca Harris executrix. Said executrix was granted administration. Sureties: John Watson, William Mumford. Date: 6 August 1772.
- bond of William Hopper, Joseph Nicholson, Jr., & James Bordley administrators dbn of Chris. Wilkinson. Sureties: Joseph Nicholson, Phillip Feddeman. Date: 20 June 1772.
- bond of John Kent administrator of Eliphalet Jacobs. Sureties: Thomas Baker, Samuel Walters. Date: 20 August 1772.

44:549
- bond of Bartholomew Tiddeman administrator of William McNess. Sureties: William Bell, William

Court Session: 1772

Purnel. Date: 20 August 1772.
- bond of Jonathan Roberts administrator of Samuel Blunt. Sureties: Jonathan Roberts, James R. Blunt. Date: 6 August 1772.
- bond of Frances Small administratrix of Richard Small. Sureties: John Caseen, Henry Downes. Date: 7 July 1772.
- bond of Hannah Bryan administratrix of Stephen Bryan. Sureties: James Hutchings, Jr., Marma. Goodhand. Date: 26 June 1772.
- bond of Elisabeth Taylor administratrix of Richard Taylor. Sureties: Benjamin Roe, James Kent. Date: 21 April 1772.
- inventory of Isaac Turner.
- inventory of William Pinder.
- inventory of Edgar Webb.
- inventory of Richard Gafford.
- inventory of Mathew Collins.
- inventory of John Glass.
- inventory of Richard Scotton.
- inventory of John Sherwood.
- inventory of Mathew Bryan.
- inventory of Rachel Chance.
- inventory of Boon Chance.
- inventory of James Meredith.
- inventory of Richard Smith.
- inventory of Hester Thompson.
- inventory of Solomon Clayton.
- inventory of John Sherwood.
- accounts on estate of Edgar Webb.
- accounts on estate of John Smith.
- accounts on estate of James Clow.
- accounts on estate of James Tolson.
- accounts on estates of Andrew Hall & Ester Hall.

44:550

31 August. T. Bowles (g, FR) exhibited:
- will of Rudey Aspey, constituting Jacob Aspey executor. Said executor was granted administration. Sureties: Henry Dice, George Casner. Date: 8 June 1772.
- will of John Orme, constituting James Orme & Lucy Orme executors. Said executors were granted administration. Sureties: Alexander Magruder, George Scott. Date: 22 May 1772.

- will of Henry Tom, constituting
  Martin Harry & Balser Gull
  executors. Said executors were
  granted administration. Sureties:
  Jonathan Hagar, C. Orendriff. Date:
  18 June 1772.

44:551 • will of Adam Stull, constituting
  Christopher Stull executor. Said
  executor was granted administration.
  Sureties: Phillip Stubbard, Henry
  Staley. Date: 17 July 1772.
- will of Westall Ridgly.
- will of Benjamin Hall.
- will of Peter Rench.
- will of George Gue.
- will of Nathan Garrett.
- will of Ann Orf [?].
- inventory of Rudolph Apey.
- inventory of James Carrick.
- inventory of Richard Cheyny.
- inventory of Joachim John.
- inventory of Edward Willett.
- inventory of John Adamson.
- inventory of Thomas Mills.
- inventory of Cathram Malet.
- inventory of David Finney.
- inventory of John Venneman.
- final accounts on estate of Joseph
  Clark.
- final accounts on estate of John
  Smith.
- final accounts on estate of Henry
  Linn.
- final accounts on estate of Thomas
  Ramsay.

44:552 24 August. Baruch Williams (CE)
  exhibited:
- will of Robert Macky, constituting
  James Mackay executor. Said
  executor was granted administration.
  Sureties: Joseph Mahafey, John
  Macky. Date: 30 June 1772.
- will of Jean Mitchell, constituting
  William Kirkpatrick executor. Said
  executor was granted administration.
  Sureties: Thomas Card, John Cather.
  Date: 9 June 1772.
- will of George Lewis, constituting
  Sarah Lewis & Joseph Ensor
  executors. Said executors were
  granted administration. Sureties:

Alexander Stuart, Hyland Price.
Date: 11 August 1772.

- will of John Husband, constituting John Ford executor. Said executor was granted administration. Sureties: Thomas Biddle, Benjamin Breward. Date: 29 May 1772.
- will of Sarah Standley. Also, bond of Thomas Savin, Sr. administrator. Sureties: Augustine Savin, Robert Lusby. Date: 18 June 1772.
- bond of Jennet Riddle administratrix of John Riddle. Sureties: John Murphy, Samuel Gray. Date: 4 July 1772.
- bond of Mary Boldin administratrix of Jesse Boldin. Sureties: James Boldin, Thomas Richardson. Date: 12 August 1772.
- bond of Eleanor Finney administratrix of Daniel Finney. Sureties: John Hall, John Stevenson. Date: 6 June 1772.

44:553
- bond of John Hall administrator of Thomas Davis. Sureties: John Veazey, Jr., Jos. Davis. Date: 5 August 1772.
- bond of Cassandra Chew administratrix of Phineas Chew. Sureties: Samuel Thomas, Richard Thomas. Date: 2 June 1772.
- bond of John Gray administrator of Richard White. Sureties: Henry Pennington, Nicholas Dorrell. Date: 18 June 1772.
- will of Thomas Crocker.
- will of Hartley Sappington.
- inventory of John Davidge.
- inventory of Dennis Nowland.
- inventory of Elias Eliason.
- inventory of John Buchannon.
- inventory of James Scott.
- inventory of James Quaile.
- inventory of John Husband.
- LoD on estate of Elias Eliason.
- LoD on estate of John Davidge.
- LoD on estate of William Bavington.
- LoD on estate of John Husband.
- LoD on estate of John Frier.
- LoD on estate of Dennis Nowland.
- LoD on estate of John Husband.
- LoD on estate of James Corbit.

44:554
- LoD on estate of John Davidge.
- LoD on estate of Moses Cockran.
- accounts on estate of William Bavington.
- accounts on estate of James Corbit.
- accounts on estate of Moses Cockran.
- accounts on estate of John Frier.
- accounts on estate of John Manley.

2 September. Jos. Nicholson (KE) exhibited:
- will of Augustine Boyer. Also, bond of Thomas Boyer & Augustine Boyer administrators. Sureties: Samuel Davis, John Wilmer. Date: 18 August 1772.
- bond of Judah Brice administratrix of Richard Brice. Sureties: William Grant, William Brice. Date: 19 January 1772.
- bond of Ann Piner administratrix of Jatin Cample. Sureties: William Geddis, William Ringgold. Date: 5 August 1772.
- bond of Hannah Usher administratrix of Andrew Usher. Sureties: Jos. Ireland, Charles Harbert. Date: 19 August 1772.
- bond of Araminta Perkins administratrix of Frederick Perkins. Sureties: John Wallis, John Brooks. Date: 5 August 1772.

44:555
- inventory of William Crew.
- inventory of Samuel Hodges.
- inventory of Isaac Boots.
- inventory of Michael Chandler.
- inventory of Robert Meeks.
- inventory of John Reed.
- inventory of Ebenezar Blackiston.
- inventory of Elisabeth Hall.
- inventory of Paul Whichcote.
- inventory of John Donaldson.
- inventory of Bridget Wise.
- final accounts on estate of Isaac Wilson.
- accounts on estate of William Crew.
- accounts on estate of Joshua Kelly.
- accounts on estate of Jos. Garnett.
- accounts on estate of John Granger.
- accounts on estate of George Williamson.

Court Session: 1772

31 July. Deputy Commissaries to examine accounts of:
- QA: John Kerr administrator of Zadock Martin.
- BA: Mary Brown executrix of Benjamin Brown.
- FR: Margaret Hickman administratrix of Joshua Hickman.
- CE: Sarah Pennington & William Withers administrators of Abraham Pennington.
- CE: Elisabeth Cunning administratrix of William Cunning.
- CE: Elisabeth Latham executrix of John Manly.
- CE: William Withers & his wife Rosannah executrix of Walter Dunn.
- SO: Chase Dorman & Sarah Dorman executors of Michael Dorman.
- SO: John Turpin administrator of Elisabeth Turpin.
- SO: Thomas Pullit administrator dbn of Christopher Dowdle.
- SO: Levin Wright executor of Solomon Wright.
- SO: David Wilson executor of Benjamin Fransway.
- SO: Elisabeth Allen executrix of Joseph Allen.
- KE: John & Sarah Smith executors of Josias Ringgold.
- petition of William Jacobs (BA). Administration bond on estate of Renaldo Monk assigned to petitioner.

7 August.
- SM: Hannah Greenwell executrix of James Greenwell.
- SM: Dorothy Ford executrix of Ignatius Ford.

10 August.
- TA: Thomas Young & his wife Rebecca administratrix of John Rice.
- TA: William Tucker & Elisabeth Tucker administrators of Noah Holmes.

14 August.
- TA: William Robinson executor of Charles Robinson.
- BA: William Robinson executor of Richard Robinson.
- BA: John Watson executor of Easter Watson.

44:556

Page 195

19 August.
- petition of Samuel Thompson (QA). Administration bond on estate of Dowdall Thompson assigned to petitioner.
- WO: Solomon Long & his wife Comfort executrix of Stephen Wright.
- WO: Avery Morgan executor of Avery Morgan.
- WO: Avery Morgan & his wife Hannah executrix of Joseph Massey.
- TA: Jonathan Downes & his wife Mary administratrix of Macklin Elbert.

21 August.
- TA: William Smith & James Ringgold Blunt surviving executors of John Smith.

22 August.
- DO: James Shaw & his wife Mary & Abner Lecompt executors of John Lecompt.

24 August.
- DO: Reuben Pennington administrator of Benjamin Pennington.
- CE: Jacob Lumon executor of Mary Lumon.

25 August.
- WO: Naomi Mumford administratrix of John Mumford.
- WO: Betty Minor administratrix of Charles Minor.
- BA: Charles Harryman administrator dbn of Isaac Raven.

29 August.
- TA: Thomas Tibley executor of Elisabeth Exley.
- TA: Ebenezar Meckie & Robert Campbell administrators of Adam Hill.

44:557 3 September. John Bracco (g, TA) exhibited:
- bond of John Dickinson administrator of John Hollyday. Sureties: John Gibson, William Besswick. Date: 29 August 1772.
- will of John Porter.
- will of William Cummins.
- will of John Mason.
- will of Francis Register.
- inventory of Rachel Willoughby.
- inventory of John Falconer.

- inventory of Rachel Willoughby.
- inventory of George Ubankes.
- inventory of Thomas Powell.
- inventory of George Lawrence.
- inventory of Solomon Palmer.
- inventory & LoD of John Harrison.
- inventory of Thomas Jenkins, Jr.
- inventory of John Debson.
- inventory & LoD of Samuel McCleland.
- inventory of Cornelius Daily.
- inventory of Macklin Elbert.
- inventory of Robert Bromwell.
- inventory & LoD of Stephen Batcliff.
- inventory & LoD of Thomas McCleland.
- inventory & LoD of John Price.
- final accounts on estate of John Price.

44:558 9 September. John Goldsborough (g, DO) exhibited:
- will of Thomas Hayward, constituting Sarah Hayward executrix. Said executrix was granted administration. Sureties: William Jones, David Covender. Date: 19 June 1772.
- will of Mathew Kirvan, constituting Judah Kirvan executrix. Said executrix was granted administration. Sureties: John Kirwan, Peter Kirwan. Date: 17 June 1772.
- will of George Hutton, constituting Mary Hutton executrix. Said executrix was granted administration. Sureties: Jacob Nunar, John Dodden. Date: 16 June 1772.
- bond of Mary Safford executrix of James Safford. Sureties: Abraham Safford, Michael Todd. Date: 12 August 1772.
- bond of Sarah Pattison executrix of Jacob Pattison. Sureties: James Hooper, Henry Hooper. Date: 24 August 1772.
- bond of Thomas Stapleford administrator of Thomas Stapleford. Sureties: Raymond Stapleford, Edward Stapleford. Date: 14 August 1772.
- bond of James Tootell administrator of Joseph Bright. Sureties: John

Stevens, Roger Jones. Date: 7 July
1772.

- bond of James Tootell administrator
of James Bright. Sureties: John
Stevens, Roger Jones. Date: 7 July
1772.

44:559 • bond of James Tootell administrator
of John Bright. Sureties: John
Stevens, Roger Jones. Date: 7 July
1772.

- bond of James Woolford administrator
of Levin Woolford. Sureties:
Benjamin Woodard, John Travillion
Stewart. Date: 7 August 1772.

- bond of Amelia Traverse & William
Traverse administrators of Thomas
Traverse. Sureties: Henry Traverse,
John Traverse. Date: 12 August
1772.

- bond of James Jones, Sr.
administrator of Levi Jones.
Sureties: Benjamin Baily, Benjamin
Baily [!]. Date: 13 April 1772.

- bond of Mary Navey administratrix of
Henry Navey. Sureties: John Navey,
Henry Navey. Date: 31 October 1772
[!].

- bond of Priscilla Traverse
administratrix of William Hick
Traverse. Sureties: Henry Traverse,
John Traverse. Date: 12 August
1772.

- bond of William Langrel, Jr.
administrator of William Langrell.
Sureties: Benjamin Todd, Leui
Willin. Date: 19 June 1772.

- bond of Esther Norman administratrix
of George Norman. Sureties: Henry
Hubbert, Nathan Bradley. Date: 17
June 1772.

- bond of Ezekiel Johnson
administrator of Solomon Matkin.
Sureties: William Dean, John Hooper.
Date: 17 June 1772.

44:560 • bond of Mary Wheeler administratrix
of John Wheeler. Sureties: William
Thomas, William Ross, Jr. Date: 6
June 1772,

- bond of Rachel Sprouce
administratrix of George Sprouse.
Sureties: Richard Collison, John
Sisk. Date: 16 June 1772.

- bond of Elisabeth Connerly administratrix of Jeremiah Connerly. Sureties: Daniel Payne, Jeremiah Connerly. Date: 16 June 1772.
- bond of Elisabeth Stewart administratrix of Joseph Stewart. Sureties: Thomas Stewart, John Travillion Stewart. Date: 28 April 1772.
- bond of Jacob Wright administrator of William Wright. Sureties: Levin Wright, Lemuel Wright. Date: 19 May 1772.
- bond of John Hurly administrator of Mark Hurley. Sureties: Daniel Waters, Mathew Hurley. Date: 20 May 1772.
- bond of Anne Errickson administratrix of John Errickson. Sureties: Daniel Chance, William Hardesty. Date: 25 May 1772.
- bond of Sarah Ennalls Nevett administratrix of John Rider Nevett. Sureties: Daniel Maynard, William Maynadier. Date: 5 June 1772.

44:561
- bond of Sarah Murphy administratrix of Thomas Murphy. Sureties: Ambrose Gosling, Lemuel Davis. Date: 18 April 1772.
- bond of Sarah Wright administratrix of William Wright. Sureties: James Wright, William Noble. Date: 27 April 1772.
- bond of Phil. Lecompt administrator of Charles Walker. Sureties: James Wing, Roger Trego. Date: 14 August 1772.
- inventory of Joseph Todd.
- inventory of Andrew Lord.
- inventory of Abner Lecompt.
- inventory of Henry Keene.
- additional inventory of Zebulon Keene.
- additional inventory of James Farguson.
- LoD on estate of John Parkerson.
- LoD on estate of Nehemiah Lecompt.
- final accounts on estate of David Shehawn.
- final accounts on estate of Richard Cole.
- final accounts on estate of John

Warren.
- final accounts on estate of William Collison.
- final accounts on estate of William Whitely.
- accounts on estate of William Woolen.
- accounts on estate of John Parkerson.
- accounts on estate of Reimour Land.
- accounts on estate of William Phillips.
- accounts on estate of Edward Williams.
- accounts on estate of William Noble.
- accounts on estate of James Sherwin.

44:562 Thomas Holbrook (g, SO) exhibited:
- will of John Disharoon. Also bond of Jos. Dasharoon acting executor. Sureties: Constant Disharoon, William Hath. Date: 19 August 1772.
- will of Samuel Cox. Also, bond of Martha Cox administratrix. Sureties: Lodowick Milbourne, Jacob Milbourne. Date: 19 August 1772.
- will of Levin Gilliss. Also, bond of Sarah Gilliss administratrix. Sureties: Joseph Gilliss, John Evans, Jr. Date: 3 August 1772.
- bond of Stephen Hopkins executor of John Hopkins. Sureties: William Winwright, Cannon Winwright. Date: 6 August 1772.
- bond of Elenor Twelly administratrix of John Twelly. Sureties: Cannon Winwright, John Winwright. Date: 31 August 1772.
- bond of Betty Handy administratrix of Thomas Handy. Sureties: William Murray, George Handy. Date: 27 August 1772.
- inventory of James Polk.
- inventory of Handy Beauchamp.
- inventory of John Paden.
- inventory of John Caldwell.

44:563 W. Young (BA) exhibited:
- will of Joseph Burgess, constituting Joseph Burgess executor. Said executor was granted administration. Sureties: James Cox, Thomas Cox.

Date: 10 August 1772.

- will of James Billingsly, constituting Ruth Billingsley executrix. Said executrix was granted administration. Sureties: William Ball, Robert Clark. Date: 31 August 1772.
- will of James Spavold, constituting Amos Garratt executor. Said executor was granted administration. Sureties: Isaac Webster, Bennett Mathews. Date: 18 August 1772.
- bond of Elisabeth Holtzinger & Marten Ezchelberger executors of Barnet Holtzinger. Sureties: Frederick Myer. Date: 4 August 1772.
- bond of Temperance Heddington administratrix of Nathan Heddington. Sureties: George Harryman, Abel Heddington. Date: 13 August 1772.
- bond of Sarah Guishard administratrix of Mark Guishard. Sureties: Abraham Wright, Henry Hendon. Date: 2 September 1772.
- bond of Catherine Anderson administratrix of John Anderson. Sureties: Abraham Whitaker, Thomas Brierly. Date: 31 August 1772.
- bond of Catharine Anderson administratrix of Edward Flanagan. Sureties: Abraham Whitaker, Thomas Brierly. Date: 31 August 1772.
- inventory of William Hitchcock.
- inventory of Garret Cruson.
- inventory of John Skipton.

44:564
- inventory of Jacob Schartel.
- inventory of James McComas.
- inventory of George Ogg.
- final accounts on estate of Robert Saunders.
- final accounts on estate of William Ogg.
- final accounts on estate of Benjamin Vantcome.
- final accounts on estate of Thomas Baily.
- final accounts on estate of Ann Howard.
- final accounts on estate of James McKowan.
- final accounts on estate of Edward

Court Session: 1772

York.

Benton Harriss (g, WO) exhibited:
- will of Robinson Lingo, constituting Smith Lingo & Joseph Dashiell executors. Said executors were granted administration. Sureties: John Purdue, James Purdue. Date: 14 May 1772.
- will of Mary Kirby. Also, bond of Sarah Kirby administratrix. Sureties: Thomas Pridix, John Miller. Date: 29 May 1772.
- will of James Cathrell, constituting James Cathell executor. Said executor was granted administration. Sureties: William Law, Daniel Pike. Date: 8 May 1772.

44:565
- will of William Fassitt, constituting Mary Fassitt executrix. Said executrix was granted administration. Sureties: John Marshall, Elisha Bredel. Date: 15 May 1772.
- will of Solomon Brittingham, constituting Mary Brittingham executrix. Said executrix was granted administration. Sureties: Samuel Ennis, Schoolfield Parker. Date: 17 April 1772.
- will of Ezekiel Porter, constituting Samuel Ennis executor. Said executor was granted administration. Sureties: William Davie, Charles Parker. Date: 8 April 1772.
- will of Isaac Meglamre, constituting Anne Meglamere executrix. Said executrix was granted administration. Sureties: David Vance, Thomas Cannon. Date: 27 June 1772.
- will of Alexander Massey, constituting John Massey executor. Said executor was granted administration. Sureties: William Fassit, Henry Franklin. Date: 10 July 1772.
- will of James Davis, constituting Sabrah Davis executrix. Said executrix was granted administration. Sureties: Samuel Davis, Stephen Beuchamp. Date: 24

April 1772.

- will of Armvell Showell, constituting Rebecca Showell executrix. Said executrix was granted administration. Sureties: Adam Bravard, William Evans. Date: 10 January 1772.
- will of John Collier. Also, bond of Tabitha Collier administratrix. Sureties: William Stephens Hill, John Jones. Date: 7 April 1772.
- will of William Crockett, constituting Elisabeth Crockett & Richard Crockett executors. Said executors were granted administration. Sureties: William Elegood, Obediah Smith. Date: 4 August 1772.

44:566 - will of George Thompson, constituting Jesse Thompson executor. Said executor was granted administration. Sureties: Isaac Jones, Charles Dorman. Date: 10 July 1772.
- will of Charles Wharton, constituting Sarah Wharton executrix. Said executrix was granted administration. Sureties: Benjamin Henderson, Solomon Webb. Date: 6 June 1772.
- will of Thomas Evans, constituting Hannah Evans executrix. Said executrix was granted administration. Sureties: Peter Chaille, Thomas Powell. Date: 29 May 1772.
- will of Solomon Russell. Also, bond of Josiah Russell administrator. Sureties: Jos. Dashiell, James Houston. Date: 27 June 1772.
- will of Jonathan Cathell. Also, bond of Daniel Cathell administrator. Sureties: Joshua Sturgis, James Perdue. Date: 14 May 1772.
- will of John Beavin. Also, bond of Mary Beavin administratrix. Sureties: William Radney, Rowland Beavens. Date: 6 April 1772.
- will of John Swain. Also, bond of Anne Swain administratrix. Sureties: Jonathan Bell, William

Swain. Date: 22 May 1772.

- will of John Hammond. Also, bond of Leah Hammond administratrix. Sureties: John Jones, George Jones. Date: 22 May 1772.
- bond of Jonathan Smith administrator dbn of John Kelly. Sureties: Jonathan Hill, Peter Callaway. Date: 5 August 1772.

44:567

- bond of Joseph Houston administrator dbn of James Houston. Sureties: Littleton Dennis, Isaac Layfield. Date: 15 May 1772.
- bond of John Rogers administrator of Mathew Rogers. Sureties: Peleg Walter, Jacob Rogers. Date: 15 May 1772.
- bond of Caleb Milbourn administrator of Michael Milbourn. Sureties: Littleton Dennis, Joseph Stephenson. Date: 19 June 1772.
- bond of Mary Houston administratrix of William Fassitt. Sureties: John Purnell, Angelo Atkinson. Date: 15 May 1772.
- bond of John Postly administrator of John Postly. Sureties: Robert McCrea, Nathaniel Rackliffe. Date: 24 April 1772.
- bond of Joseph Dickenson administrator of Levi Dickenson. Sureties: Eliakim Johnson, Jonathan West Watson. Date: 3 April 1772.
- bond of Mary Truitt administratrix of George Truitt. Sureties: William Bradford, John Jones. Date: 7 April 1772.
- will of John Bowin.
- will of Sarah Johnson.
- will of Esekiel Dubberly.
- will of Thomas Beavins.
- will of Race Clark.
- will of Rachel Kelly.
- will of Benjamin Henderson.

44:568

- inventory of James Houston.
- inventory of Daniel Young.
- inventory of Daniel Godwin.
- inventory of Thomas Evans.
- inventory of John Bibbins (alias John Beavins).
- inventory of Brickus Townshend.
- inventory of James Polk.

- inventory of Sarah Warren.
- inventory of Armwell Showell.
- inventory of Graves Bashaw.
- inventory of Joshua Langford.
- inventory of Charles Ennis.
- inventory of Benjamin Henderson.
- inventory of Isaac Brittingham.
- inventory of Priscilla Austin.
- inventory of Ephraim Christopher.
- inventory of James Porter.
- inventory of William Truitt.
- inventory of George Mumford.
- inventory of Frances Allen.
- inventory of Baxter Bennett.
- final accounts on estate of Solomon Claywell.
- final accounts on estate of Elijah Brittingham.
- final accounts on estate of Angelo Atkinson.
- final accounts on estate of Peter Corbin.
- final accounts on estate of Samuel Stephenson.
- final accounts on estate of John Townshend.
- final accounts on estate of John Stockley.
- final accounts on estate of John Richards.

44:569
- final accounts on estate of Joseph Nicholson.
- final accounts on estate of Solomon Milbourn.
- final accounts on estate of John Maglamary.
- final accounts on estate of John Long.
- final accounts on estate of John Hall.
- accounts on estate of Nathan Frames.
- accounts on estate of John Windsor.
- final accounts on estate of Stephen Seady.
- final accounts on estate of Hannah Jones.
- final accounts on estate of James Fookes.

2 September. Deputy Commissaries to examine accounts of:
- KE: Hannah Smith administratrix of

John Smith.
- KE: Charity Pratt administratrix of Phillip Pratt.
- KE: Hannah Miles administratrix of Nathan Miles.
- KE: Mary Hynson administratrix of Charles Hynson.
- KE: Samuel West administrator of Elisabeth McDermott.

3 September.
- KE: Mary Harwood administratrix of Peter Harwood.
- CH: William Warren administrator of John Gwynn.
- FR: John Cooper administrator of Mary Ann Cooper.

7 September.
- SO: William Badley administrator of William Robertson.
- SO: Benjamin Griffith & his wife Rachel executrix of T. Garthill.
- BA: John Lynch & his wife Mary executrix of John Webster.
- BA: Mary Bowen executrix of Nathan Bowen.
- WO: William Fassitt administrator of Levin Fassitt.
- SO: John Pollitt executor of Sarah Dowdle.

44:570 8 September.
- SM: Christian Taylor executrix of John Taylor.
- SM: Elisabeth Wheatly executrix of John Wheatly.
- SM: Mary Coombs executrix of John Hatton Coombs.

9 September.
- WO: John Hopkins executor of Nathaniel Hopkins Murray.
- WO: William Truit administrator of William Truit.
- WO: Prisgrave Kinnett administrator dbn of Laban Kennitt.
- WO: Agnes Gillett executrix of Jarman Gillett.
- WO: Hannah Christopher executrix of Ephraim Christopher.

10 September.
- SO: John Piper one of sureties of Mathew Piper administrator of Christopher Piper.
- SO: Isaac Collins executor of James

Quartermus.

- CE: Amos & George Alexander executors of Theophilus Alexander.
- CE: John Anderson & William Glasgow executors of John Glasgow.
- WO: Luke Morriss & George Hayward, Esq. executors of Isaac Morris.
- WO: Sarah Hall administratrix of Stephen Hall.
- KE: Richard Gresham executor of Sarah Gresham.

12 September.

- KE: John Burke administrator of John Sharpe.

14 September.

- WO: William Davis administrator of Robert Davis.
- WO: William Jordan Hall & Hannah Hall executors of Margaret Hall.
- WO: Hannah Evans executrix of Thomas Evans.
- TA: Elisabeth Harwood & Robert Harwood administrators of William Harwood.
- TA: Mary White administratrix of William White.
- TA: Joshua Clark administrator of John Scott.
- WO: Robert Dennis & his wife Esther administratrix of Palmer Spaight.
- petition of heir at law of William Pitney (CH), to prove said will.

15 September.

- KE: Hannah Tolson & Nathaniel Tolson administrators of Andrew Tolson.
- WO: Caleb Wyat administrator of William Wyat.
- WO: Abraham Cannel administrator of Benjamin Foreman.
- WO: Southy King administrator of William King.
- QA: William Wilcocks executor of Daniel Wilcocks.
- DO: John Fisher administrator of Alexander Morton.
- KE: Sarah Kinnard administratrix of Thomas Kinnard.
- KE: Mary Lorain executrix of Thomas Lorain.
- KE: William Pearce administrator of Mary Watkins.

16 September.

44:571

- CH: Mary Warden administratrix of William Warden.
- CH: Sarah Boswell administratrix of John Boswell.
- QA: Richard Manwaring & his wife Elisabeth executrix of Nathaniel Smith.
- QA: Elisabeth Leatherbury administratrix of James Dudley.
- QA: Susannah Smith administratrix of Richard Smith.

18 September.
- WO: John Parker executor of George Parker.
- CH: Elisabeth Timms administratrix of Joseph Timms.
- CH: Phoebe Evans executrix of Francis Evans.
- CH: Thomas Lomax administrator of John Lomax.

19 September.
- BA: Sarah Burke administratrix of Thomas Burke.
- BA: David Tate executor of Mary Jenkins.
- BA: Clement Lewis administrator of Joseph Lewis.
- DO: John Dickenson executor of Henry Trippe.
- DO: Jacob Wright administrator of William Wright.
- DO: Esther Norman administratrix of George Norman.
- DO: Rachel Sprouce administratrix of George Sprouce.
- DO: John Keene & Benjamin Keene, Jr. executors of Henry Keene.
- DO: Ann Smith of a copy of will annexed for Levin Smith.
- DO: Mary Hitch executrix of William Hitch.
- DO: Elijah Hatfield administrator of William Hatfield.
- DO: Elijah Green administrator of William Green.
- DO: Sarah Wright administratrix of William Wright.
- DO: John Russell executor of Thomas Wall.
- DO: Mary Snow administratrix of William Snow.
- DO: William Campbell & his wife Jane

executors of John Oldfield.

44:572
- DO: Bridget Simmons administratrix of Thomas Simmons.
- DO: Mary Smith administratrix of Edward Smith, Jr.
- DO: Mrs. Hermana Addams administratrix of Daniel Addams.
- DO: Rosanna Ferguson administratrix of James Ferguson.
- DO: Rebecca North administratrix of George North.
- DO: Elisabeth Howarth administratrix of John Howarth.
- DO: James Shaw & his wife Mary executrix of John Lecompt.
- DO: Mary Wheeler administratrix dbn of Thomas Wheeler.
- DO: Nathan Bradley administrator of Nehemiah Boxall.
- DO: Benoni Banning executor of Benjamin Clark.
- DO: Benjamin Keene administrator of Benjamin Keene.
- DO: Richard Keene executor of Zebulon Keene.
- DO: Jos. Nichols, Jr. administrator of Mary Cannon.
- DO: Edward Woolen administrator of William Woolen.
- DO: Thomas Cannon administrator of Catharine Cannon.
- FR: Barbary Joan & John Harrgereder executors of Yoachim Joan.
- SO: George Waters executor of John Waters.
- SO: John Elzey administrator of Arnold Elzey.

21 September.
- SO: Leah Gray administratrix of Jacob Gray.

22 September.
- FR: Sarah Johnson administratrix of Thomas Johnson.
- QA: James Kent administrator dbn of Robert Hawkins.
- QA: John Ruth & his wife Elisabeth administratrix of Bartholomew Jacobs.
- QA: John Young executor of John Young.

24 September.
- QA: Littleton Dennis executor of

- John Dennis.
- QA: Mary Masters administratrix of Robert Masters.
- FR: Edward Owen & Sarah Owen executors of Lawrence Owen.
- BA: Sarah McComas executrix of Aquila McComas.
- petition of Nathan Williams (CH). Administration bond on estate of Thomas Hudson assigned to petitioner.

26 September.
- BA: Nathan Giles administrator of John Giles.
- BA: John Crayton executor of Timothy McCann.

44:573   3 October.
- KE: Joseph Milton, Jr. administrator of John Milton.

5 October.
- FR: Jacob Stoner, Philip Engles, & Adam Young executors of Jacob Mullendore.

6 October.
- FR: William Debruller executor of William Debruller.
- BA: William Harwood executor of Susannah Harwood.
- BA: Clement Lewis administrator of Jos. Lewis.
- BA: Mary Aulton administratrix of Joseph Aulton.
- QA: Sophia Slay administratrix of Edward Slay.
- FR: Elisabeth Gosling & Robert Masten administrators of Ezekiel Gosling.
- CH: Raphael Boarman executor of Elisabeth Warren.

8 October.
- KE: Ann Piner administratrix dbn of John Campbell.
- KE: Nathaniel Comegys administrator of Alexander Kelly.
- BA: Rachel Jones administratrix of Jacob Jones.
- QA: Priscilla Brown executrix of Charles Brown.

12 October.
- CE: William Bavington & Argl Beedle administrators of William Bavington.
- CE: Benjamin Maulding administrator

of Francis Maulding.
- CE: Elias Eliason & Abraham Eliason executors of Elias Eliason.
- SO: Jos. Humphrys executor of Thomas Humphrys.
- SO: Jonathin Slater administrator of David Slater.

15 October.
- QA: Mathew Chilton administrator of Abel Chilton.

20 October.
- FR: Gartrude Glass administratrix of John Glass.
- KE: Michael Jobson executor of Dennis Shehawn.

26 October.
- QA: William Nevett & James Wilson sureties for Robert Wood administrator of David Robertson.
- QA: Moses Massey & Robert Little sureties for Margaret Farrow administratrix of Nathan Farrow. Note: administratrix is runaway.

27 October.
- KE: Mary McHard administratrix of Samuel McHard.
- CE: Ann Marcer executrix of Robert Marcer.
- CE: Betty Todd executrix of Benjamin Todd.
- DO: Betty Todd administratrix of Jos. Todd.
- FR: Susannah Vowles & George Stricker executors of Jacob Vowles.

44:574 30 October.
- CE: Thomas Chandler & his wife Mary administratrix of Peter Jones.
- SM: Richard Fenwick executor of Bennett Fenwick.
- SM: Nicholas Manjer & his wife Ann administrators of Frances Thompson.

2 November.
- QA: David Davis & his wife Sophia executrix of Benjamin Roberts.
- CH: Elisabeth Speak administratrix of John Speake.
- CE: Jonathan Smith executor of Peter Bayard.

6 November.
- KE: Martha Newcomb administratrix of Thomas Newcomb.

9 November.

- FR: Mary Mackall administratrix of Benjamin Mackall.
- petition of William & Arthur Bordley (KE). Administration bond on estate of Thomas Bordley assigned to petitioners.

10 November.
- DO: Samuel Skinner & his wife Catharine executrix of Thomas Alcock.
- DO: Elisabeth Bowdle executrix of Joseph Bowdle.
- KE: Rebecka Garland administratrix of John Garland.
- SO: Sarah Taylor executrix of Elias Taylor.
- FR: Ann Eason administratrix of John Eason.
- PG: Basil Wilson administrator of Lancelot Wilson.
- PG: Daniel Page administrator of George Page.
- PG: James & Zadock Moore executors of Peter Moore.

12 November.
- PG: Carolina Orrick administratrix of John Orrick.
- FR: Henry Cock executor of Susannah Beatty.

17 November.
- QA: Thomas Smyth & his wife Mary administratrix of James Routh.

20 November.
- PG: John Stonestreet executor of Thomas Stonestreet.
- CH: Thomas Jenkins administrator of Jane Jenkins.
- CH: Samuel Green & his wife Elisabeth executrix of John Jenkins.
- CH: Phillip Thomas executor of John Thomas.
- CH: Robert Thompson & his wife Ann executrix of Maximillian Mathews.
- CH: Henrietta Hamersly executrix of Basil Hamersly.

28 November.
- CH: Thomas Cooper executor of John Cooper.

44:575
- appointment of Thomas Jones, Esq. (BA) as Deputy Commissary (BA), in room of Col. William Young (late dec'd).

Court Session: 1772

1 December.
* CH: Henrietta Blackiston executrix of Ebenezar Blackiston.
* KE: John Bowers executor of Thomas Bowers.

4 December.
* QA: Hannah Turner administratrix of Isaac Turner.

7 December.
* petition of Carty Ellers (KE). Administration bond on estate of Benjamin Whaley assigned to petitioner.

8 December.
* TA: Stephen Daden & Joseph Daiden administrators of Mary Daiden.
* petition of John Moore (KE). Elisabeth Posey wife of Capt. John Posey (TA) died indebted to petitioner.

44:576 Said John Posey has not taken LoA & is removed out of the Province. Therefore, said John Posey has relinquished LoA. LoA dbn granted to petitioner.

12 December.
* SO: Hugh Porter & his wife Sarah Ann administratrix of Coventon Mezick.

14 December.
* DO: John Hignut & Daniel Hignut executors of James Hignut.
* DO: John Fisher executor of Alexander Morton.
* DO: William Byus executor of William Byus.
* DO: Mary Lane administratrix of Thomas Lane.

44:577 * DO: Mary Hayward administratrix of Francis Hayward.
* DO: John Brown executor of John Brown.
* DO: James Brown administrator of James Brown.
* DO: Arthur Whitely, Jr. executor of James Wallace.
* DO: Betty Vinson administratrix of John Vinson.
* DO: William Lecompt executor of Abner Lecompt.
* DO: Mathew Driver, Jr. administrator of Reimour Land.

15 December.

- CE: William Clark & William Stewart executors of Thomas Stewart.
- CE: Sarah Lewis & Joseph Ensor administrators of George Lewis.
- CE: Rachel David executrix of John David.

17 September. John Goldsborough (g, DO) exhibited:

- bond of Benjamin Woodard administrator of Richard Richardson. Sureties: William Jones, Henry Jones. Date: 8 September 1772.
- bond of Elisabeth Griffith administratrix of Thomas Griffith. Sureties: Levin Woolford, John Mitchell. Date: 4 September 1772.
- bond of Betty Vinson administratrix of John Vinson. Sureties: John Stevens, Peter Ratcliff. Date: 11 September 1772.
- bond of William Eccleston administrator of James Eccleston. Sureties: Charles Eccleston, William Lecompt. Date: 17 August 1772.
- will of John Salsbury.
- will of Joseph West.

44:578
- inventory of Thomas Faulkner.
- inventory of Thomas Simmons.
- inventory of William Hatfield.
- inventory of William Hitch.
- inventory of Joseph Bowdle.
- inventory of George North.
- inventory of William Green.
- inventory of William Wright.
- inventory of Josiah Stamper.
- LoD on estate of Joseph Ford.
- LoD on estate of Josiah Stamper.
- LoD on estate of William Hitch.
- LoD on estate of William Hatfield.
- LoD on estate of Thomas Faulkner.
- LoD on estate of Thomas Faulkner [!].

8 October. Col. Jos. Nicholson (KE) exhibited:

- bond of Mary Little executrix of George Little. Sureties: George Little, James Sweaney. Date: 29 August 1772.
- bond of Rebecca Garland administratrix of John Garland.

Sureties: James Cheffins, George
Blackiston. Date: 31 July 1772.

44:579 • bond of Charlotte Darrah & John
Darrah administrators of Thomas
Darrah. Sureties: James Blake,
Samuel Griffith. Date: 29 August
1772.
• will of Sarah Milton.

12 October. John Allen Thomas (g, SM)
exhibited:
• will of William Doxey, constituting
William Doxey executor. Said
executor was granted administration.
Sureties: Jessee Tennison, Samuel
Smith. Date: 30 June 1772.
• will of Mark Shadrick, constituting
Margaret Shadrick & John Shadrick
executors. Said executors were
granted administration. Sureties:
Benjamin Bean, Richard McKay. Date:
24 August 1772.
• will of John Tarlton, constituting
Anne Tarlton executrix. Said
executrix was granted
administration. Sureties: John
Reeder Younger, James Tarlton.
Date: 16 June 1772.
• will of Thomas Newton, constituting
Susannah Newton & William Newton
executors. Said executors were
granted administration. Sureties:
John Booth, John Heard, Jr. Date:
15 September 1772.
• bond of John Smith executor of James
Smith. Sureties: Thomas Griffin,
Nicholas Smith. Date: 24 March
1772.
• bond of Michael Parker Jamison
executor of Mary Smith. Sureties:
Charles Egerton, William Egerton.
Date: 21 January 1772.

44:580 • bond of James Maddox administrator
of George Vaudrie. Sureties: George
Maddox, Thomas Smoot. Date: 12
August 1772.
• bond of Anne Lucas administratrix of
John Baptist Lucas. Sureties: John
Baily, John Goddard. Date: 12 May
1772.
• bond of Joseph Collison
administrator of Isaac Fairbrother.

Surety: Daniel Sulivane. Date: 18 May 1772.
- bond of Elisabeth Howard administratrix of Cornelius Howard. Surety: John Medcalf. Date: 16 June 1772.
- bond of Elisabeth Taney & Nicholas Lewis Sewall administrators of John Frances Taney. Sureties: Walter Pye, Raph. Taney. Date: 27 July 1772.
- bond of Ann Drayden Abel administratrix of Philip Abel. Sureties: Benedict Spalding, Bazil Brewer. Date: 7 August 1772.
- bond of Thomas Alvey administrator of Richard Wheatly. Sureties: Athan. Ford, Francis Roberts. Date: 15 September 1772.
- bond of Ann Manly administratrix of Thomas Manly. Sureties: Richard Thompson, Robert Bean. Date: 24 September 1772.
- bond of Robert Watts administrator of Mark Rhodes. Surety: John Hatton Read. Date: 7 August 1772.

44:581
- bond of Elisabeth Jenifer administratrix of John Read Jenifer. Sureties: Samuel Jenifer, Cuthbert Abell. Date: 15 September <no year given>.
- will of Thomas Brome.
- will of James Coombs.
- will of Elisabeth Miles.
- will of Susannah Craycroft.
- inventory of John Baptist Lucas.
- inventory of Charles Askom.
- inventory of John Baxter.
- inventory of John Morgan.
- inventory of Peter Pain.
- inventory of James Smith.
- inventory of William Mattingley.
- inventory of George Vaudrie.
- inventory of Samuel Wright.
- inventory of Mark Rhodes.
- inventory of Richard Barnhouse.
- inventory of Ignatius French.
- inventory of George Fenwick.
- inventory of John Tewell.
- inventory of Mary Smith.
- inventory of Robert Cole.
- inventory of Francis Taney.

Court Session: 1772

44:582
- inventory of William Fraiser.
- inventory of Thomas Shanks.
- inventory of Clement Hill.
- inventory of Teresia Strutford.
- LoD on estate of Charles Askom.
- LoD on estate of Richard Barnhouse.
- accounts on estate of Mark Rhodes.
- accounts on estate of John Corsair.
- accounts on estate of John Ford.
- accounts on estate of Charles Hazeldine.
- accounts on estate of John Johnson.
- accounts on estate of Thomas Spalding.

14 October. Elie Vallette (g, AA) exhibited:
- will of Mary Thompson, constituting John Rutherford executor. Said executor was granted administration. Surety: Samuel Harvey Howard. Date: 17 July 1772.
- will of George Conaway, constituting Rachel Conaway executrix. Said executrix was granted administration. Sureties: Charles Robinson, William Maccubbin. Date: 28 July 1772.
- will of Caleb Dorsey, constituting Samuel Dorsey, Michael Pue, Milcah Dorsey, & Eloner Dorsey executors. Said executors were granted administration. Sureties: Edward Gaither, Jr., Edward Norwood, Date: 7 September 1772.
- will of Richard Sappington, constituting Margaret Sappington, John & Richard Sappington executors. Said executors were granted administration. Sureties: Mark Brewer Sappington, Richard Wheeler. Date: 23 September 1772.
- will of William Reed, constituting Eleanor Reed executrix. Said executrix was granted administration. Sureties: John Davidson, Thomas Harwood, Jr. Date: 12 October 1772.

44:583   8 October.
- will of Lawrence Shrivour, constituting Mary Shrivour executrix. Said executrix was

Page 217

granted administration. Sureties:
Lawrence Shrivour, John Shrivour.
Date: 22 June 1772.
- will of William Lux, constituting
William Lux executor. Said executor
was granted administration.
Sureties: William Russell, Daniel
Hughs. Date: 12 June 1772.
- will of Thomas Watkins, constituting
Vachel Sewel executor. Said
executor was granted administration.
Sureties: John Marriott, Jacob
Lusby. Date: 15 June 1772.
- bond of Comfort Cromwell
administrator of John Cromwell.
Sureties: Thomas Wilson, Isaac
Harris. Date: 12 June 1772.
- will of Henry Child. Also, bond of
Samuel Child & William Child
administrators. Sureties: Morgan
Jones, William Child. Date: 27
October 1772.
- will of Henry Dorsey. Also, bond of
Samuel Dorsey administrator.
Sureties: Joshua Griffith, George
Scott. Date: 13 August 1772.
- bond of Francis Scrivenor
administrator of Mary Scrivenor.
Sureties: Morgan Jones, Richard
Randall. Date: 10 August 1772.
- bond of Anthony Musgrove
administrator of Anthony Musgrove.
Sureties: Samuel Musgrove, George
Nelson. Date: 27 August 1772.
- bond of Catharine Davis
administratrix of Samuel Davis.
Sureties: Robert Tongue, William
Tuttel. Date: 18 July 1772.

44:584
- bond of Stephen Stewart & Kensay
Johns administrators of Robert
Norris. Sureties: Isaac Hall,
Gassaway Watkins. Date: 15 June
1772.
- will of Col. Charles Hammond.
- will of Augustine Marriott.
- inventory of Thomas Watkins.
- inventory of Mark Brown.
- inventory of Francis Oneal.
- inventory of Ann Dorsey.
- inventory of Thomas Sappington.
- LoD on estate of Thomas Sappington.
- LoD on estate of Nicholas Hammond.

Court Session: 1772

- LoD on estate of Nathaniel Adams.

15 October. Exhibited from TA:
- exemplification of will of Matthias Gale & PoA.
- bond of Mathias Gale administrator of Matthias Gale. Sureties: William Hayward, Henry Jackson. Date: 23 September 1772.

Exhibited from AA:
- will of James Esdale.

Exhibited from BA:
- inventory of John Ridgely in BA & AA.

44:585
- bond of John Bailey administrator of Jabez Bailey. Sureties: Thomas Johnson, Elam Bailey. Date: 21 August 1772.
- bond of John Bailey administrator of Maclean Bailey. Sureties: Robert Johnson, Elam Bailey. Date: 21 August 1772.
- bond of John Whelsh administrator dbn of Robert Gilcrash. Sureties: Clement Brooke, Thomas Lingan, Jr. Date: 2 September 1772.
- accounts on estate of Renaldo Monk.
- will of Barnet Holtzinger.
- will of Hellen Gilcrash.

Exhibited from CV:
- will of Josias Sunderland.
- accounts on estate of Mary Laurence.
- inventory, accounts, & additional accounts of Joseph Wilson.

Exhibited from FR:
- inventory of Meriam Richardson.
- accounts on estate of Meriam Richardson.
- will of George Reid, Sr.
- will of Sarah Needham.
- inventory of Thomas Harriss.
- final accounts on estate of Absalom Warfield.

44:586 Exhibited from QA:
- accounts on estate of William Price.
- LoD & accounts on estate of John Pratt.

- accounts on estate of David Nevill.
- accounts on estate of Edward Brown.
- accounts on estate of John Brown.

Exhibited from KE:
- LoD & final accounts on estate of Samuel Hodges.
- final accounts on estate of Dorothy Hodges.

Exhibited from PG:
- bond of George Scott administrator of George Scott. Sureties: Jacob Young, John Cary. Date: 25 May 1772.

Exhibited from SM:
- bond of Philip Key administrator of Thomas Key. Sureties: James Jordan, Thomas Bond. Date: 6 July 1772.

Exhibited from CE:
- bond of Baruch Williams as Deputy Commissary (CE). Sureties: William Baxter, Richard Thomas. Date: 23 May 1772.
- final accounts on estate of Richard Gready.

44:587 Exhibited from DO:
- bond of William Murray administrator of John Murray. Surety: William Adams. Date: 17 July 1772.

Exhibited from AA:
- additional inventory & accounts of Richard Chew.
- final accounts on estate of John Waters.
- final accounts on estate of Jos. Williams.
- final accounts on estate of Yate Plummer.
- final accounts on estate of Thomas Welsh.
- final accounts on estate of James Thompson.
- final accounts on estate of William Black.
- LoD & accounts on estate of Benjamin Welsh.
- accounts on estate of Thomas Welsh

Court Session: 1772

(collier).
- accounts on estate of Joshua Ridgely.

16 October. Walter Hanson (g, CH) exhibited:
- will of Mary Semmes, constituting Henrietta Semmes executrix. Said executrix was granted administration. Sureties: George Jenkins, Henry Hagan. Date: 23 September 1772.
- will of Joshua Mills, constituting Joshua Mills executor. Said executor was granted administration. Sureties: Joseph Lancaster, Joseph Bowling. Date: 8 October 1772.

44:588
- bond of Sarah Bozwell & Charles Mankin administrators of John Bozwell. Sureties: John Carrington, A. Robey. Date: 3 October 1772.
- bond of Stephen Chandler administrator of John Chandler. Sureties: Charles Ford, Stephen Chandler, Sr. Date: 18 September 1772.
- will of Catharine Price.
- will of Priscilla Gray.
- inventory of John Gray.
- inventory of Jacob Forey.
- inventory of Miles McDaniel.
- inventory of Boles Tyer.
- inventory of Humphrey Berry.
- inventory of John Martens.
- inventory of Edward Ford.
- inventory of Elisabeth Ford.
- accounts on estate of John Martin.
- accounts on estate of John Boswell.
- accounts on estate of William Warder.
- accounts on estate of Robert Candle.

44:589 14 November. Thomas Wright (g, QA) exhibited:
- bond of Robert Walters administrator of Robert Walters. Sureties: Elijah Bishop, John Watson. Date: 31 August 1772.
- bond of Thomas Smyth administrator of John Bennett. Surety: William Ringgold. Date: 1 December 1772.
- bond of Margaret Price

administratrix of Nicholas Price.
Sureties: Hepzibah Guild, Francis
Orrell. Date: 12 September 1772.
- bond of Esther Pratt administratrix
of Henry Wright Pratt. Sureties:
William Price, Elisabeth Downe.
Date: 15 September 1772.
- bond of Margaret Derochbrune
administratrix of Francis
Derochbrune. Sureties: Jonathan
Roberts, Joseph Derochbrune. Date:
19 September 1772.
- bond of Rachell Meeds administratrix
of Rachell Meeds. Sureties: James
Webb, John Dwygens. Date: 12
September 1772.
- will of Thomas Meads.
- will of William Callaghane.
- inventory of Andrew Phoenix.
- inventory of William Webb.
- inventory of William Kirkham.
- inventory of John Atkinson.
- inventory of William Haley.
- inventory of Edward Slay.
- inventory of John Brice.
- inventory of James Garner.
- accounts on estate of Solomon
Jadwin.
- final accounts on estate of William
Elliott.
- final accounts on estate of John
Sherwood.
- final accounts on estate of Thomas
Baily.
- accounts on estate of John Meredith,
Jr.
- final accounts on estate of John
Emory.
- accounts on estate of Joseph Brewer.

W. T. Wootton (g, PG) exhibited:
- bond of Shadrack Searce
administrator of Catharine Searce.
Sureties: Michael Lowe, Jos. Hurly.
Date: 25 September 1772.
- bond of Josias Tennely administrator
of Eleanor Brook. Sureties: Elisha
Lanham, Daniel Fraiser. Date: 7
November 1772.
- bond of Elisabeth Owden
administratrix of Jonathan Oden.
Sureties: Walter Williams, Jos.

44:590

44:591 • Brashear. Date: 26 August 1772.
bond of Elisabeth Whittaker & Robert
Whittaker administrators of Henny
Whittaker. Sureties: William White,
Alexander Whitaker. Date: 1
September 1772.

• bond of John Addams administrator of
John Kelly. Sureites: John Dunn,
Jonathin Turner. Date: 15 August
1772.

• will of Richard Hatton.

• will of John Hawkins.

• inventory of James Fry.

• inventory of Francis Green.

• inventory of William Wells.

• inventory of John Cox.

• LoD on estate of John Cox.

• accounts on estate of Lancelot
Wilson.

• accounts on estate of Peter Moore.

• accounts on estate of George Page.

Th. Bowles (g, FR) exhibited:

• bond of Catherine Myer
administratrix of John Myer.
Sureties: Jacob Schley, Tobias
Risiner. Date: 7 September 1772.

44:592 • bond of Moses Chapline administrator
of Josiah Chapline. Sureties: John
Shirly, Joseph Boyer. Date: 19
October 1772.

• bond of Ambrose Cook administrator
of John Cook. Sureties: Charles
Griffith, Na. Pigman. Date: 23
August 1772.

• bond of Barbarah Gryder
administratrix of John Gryder.
Sureties: Jacob Lemon, Andrew Young.
Date: 7 November 1772.

• inventory of Thomas Jones.

• inventory of Jacob Mallendore.

• inventory of Jacob Trout.

• inventory of John Boyd.

• inventory of Smith Cornall.

• inventory of Adam Stull.

• LoD on estate of Smith Cornall.

• LoD on estate of Jacob Mallendore.

• final accounts on estate of Peter
Storp.

• final accounts on estate of Mary
Linn Cooper.

• final accounts on estate of Nicholas

Roper.
- final accounts on estate of Jacob Auld.
- final accounts on estate of Jacob Mallendore.
- final accounts on estate of Samuel Skinner.
- final accounts on estate of Robert Masters.
- final accounts on estate of Thomas Johnson.
- final accounts on estate of Ezekiel Gosling.

44:593 1 December. Col. J. Nicholson (KE) exhibited:
- will of Rudolph Moore, constituting Ealie Moore executrix. Said executrix was granted administration. Sureties: Joseph Ireland, Moses Tennant. Date: 22 October 1772.
- bond of Thomas Smith administrator of Henry Evans. Surety: T. B. Hands. Date: 5 November 1772.
- bond of Francis Levan administrator of John McGinnis. Sureties: Peter Massey, Cornelius Vansant. Date: 23 October 1772.
- bond of Priscilla Worrall administratrix of Simon Worrell. Sureties: Alexander Calder, James Hackett. Date: 18 November 1772.
- bond of Jerom Cannel & Isaac Cannel administrators of Abraham Cannel. Sureties: Henry Freelock, Robert Peacock. Date: 9 November 1772.
- will of Thomas Jones.
- inventory of Thomas Darrach.
- inventory of Andrew Usher.
- inventory of George Greenwood.
- inventory of Caleb Johnson.
- inventory of Thomas Bowers.
- inventory of Stephen Bordley.
- inventory of Richard Brice.
- LoD on estate of Thomas Kennard.
- LoD on estate of Isaac Boots.
- LoD on estate of Henry Glasford.

44:594
- accounts on estate of Stephen Bordley.
- final accounts on estate of Henry Glassford.

- final accounts on estate of John Campbell.
- final accounts on estate of Charles Hynson.
- final accounts on estate of Josias Ringgold.
- final accounts on estate of Thomas Sealey.
- final accounts on estate of Thomas Kennard.

4 December. Thomas Wright (g, QA) exhibited:
- bond of Henry Elbert administrator dbn of Hawkins Downes. Sureties: Elbert Downes, James Croney. Date: 19 November 1772.
- inventory of William Ridgaway.
- inventory of John Cooper.
- inventory of Stephen Bryan.
- inventory of William Arlett.
- LoD on estate of John Smith.
- accounts on estate of John Smith.
- accounts on estate of Sarah Goodman.

44:595 W. T. Wootton (g, PG) exhibited:
- will of William Willett, constituting Mary Willett executrix. Said executrix was granted administration. Sureties: Richard Simmons, William Willett. Date: 26 November 1772.
- will of Elisabeth Hawkins, constituting George Frazier Hawkins executor. Said executor was granted administration. Sureties: Allen Bowie, William Barnes. Date: 26 November 1772.
- bond of Jemima Burnes & Thomas Bevines administrators of James Burnes. Sureties: Enoch Jenkins, James Wilson. Date: 26 November 1772.
- will of Robert Bradley.
- LoD on estate of William Wells.

12 December. Col. W. Young (BA) exhibited:
- bond of Rebecca Boyce executor of Roger Boyce. Sureties: J. Beale Howard, James Gittings. Date: 7 November 1772.

44:596
- bond of Mary Hall executrix of Elisha Hall. Sureties: Thomas Franklin, Mordecai Grist. Date: 6 November 1772.
- bond of Ann Legate administratrix of John Legate. Sureties: James Greenfield, Thomas Nichols. Date: 2 November 1772.
- bond of Jane Stoane administratrix of James Stone. Sureties: Benjamin Richardson, Ephraim Johnson. Date: 26 October 1772.
- bond of Mary Divers administratrix of Frances Divers. Sureties: John Walters, Stephen Walters. Date: 20 October <no year given>.
- bond of Ruth Carter administrator of William Carter. Sureties: Luke Trotten, Edward Sweeting. Date: 2 November 1772.
- bond of James Gallion administrator of William Gallion. Surety: John Gallion. Date: 17 October 1772.
- inventory of William Ramsey.
- inventory of Mary Beck.
- final accounts on estate of John Webster.
- accounts on estate of Susannah Harrod.
- final accounts on estate of Richard Robinson.
- accounts on estate of Charles Robertson.

GENERAL INDEX
and
INDEX OF EQUITY CASES

Volume XXXVIII: 1771-1772

Liber: 44 (pp. 203-596)

GENERAL INDEX

John 99
Anderson
  Adam 16, 20
  Andrew 53
  Catharine 201
  Catherine 201
  Elisabeth 16, 20,
    53
  James 2, 68
  John 14, 27, 33,
    60, 82, 92, 159,
    173, 201, 207
  Rachel 25, 58, 155
  William 25, 58, 155
Ankim
  Archibald 158
Ankrim
  Archibald 26, 59
  George 26, 59, 158
Anthony
  Eleanor 137
Apey
  Rudolph 192
Arescott
  Richard 17
Arlett
  William 225
Armstrong
  Ann 15
  Archibald 15
  James 49, 96
  John 83
  Martha 75, 77
  Mary 161
  Richard 117
  Robert 75, 77, 161
Arnold
  David 30
  Elisabeth 43
  Rebecca 30
  William 187
Artlett
  Frances 110
  William 110
Ashpaw
  Henry 73
  John 73
Askom
  Charles 125, 216,
    217
  Margaret 125
Aspey
  Jacob 191
  Rudey 191

Atkinson
  Angelo 35, 105,
    204, 205
  Comfort 13, 98
  Isaac 46, 140
  John 92, 110, 136,
    222
  Levi 18
  Levy 34, 105
  Milby 18, 105
  Samuel 105
  Sarah 105
Auld
  Jacob 224
Ault
  Jacob 94, 107
  Robert 150
Aulton
  Joseph 210
  Mary 210
Austin
  John 92
  Mathias 101, 106
  Priscilla 97, 101,
    205
  Sarah 106

Badley
  William 8, 206
Bailess
  Samuel 43
Bailey
  Elam 219
  Esme 36
  George 90
  Jabez 219
  John 219
  Maclean 219
  Newton 90
  Thomas 10, 57, 71,
    138
Baily
  Benjamin 198
  Hannah 151
  John 215
  Thomas 71, 96, 140,
    141, 151, 187,
    201, 222
Bainbridge
  Peter 63
Baker
  Charles 120
  Isaac 1

Sarah 93, 110
Thomas 92, 190
Baley
  Hannah 57
Ball
  William 201
Ballard
  Jarvis 43
Balley
  George 113
Banning
  Benoni 76, 209
Barber
  Barnet 161
  Barnet White 89
  Edward 89, 161
Barnaby
  John 117
Barnes
  Job 2
  William 225
Barnett
  Barbara 93
  Rebecka 93
Barnhouse
  Jane 104
  Jean 37
  Richard 37, 104,
    216, 217
Barret
  Jeruliah 154
  Jonathan 154
Barrett
  Jerutiah 24, 58
  John 24
  Jonathan 58
Barron
  Thomas 21
Barrow
  Thomas 55, 189
Barton
  James 130
Bashaw
  Graves 101, 205
Basnett
  Charles 137
Batcliff
  Stephen 197
Bateman
  Esther 16
  John 114
  William 16, 117
Bavington
  John 106

William 106, 116,
    193, 194, 210
Baxter
  Benjamin 72
  Elisabeth 125
  Francis 160
  John 125, 216
  Rachel 71
  William 160, 220
Bayard
  Eleanor 12, 27
  James 117
  James Ashton 116
  Peter 211
  William 12, 27
Bayly
  George 146
  Hannah 140
  Newton 146
Beachamp
  Handy 113
  Mary 113
Beachford
  Levy 89
  Sara 89
Beall
  Alexander 7
  Basil 134
  James 7
  John 94, 150
  Jos. 6
  Joseph 13
  Richard 134
  Thomas 7, 42, 44,
    150
  William 127
  William Murdock 63
Bean
  Benjamin 215
  Robert 216
Beard
  James 115
  John 38, 70, 136,
    184
  Joseph 184
  Lewis 115
  Mary 115
  Richard 185
  Stephen 184
  Thomas 115, 116
Bearman
  Joseph 178
  William 178
Beaston

Zebulon 115
Beatty
  C. 135
  Charles 70
  Esther 59, 158
  George 59, 158
  John 59, 158
  Sarah 59, 158
  Susannah 105, 212
  Thomas 59, 158
Beauchamp
  Handy 200
  Levin 6, 113
Beavans
  Benjamin 41
Beavens
  Rowland 203
  Sarah 101
  William 101
Beavin
  John 203
  Mary 203
Beavins
  John 204
  Rowland 101
  Thomas 204
  William 101
Beazeley
  Peter 100
Beazley
  Peter 100
Beazly
  (N) 175
Bebber
  Isaac Van 60
Beck
  Charles 10
  Mary 131, 226
  Sarah 131
Beckett
  John 167
Beedle
  Agustine 159
  Argl 210
  Aug. 115
  Augustine 26, 60,
    106
  John 26, 60, 116,
    159
Beemsly
  Thomas 175
Beezly
  (N) 175
Bell

Jonathan 203
  William 190
Bellwood
  Samuel 36
Belt
  Jeremiah 74, 127
Belwood
  Samuel 37
Benet
  Joseph 77
Bennet
  Elisabeth 77
Bennett
  Baxter 33, 205
  Charles 34
  Elisabeth 77
  James 18, 33
  John 221
  Joseph 77
  Mary 34, 35
Benonson
  Thomas 66
Benson
  Isaac 116
Benston
  John 113
Bentley
  John 71, 72
  Tamar 71
Benton
  Vinson 22
Berry
  Anne 95
  Humphrey 221
  Humphry 95
  William 127
Besswick
  William 196
Betty
  Esther 26
  George 26
  John 26
  Sarah 26
  Thomas 26
Beuchamp
  Stephen 202
Bevans
  Richard 41, 68
Bevines
  Thomas 225
Bewley
  Joseph 44
Bibbins
  John 204

Biddle
　Thomas 193
Billingsley
　Ruth 201
Billingsly
　James 201
　Rachel 37
Birkhead
　Chris. 92
Birmintine
　James 100
Birstall
　John 22
Biscoe
　Basil 27, 76
　Bazil 160
　Bennett 27, 76, 160
　James 27, 76, 160
　John 78
　Joseph 36
　Leonard 161
　Mary 27, 76, 160
Bishop
　Elijah 221
　Ely 111
　Robert 123
Black
　John 125
　William 73, 220
Blackiston
　Ann 64, 99
　Ebenezar 119, 194,
　　213
　George 215
　Hance 99
　Henrietta 119, 213
　James 64
　Michael 14, 64
　Rachel 14
Blades
　Esther 12
　George 12
　Joseph 12, 70
Blake
　Charles 3, 22, 48,
　　56, 150
　James 119, 215
　John Sayer 5, 48,
　　106
　Richard 100
　Sarah 3, 22, 48,
　　56, 150
　Thomas 71
Blaker

Charles 48
John Sayer 48
Blandford
　John 62
Blues
　Richard 6
Blunt
　James R. 191
　James Ringgold 108,
　　153, 196
　Samuel 5, 191
Blyth
　John 148
　Sophia 148
Blythe
　John 11, 21, 55
　Sophia 11, 21, 56
Boarman
　Edward 29, 78, 164
　Gerrard 68
　Raphael 210
Body
　John 15, 25, 58,
　　155
　Peter 15, 24, 58,
　　155
Boidel
　Henry 150
Boldin
　James 193
　Jesse 193
　Mary 193
Bolthrop
　Ann 121
　Boles Tyer 121
Bolton
　John 71
BomGardner
　Eve 104
　Everhart 104
Bomgarner
　Everhart 136
Bond
　Ann 16
　Benjamin 119
　Benson 30
　Elisabeth 12, 49,
　　83
　Jacob 4, 49, 112,
　　138
　John 33, 119
　Joshua 16
　Mary 30
　Richard 71

Page 230

Thomas 16, 20, 33,
  53, 71, 145, 220
William 12, 16, 45,
  49, 61, 83
Zachariah 126
Bonsom
  Laurence 32, 80,
    169
  Philipania 32
  Philipina 80, 169
Booker
  Lambert 11, 92
Boon
  Jacob 40, 93
  William 93
Boone
  Humphry 74
  Jacob 93
  Nathan 74
Booth
  Anthony 118
  John 215
Boots
  Isaac 133, 194, 224
  Rebecca 133
Bordley
  Arthur 35, 212
  Hannah 24
  James 22, 136, 190
  Stephen 24, 35, 224
  Thomas 212
  William 35, 44, 212
Bosley
  John 131
Boswell
  John 41, 68, 208,
    221
  Sarah 41, 208
Boteler
  Henry 188
Bounds
  Comfort 51
  James 87
  Jonathan 9, 87, 113
  Richard Steph. 53
  Richard Stephen 19
  Richard Steven 145
  Richard Stevens 91
Bourn
  George 74
Bourne
  Esther 73
  George 12, 30, 79
  Jacob 73

  Margaret 30, 79
Bouth
  Sarah 14
  William 14, 91
Bowdle
  Elisabeth 122, 212
  Henry 87
  Joseph 122, 212,
    214
Bowen
  Benjamin 178
  Littleton 16, 18,
    52, 142
  Mary 178, 206
  Nathan 178, 206
  Parker 73
  Purnel 16, 52, 142
  Purnell 18
Bower
  Timothy 39
Bowers
  John 1, 213
  Thomas 63, 64, 99,
    213, 224
Bowes
  Richard 6, 169
Bowie
  Allen 225
  William 30
Bowin
  Jesse 34
  Jethro 34
  John 204
Bowles
  T. 191
  Th. 223
  Thomas 1, 42, 63,
    70, 89, 94, 134
Bowling
  Joseph 221
Bowman
  Ann 11, 106
  Samuel 2, 11, 106,
    190
Boxall
  Mary 122
  Nehemiah 209
Boxwell
  Nehemiah 41, 124
Boyce
  Rebecca 225
  Roger 128, 225
Boyd
  Archibald 120

Fran. 25, 26, 158
Francis 59, 158
John 135, 176, 223
Susannah 135
Boyer
Augustine 194
Joseph 223
Paul 1
Thomas 120, 194
Boyerly
Lodowick 1
Bozman
Nehemiah 91, 186
Nelly 91
Philemon 14
Rachel 14
Bozwell
John 221
Sarah 221
Bracco
John 7, 43, 66, 92,
117, 118, 188,
196
Bradford
William 204
Bradley
Charles 92
Henry 123
Nathan 41, 198, 209
Nathaniel 92
Robert 225
Brandt
Charles 13, 133
Brashear
Jos. 223
Brashears
Weymack 39
Bravard
Adam 203
Bredel
Elisha 202
Breward
Benjamin 193
Brewer
Bazil 216
John 73
Joseph 39, 73, 130,
222
Nicholas 73
Brice
Francess 39
John 222
Judah 194
Richard 194, 224

Robert 39
William 194
Brierly
Thomas 201
Bright
Ann 46, 104, 152
Francis 46, 104,
137, 152
James 45, 198
John 69, 198
Joseph 45, 197
Briscoe
Leonard 27, 77, 105
Bristow
William 114
Brittingham
Elijah 18, 52, 108,
142, 205
Isaac 34, 102, 205
Mary 202
Peggy 102
Samuel 18, 52, 108,
142
Solomon 103, 202
Broad
Ann 49, 82, 174
Broadus
Edward 12
Elisabeth 12
Moses 107, 123
Broadwater
Betty 47, 89
James 47, 89
Broadway
Betty 52, 142
James 52, 142
Brodess
Edward 123
Brody
Margaret 190
Robert 190
Brome
Thomas 216
Bromwell
Edward 66
Mary 66
Robert 66, 197
Brook
Ann 119, 132
Barbara 119
Basil 95, 163
Boz 119
Eleanor 222
Elisabeth 119

John 119
Roger 119
William Harrison 92
Brooke
Ann 76, 100
Barbara 167
Basil 46
Clement 219
Elisabeth 67
Henrietta 46
Henry 109
John 9, 120, 167
Leonard 132
Lucy 169
Raphel 132
Richard 169
Roger 76
Sarah 9
Thomas 67
William 9, 95
Brookes
Roger 74
Brooks
Benjamin 127
Daniel 129
John 194
Brower
Thomas 73
Brown
Absalom 82, 173
Absolom 33
Adam 3, 21, 55,
118, 119
Ann White 123
Basil 65
Benjamin 195
Charles 146, 210
Christ. 13
Christopher 111,
140
Edward 22, 154, 220
George 171
Henry 171
Jacob 112
James 51, 65, 85,
107, 123, 213
Jane 91
John 15, 22, 56,
107, 123, 126,
136, 151, 213,
220
Joseph 39, 93
Littleton 98
Margaret 12, 33,

82, 173
Mark 51, 85, 182,
218
Mary 3, 21, 55,
171, 195
Nathan 136
Priscilla 210
Robert 51, 85
Samuel 4, 23, 56,
104, 150
Valentine 52, 86,
182
William 9
William Chew 62
Browne
Robert 17
Browning
Sarah 89
Wilson 134
Wrightson 89
Writson 134
Bruce
Normand 127, 163
Richard 133
Bruff
J. E. 99
Joseph 117, 189
Thomas 111, 117
Brumagen
John 107
Bryan
Hannah 191
John 23, 57, 151
Mathew 191
Stephen 191, 225
Susanna 96
Tabitha 23, 57, 151
William 29, 78, 163
Bryarly
Robert 112
Bryon
Mathew 48
Matthew 106
Buchanan
Andrew 175
Robert 35, 133
Buchannon
John 193
Buck
John 187
Buckanan
Armstrong 131
Buckhairair 37
Buckhanan

John 134
Buckhannon
  John 114
Buckingham
  John 88
Bullen
  Charles 21
  Elisabeth 7
Bungay
  Samuel 96
Burch
  Leonard 1
Burck
  Judah 170
  Patrick 170
  Sarah 72
  Thomas 72
  Ulrick 72
Burer
  Magdalen 143
  Solomon 143
Burgess
  Hugh 89, 177, 187
  Jos. 88
  Joseph 107, 177,
    200
  Thomas 88, 177
  William 136
Burk
  James 110
  John 64
  Jonathan 67
  Thomas 72, 187
Burke
  John 207
  Sarah 208
  Thomas 208
Burkett
  James 110
Burkham
  John 117
Burn
  Magdalene 19, 53
  Solomon 19, 53
  Sweatnam 5
Burnes
  James 225
  Jemima 225
Burnet
  Elijah 34
Burrough
  Elisabeth 38
Burroughs
  Hezekiah 28

Richard 28, 38
Burt
  Joseph 36
Burton
  William 45
Busley
  William 94
Bussey
  Hezekiah 139
Bussic
  Richard 69
Butler
  Jane 10
  Peter 10
Byerly
  Lodowick 32
Byrn
  James 73
Byus
  William 122, 124,
    213

Cade
  Robert 89, 137
Cahill
  Rebecka 93
Calder
  Alexander 224
Caldwell
  Elverton 142
  John 43, 142, 200
  Leah 19, 52, 143
  Samuel 75, 126
  William 19, 53, 143
Calender
  William 116
Callaghane
  William 222
Callaway
  Peter 204
Callender
  John 27, 60, 159
  William 12, 26, 60,
    159
Calloway
  John 98, 145
  Siner 145
Cambden
  Henry 139
  Joseph 73
Cambley
  James 113
Camehill

Carlton 135
Campbell
  Alexander 39, 52,
    86, 182
  En. 134
  Jane 208
  John 14, 15, 130,
    210, 225
  Mary 52, 86, 182
  Robert 196
  William 208
Camper
  Philadelphia 11
  Solomon 11
Cample
  Jatin 194
Candle
  Edward 165
  Robert 165, 221
Cannel
  Abraham 207, 224
  Isaac 224
  Jerom 224
Cannon
  Catharine 209
  Hughlit 69
  James 123, 130
  Jesse 69
  John 75, 138
  Mary 69, 124, 209
  Thomas 186, 202,
    209
  William 69, 111
Carbery
  John Baptist 37
  Peter 37
Carbury
  John Bapt. 38
Card
  Thomas 192
Carey
  Henry 190
Carlile
  David 138
Carlisle
  David 108, 178
  Mary 108, 178
  Peter 48, 82, 173
Carnall
  Smith 134
Carnan
  Christopher 176
  Elisabeth 176
  Rowland 33, 82, 173

Carnhart
  Catharine 42
Carpenter
  William 136
Carradine
  James 153
  Thomas 137
  William 111, 137
Carrick
  James 171, 192
  Samuel 94
Carrico
  Margaret 29, 78,
    164
  Peter 29, 78, 164
Carrington
  John 221
Carslake
  Henrietta Maria 21,
    55, 75, 148
  John 21, 55, 75,
    148
Carson
  Thomas 115
Carter
  George 121
  Richard 138
  Ruth 226
  William 138, 226
Cartwright
  John 37, 125
  William 125
Carty
  John 39
Carvill
  John 35
Cary
  John 135, 157, 171,
    220
Case
  Sam 1
Caseen
  John 191
Casner
  George 191
Cason
  Ann 94
  John 94
Casson
  John 92, 93
  Robert 111
Cathell
  Daniel 203
  James 202

Chick
  Mary 114
Chiffin
  James 24, 58, 154
Chilcote
  Humphry 71
  James 179
  John 179
  Sarah 179
Child
  Henry 218
  Samuel 218
  William 218
Chilton
  Abel 211
  Mathew 211
Chisel
  Joseph 116
Chissel
  Jos. 157
  Joseph 59
Chissell
  Joseph 25
Christopher
  Ephraim 34, 205,
    206
  Hannah 34, 206
Chuck
  Joseph 114
Clagett
  Ann 31
  John 31
  Thomas 187
Clagget
  John 6
  Thomas John 67
Clapham
  John 84
Clare
  Edmund 74
Clark
  Abraham 4, 76
  Benjamin 209
  Caleb 7
  Capt. 180
  Daniel 109
  George McCaul 125
  Henry 7
  J. Atta 163
  John 50, 71, 83,
    120, 142, 174
  Jos. 105
  Joseph 192
  Joshua 7, 110, 111,

    136, 207
  Race 204
  Robert 27, 76, 201
  Sophia 49
  Thomas 76
  William 115, 214
Clarke
  Matthew 105
  William 17
Clarkson
  Dorcas 139
  Henry 139
Clayland
  John 23, 90, 137
  Susa 57
  Susannah 23, 151
  Thomas 5, 23, 57,
    151
Claypole
  James 7, 35, 36
Clayton
  Edward 23, 110
  Hannah 110
  John 181
  Mary 22, 56
  Solomon 22, 56, 191
Claywell
  Peggy 89
  Solomon 89, 205
Cleaver
  Ann 156
  William 156
Clem
  George 63, 94
  Margaret 63
Clement
  Jacob 1
Clements
  Caleb 154
  Elisabeth 67, 95
  George 67
  John 67, 88
  Rebecca 154
  Thomas 67
Clifton
  Daniel 34
Clinkscales
  Frances 95
  John 95
Clouds
  Nicholas 5, 22
  Ruth 22
Clough
  James 17

Clow
   James 90, 191
Clowse
   William 96
Coal
   Broad 82
   Frederick 96
   James 187
Coburn
   William 149
Cochran
   William 136
Cock
   Henry 105, 212
Cockran
   Moses 194
   William 136
Cole
   Broad 49, 174
   Dennis 141
   Dennis Garret 141
   Edward 67, 162
   James 107, 187, 188
   Jane 187
   John 10, 66
   Mary 141, 177
   Richard 107, 123,
     199
   Richard Miller 33,
     172
   Robert 64, 216
   Sarah 107
   Thomas 45
   William 141, 177
Coleson
   George 76
   Richard 76
   Sarah 76
   William 41, 76
Coley
   Edward 133
Collet
   Daniel 72
   Moses 72
Collier
   John 203
   Tabitha 203
Collings
   Ebenezar 101
   Mary 101
Collins
   Abigail 12, 19
   Abigal 53
   Elisabeth 92

   Isaac 75, 206
   John 12, 18, 19, 53
   Mathew 92, 191
   Thomas 132
Collison
   Joseph 215
   Richard 198
   William 200
Colson
   Peter 76
   Priscilla 76
Colston
   Jeremiah 136
Comegys
   Ann 151
   Edward 71
   Elisabeth 141
   Jacob 157
   John 151, 152
   Nathaniel 3, 17,
     88, 120, 141,
     210
Compton
   Mathew 46, 65
   Rachel 46
Conaway
   George 217
   Rachel 217
Condon
   Mr. 185
   William 184
Conely
   James 44
Connant
   Charles 73
Connaway
   Hannah 142
   Phillip 142
Connelly
   Thomas 8
Conner
   Caleb 52, 86, 182
   Elijah 8
   Isabella 8
Connerly
   Elisabeth 199
   Jeremiah 199
Connor
   Elijah 91, 141
   Isabella 141
Connoway
   Hannah 18, 52
   Phillip 18, 52, 98
Conoway

Hannah 14
Phillip 14
Constable
  Thomas 88
Contee
  Thomas 133
Coode
  Thomas 27, 38
Cook
  Ambrose 223
  Benjamin 138, 178
  John 31, 80, 167,
    223
  Thomas 5
Cooke
  Benjamin 88, 138
  William 86
Cookrah
  Mary 106
  Moses 106
Cooksay
  Samuel 45
Coombs
  James 216
  John Hatton 206
  Mary 206
  William 1
Coome
  Nicholas 135
Coonce
  Adam 94
  Anna Maria 94
  Nicholas 94
Cooper
  John 26, 59, 127,
    136, 154, 206,
    212, 225
  Mary Ann 206
  Mary Linn 223
  Rebecca 26
  Rebeccah 59
  Solomon 93
  Thomas 26, 59, 136,
    212
Copeland
  Peter 71
  William 113
Copper
  William 64
Corbin
  Betty 18
  Peter 47, 89, 205
Corbit
  James 26, 60, 104,

    115, 159, 193,
    194
  Jane 104
Cord
  John 108
  Joseph 108
Cordery
  Jonathan 109
Cornall
  Richard 134
  Smith 223
  William 134
Corsair
  John 141, 162, 217
  Sabra 141, 162
Corse
  John 141, 156
  Samuel 7, 141, 156
Cosden
  Alphonso 114
  James 114
Coskery
  Arthur 175
Costin
  Henry 16
  Lydia 16
  Richard 136
Cotterell
  Thomas 133
Cottingham
  Charles 103
  Thomas 103
Cottrell
  James 132
Couden
  Robert 129
Coughran
  James 94
  William 94
Coulborn
  Rachel 74
Coursey
  Ann 5
  Edward 17
  William 5, 17
Covender
  David 197
Cover
  Daniel 170
  Eve 170
Covington
  Levin 67
  Thomas 91
Cowarden

John 22
Jonathan 56, 151
William 22, 56, 151
Cullumber
John 100
Cummins
William 196
Cunning
Elisabeth 115, 195
William 115, 116,
195
Cunningham
George 26, 59, 105,
158
Hannah 90
Sarah 26, 59, 105,
158
Thomas 90
Curmeen
Anne 11
John 11
Curry
Eleanor 87
John 87
Cutler
Michael 6

Dade
Elisabeth 1
Daden
Stephen 213
Daiden
Joseph 213
Mary 213
Dailey
Cornelius 22
Daily
Cornelius 56, 150,
197
Dalton
Margaret 138
Thomas 138
Dames
John 93
William 93
Darby
John 122
William 109
Darden
Joseph 92
Mary 92
Stephen 92
Darnall

Henry 5, 23
Darrach
Thomas 224
Darrah
Charlotte 215
John 215
Thomas 215
Dasharoon
Jos. 200
Dashiel
Rebecca 20, 43, 53
Rebeccah 12
Thomas 27, 36
William 18
Dashiell
C. 186
George 91
Jos. 203
Joseph 202
Josiah 109, 132
Levin 185
Daughaday
Richard 45
Daugherty
Edward 25
David
David 43
John 214
Rachel 214
Davidge
John 114, 193, 194
Rachel 114
Davidson
John 39, 217
Davie
William 202
Davis
Ann 32, 81, 169
B. 113
Catharine 218
Clement 171
Cornelius 128, 165
David 87, 179, 211
Francis 179
James 91, 121, 202
John 86, 111, 183
Jos. 193
Joseph 39
Lemuel 199
Levin 102
Littleton 102
Luke 39, 130
Mary 49, 83, 170,
171, 174, 184

Dinney
  Benjamin 71
Dinny
  Benjamin 45
Disharoon
  Constant 200
  John 200
Divers
  Frances 226
  Mary 226
Divin
  Walter 105
Dixon
  Benjamin 12
  David 4
  James 4, 10
  Mary 12
  Robert 17, 40
Dixson
  Benjamin 74
Dobinson
  Ralph 129
Dobson
  George 118, 119
  John 21, 55, 88,
    149, 190
Dodden
  John 197
Dolan
  James 5, 92, 111
  Rebecka 92, 111
Donaldson
  John 99, 194
Done
  John 132
Donehoe
  Gilbert 49
Donellan
  James 7
Donoho
  Joshua 115
Donohoe
  Gilbert 45, 83, 174
  John 27, 60, 159
  Mary 27, 60, 159
Dorman
  Charles 203
  Chase 36, 195
  Esayah 36
  Michael 36, 186,
    195
  Sarah 195
Dorrell
  Nicholas 193

Dorrey
  Elisha 43
Dorset
  John 80, 167
Dorsett
  John 31
Dorsey
  (N) 83
  Ann 72, 218
  Caleb 39, 72, 129,
    217
  Edward 39, 50, 51,
    85, 129, 181
  Eloner 217
  Ely 50, 85, 181
  Greenbury 83, 142,
    174
  Henrietta Maria 51,
    85, 181
  Henry 73, 218
  John 39, 129
  John Hammon 33
  John Hammond 82,
    172
  Jonathan 149
  Joseph 129
  Joshua 72
  Mary 149
  Milcah 217
  Nathan 50
  Philemon 129
  Richard 130
  Samuel 73, 217, 218
  Sophia 83, 142, 174
  Thomas 72
  Thomas Beal 39, 85
  Thomas Beale 51, 72
  Thomas Beall 50
Dossey
  Levin 40
Dougherty
  Barnaby 189
  Edward 59, 157
  John 99, 189
Douglass
  Ann 120
  Benjamin 120, 132,
    188
  Joseph 132
  William 3, 10
Dovin
  William 127
Dowden
  John 135

Dowdle
    Christopher 96,
        186, 195
    Sarah 95, 113, 206
    Thomas 96
Dowell
    Harrison 30
Dowie
    William 45, 68, 79
Downe
    Elisabeth 222
Downes
    Elbert 225
    Elisabeth 185
    Frances 137
    Hawkins 15, 94, 225
    Henry 124, 136,
        137, 191
    James 137
    John 5
    Jonathan 196
    Mary 196
Downey
    John 111
Downie
    John 125
Downing
    John 110
Downs
    Elisabeth 185
    John 47
Downy
    William 135
Doxey
    William 215
Doyne
    Jane 29, 78, 163
Driver
    Mathew 108, 213
Drugan
    Edward 24, 58, 108,
        154
    Thomas 154
Drummond
    Sarah 105
    William 105
Drury
    Michael 37
    Peter 36, 38, 126
Dubberly
    Esekiel 204
Ducker
    Jeremiah 129
    John 129

Duckett
    Richard 185
    Thomas 185
Dudley
    George 188
    James 208
Dudly
    James 48
Duffey
    Absolom 64
Duhamel
    James 40
Duke
    James 30, 74, 79
    Mary 30, 79
Dundass
    James 39
Dunn
    John 223
    Robert 10, 49, 83,
        174
    Sarah 49, 83, 174
    Walter 195
Dutton
    Gerr. 67
    Robert 45, 72
Duval
    Alice 85
    Lewis 85
Duvall
    Alice 51, 182
    Lewis 182
    Mareen 187
Duy
    Robert 2
Dwigan
    John 124
Dwiggens
    John 110
Dwygens
    John 222
Dyson
    Bennet 139
    Bennett 164
    Dorcas 164
    Joseph 139, 164

Eagle
    Mary 153
    Solomon 136
Eareckson
    John 40
Earl

Page 244

Jos. 160
Michael 160
Earle
    Benjamin 92, 99
    John 99
    Jos. 26, 158
    Mary 99, 163
    Michael 60
Eason
    Ann 212
    John 212
Eastwood
    Benjamin 31, 80,
        167
    Elisabeth 31, 80,
        167
Eccleston
    Charles 214
    James 214
    William 214
Eddelin
    John 164
    Susa 164
Eddeline
    Christopher 126
Edelen
    Christopher 171
Edelin
    Christopher 42, 63
    James 29, 78, 108
    Susa 78, 108
    Susanna 29
Edeline
    Christopher 98
    Jane 98
    John 98
    Thomas 98
Eden
    James 65
    John 65
Edge
    Thomas 111
Edgele
    Daniel 122
Edmondson
    Mary 8
    Peter 69
    Thomas 69
    William 69
Edmonson
    Pollard 189
Edwar
    Richard Swan 161
Edward

Robert 38
Edwards
    Martha 28
    Richard Swan 28,
        75, 77, 126
Egerton
    Charles 215
    William 215
Eichelberger 201
    Frederick 2
    Jacob 2
Elbert
    Henry 189, 225
    Lodman 15, 92, 189
    Macklin 149, 196,
        197
Elder
    John 129
Elegood
    William 203
Eliason
    Abraham 114, 115,
        140, 211
    Cornelius 114
    Elias 114, 140,
        193, 211
    John 114, 115
    Lydia 115
Ellers
    Carty 213
Elliot
    Benjamin 26, 59
    Elisabeth 153
    Honour 16
    Susannah 26, 59
    Thomas 52
    William 16, 104,
        153
Elliott
    Benjamin 92, 116,
        136, 158
    Elisabeth 111, 137
    George 93
    Henry 140
    Susannah 158
    Thomas 88
    William 140, 222
Elloiot
    Daniel 34
Ellsbury
    Frederick 26, 46,
        59
    Rebecca 26
    Rebeccah 59

Ellston
Mary 54, 147
William 54
Ellts
Benjamin 74
Elms
Richard 1
Elsey
Job 186
Elson
Richard 29
Sarah 90, 169
William 90, 126,
169
Elston
Mary 20
William 20
Elt
Ann 3
Benjamin 3
Elzey
Arnold 106, 139,
209
John 106, 209
Emmitt
Samuel 94
Emory
Ann 14, 22, 56, 90,
142, 150
Arthur 14, 16, 22,
56, 90, 142,
150, 154
Charles 154
Gideon 14, 87
John 14, 22, 56,
90, 142, 150,
154, 222
Thomas 14, 16, 87
Endsworth
Benjamin 87, 137
Engell
Charles 104
Engler
Philip 70
Engles
Philip 210
Ennalls
Henry 147
Joseph 123
Mary 123
Thomas 123
Ennis
Charles 103, 205
Elisabeth 103

James 138
John 34
Samuel 34, 202
Ensor
Elisabeth 71
George 71
Joseph 61, 115,
192, 214
Erbach
Balser 42
Errickson
Anne 199
John 199
Esdale
James 219
Etherington
Bartholomew 114
Eubank
Rebeccah 189
Eubankes
George 189
Evans
Amos 116
Elisabeth 168
Elisha 14, 15, 98
Francis 68, 121,
188, 208
Hannah 203, 207
Henry 224
James 189
John 11, 47, 139,
200
Phoebe 121, 208
Robert 42
Thomas 139, 203,
204, 207
Victoria 11, 47,
139
Walter 168
William 56, 111,
203
Evenly
John 75
Everhart
George 75
Ewen
John 40
Ewing
William 114
Exley
Elisabeth 47, 196
Ezchelberger
Marten 201

Fairbrother
  Elisabeth 190
  Isaac 215
  Richard 190
Fairfax
  William 9
Falconaner
  Hannah 189
Falconar
  Gilbert 64
Falconer
  Gilbert 64, 133
  John 189, 196
  Salathiel 123
  Sarah 124
Falls
  David 64
Fanning
  Anne 37
  John 37, 65, 104
Farguson
  Abraham 45
  James 8, 69, 199
  Jane 4
  Rosannah 45
  Thomas 4, 70
Fargusson
  James 4
Fariss
  Jos. 48
Farr
  Ann 121
  George Thomas 121
  John 9, 75
  Samuel 68, 121, 133
  William 9, 75
Farrel
  Daniel 99
Farris
  John 95
Farriss
  Joseph 42
Farrow
  Margaret 152, 211
  Nathan 152, 211
Fassit
  William 202
Fassitt
  Levin 103, 206
  Mary 202
  William 101, 202,
    204, 206
Faulconer

John 123
  Nathan 123
  Thomas 123
Faulkner
  Thomas 214
Feddeman
  Ann 12, 21, 55, 148
  Daniel 12, 17, 21,
    55, 148
  Phillip 190
Feild
  John 162
Fell
  Edward 84, 176
Fennally
  Philip 31
  William 31
Fenwick
  Benedict 163
  Bennett 36, 38, 211
  Cuthbert 125
  Enoch 162
  George 125, 216
  Igna. 125
  Ignatius 65, 119
  Jane 125
  John 12
  Richard 36, 211
  William 36, 163
Ferguson
  Alexander 39, 61
  James 209
  Rosanna 209
Ferrall
  Kenedy 94
Ferrill
  John 23
  Mary 23
Ferry
  Elisha 160
  William 160
Ffrisby
  George 115
Fiddeman
  Daniel 119
Finissey
  John 98
Finney
  Daniel 193
  David 192
  Eleanor 193
Fisher
  John 107, 207, 213
Fitch

Henry 224
Freeman
   Abraham 16
   Jacob 16
   William 24, 57, 154
French
   Arena 178
   Ignatius 125, 162,
     216
   Jacob 86, 182
   James 1, 125, 130
   John 125, 162
Frier
   John 193, 194
Frisby
   Cordelia 47
   Richard 99
   William 47, 99, 100
Fry
   James 188, 223
Fryer
   Jane 114, 116
Fullerton
   Charles 8
   Joshua 8
   Mary 8, 18
Fulton
   Ann 114
   David 179
   Francis 114
Furlaid
   Joseph 110
Furnis
   William 43
Furroner
   Edward 115
   Elisabeth 115

Gafford
   Richard 93, 191
Gaither
   Edward 51, 85, 217
   John 51, 85
   Sarah 51, 62, 85
Gale
   George 95
   Levin 95
   Mathias 219
   Matthias 219
Gallion
   James 226
   John 226
   William 44, 226

Galt
   James 170
Gambril
   William 130
Gantt
   Edward 61
Gardin
   Jane 2
Gardiner
   Clement 125
   James 72
   John 29, 78, 164
   John Thomas 161
   Jos. Thomas 77
   Joseph 129
   Richard 129
Gardner
   John 100
   Kinsey 100
   Robert 100
Gardwin
   James 2
Garey
   Mary Ann 66
Garford
   Richard 124
   Sarah 124
Garland
   John 212, 214
   Rebecca 214
   Rebecka 212
   Stephen 20, 53
Garner
   Alice 137
   Benjamin 121, 133,
     165
   James 137, 222
Garnett
   George 91, 93
   Jos. 194
   Joseph 108
   Mary 11, 87
   Thomas 11, 87
Garratt
   Amos 201
Garret
   Amos 61
Garretson
   Cornelius 130
   Garet 44
   Job 61, 71, 72, 86,
     179
   Martha 10
Garrett

Amos 130
John 184
Nathan 192
Garrott
John 184
Garthill
T. 206
Gartrill
John 46
Gary
Gideon 129
Gash
Thomas 72
Gastineau
George Lewis 91
Gastineaux
George Lewis 14,
19, 53
Job 14, 53
Gastineax
Job 19
Gates
Joseph 113
Gay
Hugh 115
Nicholas Ruxton
107, 128, 177
Gear
Henry 110, 168
Geary
John 66, 184, 185
Mark 184, 185
William 66, 189
Geddes
William 99
Geddis
William 194
Geist
Samuel 73
George
Hanna 57
Hannah 24, 154
Joshua 24, 57, 154
Gerber
Martin 70
Gibbs
Isaac 115
Gibson
Frances 15, 21, 55,
148
Francis 15, 21, 55
Jacob 189
James 43, 49, 83,
174, 189

John 37, 118, 196
Joshua 37
Peter 148
William 42
Gilchrist
Helen 174
Hellen 49, 83
Robert 49, 83, 174
Gilcrash
Hellen 219
Robert 219
Giles
Ann 84, 176
Jacob 49, 83, 174
James 84
John 176, 210
Nathan 210
Thomas 18
Gill
Henry 78
Gillespy
Samuel 113
Gillett
Agnes 206
Jarman 206
Gillispy
Samuel 115
Gilliss
Benjamin 186
Ezekiel 186
Joseph 200
Levin 200
Sarah 200
William 186
Gilpin
Thomas 88
Gist
Mordecai 71, 176
Gittings
James 225
Givan
John 1
Gladen
Howel 89
Sarah 89
Gladman
Michael 177
Thomas 177
Gladstone
Obediah 103
Turvill 103
Glasford
Henry 224
Glasgow

John 27, 60, 116,
159, 207
Patrick 102
William 27, 60,
159, 207
Glass
Gartrude 211
John 191, 211
Rebecka 140
Thomas 140
Glassford
Henry 224
Gleaves
John 23, 57, 154
Goddard
John 215
Goddart
Jane 6
Godwin
Daniel 102, 204
Mary 102
Thomas 102
Gody
Cloe 45, 68
Golder
John 50, 84
Phillip 180
Goldsborough
Foster 189, 190
Henrietta Maria 66,
189
Ignatius 27, 76,
160
Jane 76, 160
John 4, 8, 17, 21,
27, 40, 68, 122,
197, 214
Nicholas 21, 44, 55
Sarah 55
Thomas 189, 190
Goldsmith
John 104
Mary 104
Goodhand
Marma. 191
Goodman
Sarah 94, 225
Goodrick
Charles 1
Francis 28
Gordon
Charles 60, 88, 160
James 113
John 66

Thomas 10
Gorsuch
Charles 84
Goslee
Samuel 30
Gosling
Ambrose 199
Elisabeth 210
Ezekiel 210, 224
Gossage
Charles 175
Mrs. 176
Sarah 175
Gough
John 2
William 33, 82, 173
Gould
James 5
Govane
William 43, 50, 83,
141, 174
Gover
Elisabeth 105, 176
Ephraim 105, 176
Grace
Abel 8, 70
Grafton
William 47, 96, 138
Graham
Andrew 92
Ann 185
Daniel 2, 10, 71
Elisabeth 2, 72
Ezekiel 186
Henry 185
Granger
Benjamin 123
John 194
Joseph Thomas 28
Grant
Eleanor 157
Elisabeth 167
George 167
William 87, 100,
157, 194
Gravenor
William 186
Graw
(N) 79
Gray
Ann 30, 79
George 108, 138
Jacob 209
James 10, 138

Jeremiah 188
John 30, 74, 79,
    100, 108, 138,
    188, 193, 221
Leah 209
Priscilla 221
Samuel 193
Sarah 113
Stephen 188
William 4, 113
William H. 188
Grayless
  Jesse 123
Gready
  Richard 220
Greaves
  Ann 79
  Driver 79
  John 79
Green
  Ann 14
  Benjamin 4, 49
  Elijah 208
  Elisabeth 46, 109,
    123, 212
  Ezekiel 19, 53, 143
  Francis 109, 223
  Isaac 15, 19, 20,
    53, 88, 145
  John 110
  Michael 93, 110
  Richard 15, 20, 53,
    88, 132, 145
  Samuel 46, 212
  Sarah 110
  William 4, 14, 19,
    70, 123, 208,
    214
Greenfield
  James 226
Greenwell
  Hannah 195
  James 38, 195
  Justinian 37, 126
  Margaret 37
Greenwood
  George 139, 224
Greeves
  Ann 30
  Driver 30
  John 30
Gresham
  John 127, 133, 156
  Richard 133, 207

Robert 133
Sarah 207
Greves
  John 74
Griffin
  Ann 36
  Nehemiah 36
  Nicholas 126
  Thomas 36, 215
Griffith
  Benjamin 46, 206
  Charles 72, 223
  Elisabeth 214
  Hen. 84
  Henry 50
  John 72, 100
  Joshua 128, 218
  Rachel 46, 206
  Robert 8
  Samuel 120, 215
  Thomas 214
Grindle
  P. 135
Gripe
  Jacob 1
Grist
  Mordecai 131, 226
Groom
  Samuel 61, 179
  Thomas 179
Groome
  Samuel 86, 179
Grosh
  Peter 63, 135
Grove
  Ebsworth 29, 79,
    163
  Elisabeth 29, 79,
    163
  Mary 121
  Matthew 121, 133
Groves
  Matthew 188
  Posthuma 41, 87,
    121
Grub
  Jacob 135
  James 171
Grubb
  James 106
Gryder
  Barbarah 223
  John 223
Gue

George 192
Guild
  Hepzibah 222
Guishard
  Mark 201
  Sarah 201
Guither
  William 28, 75
Gull
  Balser 192
Guthrie
  Francis 38
Guyther
  Grace 125
  Thomas 162
  William 77, 125,
    161, 162
Gwynn
  John 46, 206

Hacket
  James 7, 134
  Oliver 122
Hackett
  Isaac 90
  James 90, 224
  William 110
Hadley
  Mary 17, 23, 56
Hagan
  Basil 1, 29, 78,
    108
  Bazil 164
  Henry 1, 9, 221
  Sarah 1
Hagar
  Jonathan 192
Hagen
  Henry 1
Haines
  Daniel 16, 63
  Mary 16
  Nathan 16
Hale
  James 70
Haley
  Elisabeth 75
  Henrietta 64
  Samuel 75
  Thomas 75
  William 35, 64,
    111, 222
Hall

Andrew 4, 23, 56,
  104, 150, 191
Benjamin 192
Christopher 120
Cordelia 48
Daniel 89, 144
Edward 49, 82, 104,
  128, 174
Elisabeth 120, 194
Elisha 84, 144,
  175, 176, 226
Ester 191
Esther 4, 23, 56
Hadrick 34
Hannah 207
Henry 39, 62, 128
Isaac 130, 218
John 2, 3, 34, 48,
  61, 89, 117,
  144, 189, 193,
  205
Joshua 108
Margaret 207
Mary 175, 176, 226
R. 118
R. B. 185
Richard B. 109
Robert 144
Samuel 34, 35
Sarah 19, 52, 143,
  175, 207
Sophia 108
Stephen 19, 52, 97,
  143, 207
Thomas 124
William 6, 40, 48
William Jordan 207
Halsey
  William 42
Hambleton
  Alexander 1
  Ignatius 68
Hamersley
  Basil 9
Hamersly
  Basil 212
  Francis 126
  Henrietta 212
Hamil
  Hugh 9
Hamill
  Hugh 30, 79, 164
  John 79, 164
Hamilton

Bassil 121
Gavin 115
John 126
Kerenhapuch 177
William 177
Hammell
   John 76
Hammill
   John 30
Hammon
   Hamutal 130
Hammond
   Ann 50, 84
   Caroline 130
   Charles 50, 84,
     180, 218
   Hamutal 130
   John 50, 84, 180,
     204
   Leah 204
   Mary 73
   Nathan 130
   Nicholas 218
   Philip 84
   Phillip 50, 180
   Richard 89, 137,
     152
Hamond
   John 111
Hance
   Chris. 139
Hands
   T. B. 224
   Th. B. 133
Handy
   Benjamin 102
   Betty 200
   Esther 186
   George 200
   Isaac 186
   John 17, 46, 102
   Samuel 141
   Thomas 8, 200
Haner
   Robert 189
Hannan
   John 133
Hannon
   John 79
Hanson
   Frederick 64, 99,
     119
   Hanse 64
   Mary 119

Robert 47, 87, 121
Theo. 9
Theophilus 45
Walter 1, 9, 41,
   67, 95, 120,
   121, 132, 188,
   221
William 45, 68
Hansworth
   Thomas 38
Hanworth
   Mary 37
   Thomas 37
Har
   Ann Maria 139
   Phillip 138, 139
Harbert
   Charles 194
Hardcastle
   Robert 111
   Thomas 87, 93, 111,
     137
Harden
   Charles 81, 170
   Elias 170
   Elisabeth 170
Hardesty
   Priscilla 90, 167
   William 199
Hardey
   George 187
Harding
   Charles 183, 184
   Eleanor 184
   Elias 63, 183, 184
   Elisabeth 184
   Mary 75, 106
   Richard 75, 106
Hardman
   Catharine 134, 135
   Michael 135
Hardy
   Ann 105, 132
   Anthony 66
   George 105
   Lucy 187
Harman
   Grace 29
   John 29, 107
Harper
   Catharine 103
   David 122, 147
   John 103
   Josias 32

Robert 32
Harrgereder
    John 209
Harrington
    J. 117
    Nathan 89, 152, 153
    William 104, 137,
        190
Harriot
    Susannah 81, 172
    William 81, 172
Harriott
    William 33
Harris
    Aaron 172
    Benton 97, 100
    Edward 2
    Elisabeth 93
    Isaac 218
    James 19, 53
    Nathaniel 135
    Nehemiah 113
    Rebecca 190
    Sarah 12, 19, 53
    Thomas 135, 172
    William 93
Harrison
    Edward 189
    Elisha 180
    Francis 74
    J. H. 188
    John 21, 55, 140,
        148, 197
    Joseph 165
    Kellelen 76
    Kenelm 27, 160
    Richard 121, 165
    Thomas 117
    William 21, 55,
        140, 148
Harriss
    Benton 33, 202
    Francess 3
    James 12, 18
    Nathaniel 172
    Thomas 219
Harrisson
    Isaac 7
    William 66
Harritt
    Susannah 33
Harrod
    Susannah 226
Harry

John 48
    Martin 192
    Thomas 48
Harryman
    Charles 2, 196
    George 201
Hars
    Philip 138
Hart
    Elisabeth 35
    John 2
Harvey
    David 3
    Levin 97
Harwood
    Elisabeth 3, 21,
        55, 148, 207
    Mary 21, 55, 148,
        206
    Peter 21, 55, 148,
        206
    Robert 3, 21, 55,
        148, 207
    Susannah 210
    Thomas 73, 129,
        130, 217
    William 3, 21, 55,
        148, 207, 210
Haslet
    Jos. 153
    William 17
Hasselbach
    Catharine 72
    Nicholas 72
Hasty
    Ann 29
    Clement 29
Hatfield
    Elijah 123, 208
    William 123, 208,
        214
Hath
    William 200
Hatton
    Catharine 138
    China 138
    Jo. 9
    John 10, 48, 96
    Richard 223
    Thomas 48, 71, 138
Haun
    George 104, 136
Hawkins
    Alexander Smith 1,

Page 255

29, 47, 78, 107,
133, 164
Elisabeth 225
George Frazier 225
Hen. Smith 78
Henry 12, 104, 133,
166
Henry Smith 29, 47,
107, 164
John 111, 130, 183,
223
John Stone 62
Josiah 12
Josias 104, 166
Mary 30, 79, 164
Robert 152, 209
Rudolph Moris 79
Rudolph Morris 30,
164
Thomas 2, 29, 32,
47, 78, 107,
164, 183
Haws
Ann Statia 173
Daring 33, 82
Hay
Abraham 48
Haydon
Basil 65
William 65
Hayes
Thomas 90
Hayman
David 97
Isaac 105, 139, 146
James 97
John 97
Joshua 105, 146
Liddy 105
Lydia 146
Margarett 97
William 35, 103
Haynie
Judith 131
Samuel 131
Hayter
Abraham 81
Hayward
Francis 123, 213
George 97, 109, 207
Mary 123, 213
Sarah 197
Thomas 197
William 126, 189,
219
Hazel
Sarah 88, 156
William 88, 133,
156
Hazeldine
Charles 217
Hazelfine
Charles 107
Headshoe
Catharine 96
Phillip 96
Heard
Barbara 28
Bennet 163
James 65
John 28, 37, 39,
163, 215
Mark 37, 126
Mathew 37
Richard 28, 38, 39
Susannah 37
Hearn
Benjamin 17
Jonathan 131
Samuel 132
Heason
John 129
Heath
Charles 163
Daniel 163
Daniel Charles 62
Hester 92
James 115
Mary 163
William 92, 137
Heddington
Abel 201
Nathan 201
Temperance 201
Heighe
Mary 47
Thomas Holdsw. 74
Thomas Holdsworth
47
Helestine
Charles 77
Elisabeth 77
Hellen
Jane 73, 119
Henderson
Benjamin 203, 204,
205
Ephraim 11

John 11, 98
Rhoda 11
Thomas 114
Hendly
John 125
Hendon
Henry 201
Hendrickson
Augustine 114
John 96, 105, 114,
177
Henesey
Andrew 57
John 57
Henley
Henrietta 77
James 77, 78
Hennesey
Andrew 151
John 151
Hennessey
Andrew 23
John 23
Henney
Thomas 150
William 150
Henrickson
Henry 114
Henry
Adam 172
Michael 96
Sarah 172
Hergareder
John 42
Heron
John 26, 59
Martha 26, 59
Herring
David 5, 94
Elisabeth 5
Herron
John 158
Martha 158
Heselius
Mr. 185
Heseltine
Charles 28
Elisabeth 28
Hewet
Thomas 5
Hewett
Thomas 23
Hezeltine
Charles 65, 66

Hickman
Andrew 25, 106
Elisabeth 106
Hickman Rachel 25
Joshua 195
Margaret 195
Selby 35
Hicks
Giles 22, 56, 150
James 190
John 8, 20, 54, 70
Sarah 20, 53
Higdon
Thomas 10
Hignut
Daniel 213
James 213
John 213
Hill
Adam 196
Anne 65
Clement 65, 217
Darky 183
Elisabeth 41
John 3, 48
Jonathan 204
Joshua 102
Rosannah 48
Samuel 102
Thomas 44
William 43
William Stephens
203
Hilleary
Henry 98
Thomas 98, 188
Hindman
James 127
Hissey
Charles 2
Hitch
Joseph 6, 89, 132
Joshua 15, 17, 89
Mary 123, 208
Robert 17
Sarah 17
Spencer 123
Whittenton 123
William 122, 208,
214
Hitchcock
Josias 44
William 112, 201
Hodges

Robert 34
Stephen 95, 113,
   200
Hopper
  William 136, 190
Hoskins
  John 125
Houston
  James 102, 145,
   203, 204
  Joseph 204
  Mary 102, 204
Hoverton
  John 104
How
  Priscilla 4
Howard
  Ann 10, 131, 142,
   201
  Benjamin 10, 16,
   23, 45, 57, 96,
   99, 142, 155
  Cornelius 39, 71,
   130, 216
  Elisabeth 216
  J. Beale 225
  John 51, 85, 181
  Samuel 51, 76, 85,
   181
  Samuel Harvey 73,
   217
Howarth
  Elisabeth 8, 209
  John 8, 69, 209
Howe
  Priscilla 17, 20
Howell
  John 99
  Nathaniel 99
  William 99
Howerton
  John 119
Hubbard
  Elisabeth 147
Hubbert
  Elisabeth 147
  Henry 198
  Titus 41
Hubert
  Benjamin 187
Hudson
  David 102
  John 102
  Richard 165

Samuel 121
Thomas 210
Huffington
  John 109
  Levin 109
Hugh
  Andrew 134
Hughes
  J. 115
Hughlet
  Thomas 17
  William 17
Hughlett
  William 93
Hughs
  Daniel 218
  Hannah 178
  James 115
  Samuel 96
Humberstone
  George 27, 60, 159
  Jonathan 27, 60,
   159
Humphreys
  Joseph 106
  Thomas 106
Humphris
  Joseph 186
  Thomas 18, 132
Humphrys
  Jos. 211
  Thomas 211
Hungerford
  Barton 10
Hunt
  Joseph 1
  Peter 13, 17
  Thomas 95
Hunter
  Anthony 33, 81, 170
  David 32, 81, 170
  Ezekiel 92
Hur
  Anna Maria 96
  Phillip 96
Hurley
  Mark 199
  Mary 76
  Mathew 199
  Roger 41, 69, 76
Hurly
  John 199
  Jos. 222
Hurt

Henry 7
Husband
John 193
Hutchcraft
Thomas 128
Hutcheson
Ann 47, 87, 122
Gaving 116
James 87
Hutchings
Benedict 118
Dorothy 153
James 191
Ris 153
William 39
Hutchinson
Elisabeth 80
John 80
Hutchison
Ann 25, 58, 155
Elisabeth 30
James 48
John 25, 30, 58,
155
Hutton
George 197
Mary 197
Hyde
Thomas 73
Hyland
John 116
Mathew 117
Hynasy
John 118
Hynson
Andrew 91
Charles 91, 118,
206, 225
James 91
John 63
Martha 64, 71, 99
Mary 63, 91, 206
William 15, 25, 58,
64

Iiams
John 52
Imbert
Rachel 4, 141
Thomas 5, 17, 141
Ireland
Jos. 194
Joseph 224

William 100
Irons
Aaron 102
Jane 102, 103
Irving
George 185
Mary 141
Thomas 141, 185
Irwin
Constant 180
Isaack
Joseph 128
Isaacke
Jos. 30

Jaboe
Ann 46
Athinasius 46
Jackson
Henry 95, 186, 219
John 52, 86, 128
Jacob
Samuel 86
Jacobs
Bartholomew 209
Benjamin 6, 48
Eliphalet 190
Jacob 115
Jemima 6
Mordecai 6, 127
Samuel 52
William 5, 195
Jacquery deSales
Mary 112
Samuel 112
Jadwin
John 40
Solomon 40, 94, 222
James
Alexander 11
Ezekiel 18
Javis 118
Richard 131
Sarah 118
Thomas 35
Jameson
Henry 31, 164
Jamison
Michael Parker 215
Janson
John 62
Jarratt
James 70

Mary 70
Jarrett
   Abraham 130
Jehosaphat
   Arthur 35
Jenifer
   Daniel 41, 76, 120
   Elisabeth 216
   John Read 216
   John Richard 125
   Samuel 216
Jenkins
   Edward 98
   Enoch 225
   George 221
   Jane 121, 188, 212
   John 46, 212
   Lurena 92
   Mary 208
   Thomas 92, 121,
     132, 197, 212
   William 3, 36
Jenners
   Daniel 73
Jennings
   Mr. 185
   Thomas 175, 179,
     184
Jerrum
   Thomas 118
Joan
   Barbara 42
   Barbary 209
   Joahim 42
   Yoachim 209
Jobson
   John 8
   Michael 107, 211
John
   Joachim 192
   Yocham 136
Johns
   Acquila 82
   Aquila 173
   Aquilla 49
   Kensay 218
   Kinsey 50, 84
   Richard 189
   Sarah 49, 82, 173
   Susa 50
   Susannah 84
Johnson
   Ann 50, 84, 180
   Archibald 31, 72,

     80
   Barnet 2
   Beatrise 58
   Beatrix 24, 46, 155
   Caleb 224
   Eleanor 27, 76, 160
   Eliakim 204
   Ephraim 226
   Ezekiel 198
   Hester 2
   James 29
   John 2, 27, 29, 34,
     70, 76, 160,
     161, 217
   Leonard 101
   Lydia 185
   Moses 44
   Nathan 112, 175
   Robert 29, 50, 73,
     84, 180, 219
   Samuel 44, 113
   Sarah 32, 76, 81,
     204, 209
   Thomas 2, 24, 32,
     65, 76, 81, 138,
     175, 209, 219,
     224
   William 2, 76
   Zachariah 29
Jones
   Benjamin 33, 82,
     173
   Bethridge 51, 86
   Charles 33, 82, 173
   Daniel 5, 76
   Ephraim 131
   George 204
   H. Jacob 187
   Hannah 141, 205
   Henry 214
   Isaac 39, 41, 62,
     76, 203
   Jacob 63, 72, 187,
     210
   James 198
   John 203, 204
   Levi 198
   Mary 4, 69
   Mathias 62
   Morgan 218
   Moses 116
   Peter 26, 60, 159,
     211
   Rachel 72, 210

Richard 105, 177
Roger 198
Thomas 40, 50, 86,
   97, 117, 135,
   141, 179, 212,
   223, 224
William 51, 86,
   117, 122, 197,
   214
Jordan
   Charles 65
   James 37, 65, 163,
      220
   John 187
   John Mortan 39
   Mildred 28, 65, 77
Joy
   William 1, 41
Jump
   Elisabeth 150
   Sarah 89, 152
   Vaughan 89, 152

Keen
   Ezekiel 122
Keene
   Benjamin 14, 69,
      122, 208, 209
   Edward 40
   Henry 122, 199, 208
   John 93, 122, 208
   Richard 40, 209
   Samuel 93
   Zebulon 40, 69,
      199, 209
Kellar
   Rudolp 94
Keller
   Abraham 32, 42
   Margaret 32
Kelleson
   Robert 85
Kelley
   Alexander 3, 64
   James 84, 112
   Sarah 24, 58
Kellum
   Daniel 118
Kelly
   Alexander 210
   Hannah 140
   James 175
   John 204, 223

Joshua 140, 194
Mary 175
Rachel 204
Kemp
   Christian 94
   Mathew 15, 19, 53,
      145
   Thomas 6
Kennard
   John 13
   Sarah 35
   Stephen 35
   Thomas 35, 91, 224,
      225
Kennedy
   Robert 112
Kennely
   William 186
Kennett
   Kinal 144
   Martin 103, 144
   Presgrave 144
Kenney
   Joseph 15
   William 15
Kennitt
   Laban 206
Kensey
   James 88
Kent
   James 152, 191, 209
   John 93, 136, 190
Kenton
   James 153
Kerr
   John 92, 153, 195
Kerrick
   Elisabeth 16
   Hugh 16, 68
   James 121
Kersey
   Mary 1
   Thomas 1, 41
Kersner
   Jacob 63
Key
   James 120
   Philip 220
   Phillip 13, 127
   Susannah 13, 163
   Theodosia 127
   Thomas 220
Kibble
   Elisabeth 132

George 87, 132
William 9, 87, 132, 186
Kibles
  Michael 104
Killiam
  John 186
Killum
  John 8
Kilpatrick
  James 96
  John 35
Kimbol
  John 171
  Loline 171
King
  Charles 27
  Ephraim 3, 46, 95, 105
  Ezekiel 107
  Frances 19
  Francis 67
  John 95
  Nathaniel 153
  Nehemiah 19
  Robert 101
  Southey 19
  Southy 53, 143, 207
  Susannah 27
  Thomas 51, 85, 181
  William 19, 53, 143, 207
  Zorobable 95
Kinnard
  Ann 99
  Daniel 99
  John 99, 133
  Sarah 207
  Thomas 207
Kinnesbrick
  John 135
Kinnett
  Prisgrave 206
Kinney
  William 91
Kinsey
  James 113
Kirby
  Benjamin 22
  Mary 202
  Sarah 202
Kirchner
  Caspar 177
  Christiana 177

Kirk
  Alexander 114
Kirkham
  William 222
Kirkland
  Leah 52
  William 12, 52
Kirkman
  William 136
Kirkpatrick
  William 192
Kirkshaw
  James 73
  John 73
  Sarah 73
Kirshner
  John 42
  Marlin 42
Kirvan
  Judah 197
  Mathew 197
Kirwan
  John 197
  Peter 197
Kissick
  Jane 169
  Robert 169
Kitten
  Theophilus 45
  Thomas 45, 108
Knote
  Hannah 22
  Harman 22
Knotts
  Hannah 56
  Harman 56
  Nathaniel 22, 56
Kollock
  Cornelius 103

Lacorure
  Mary 90
Lake
  Henry 69
Lamb
  John 99
Lambdin
  John 40
Lancaster
  Joseph 221
  Thomas 127
Land
  Ramour 108

Reimour 200, 213
Reymour 8
Lane
    Benjamin 51, 85,
        181
    Harrison 168
    Harrisson 52
    John 72
    Mary 76, 213
    Nathan 72
    Richard 72
    Robert 64
    Samuel 51, 72, 85,
        181
    Thomas 41, 51, 63,
        76, 85, 124,
        181, 213
    William 103
Langford
    David 113
    Joshua 145, 205
    William 91
Langley
    William 37
Langrel
    William 198
Langrell
    William 198
Lanham
    Edward 66
    Elisha 67, 222
    Winefred 66, 110
Lankford
    David 9
    William 9
Lansdale
    Isaac 127
Latham
    Elisabeth 115, 195
    John 115
Latherbury
    Jonathan 118
Lathinghouse
    William 100
Lathom
    Elisabeth 90
Laurence
    Elisabeth 117
    George 32, 81, 117,
        170
    Mary 32, 81, 100,
        167, 170, 219
Lavall
    William 13

Law
    William 202
Lawrence
    George 197
Laws
    Elijah 103
    Robert 64
Lawson
    Alexander 180
Lawther
    Francis 12
Layfield
    George 140
    Isaac 140, 204
Layton
    James 45
Lease
    Jacob 135
    William 135
Leatherbury
    Charles 48, 110
    Elisabeth 48, 110,
        208
    Jonathan 133
    Peregrine 133
Leaveille
    John 108
Lecompt
    Abner 196, 199, 213
    Charles 122
    John 108, 147, 196,
        209
    Nehemiah 108, 199
    Phil. 199
    Philemon 124
    William 122, 213,
        214
Lecompte
    Abner 4, 11, 20, 54
    John 11
    Nehemiah 17
    Philemon 4, 20, 54,
        76
    William 4, 20, 54,
        76
Lee
    Charles 162
    George 133
    John 46
    Joseph 78
    Mary 162
    Thomas 6, 31, 80,
        167
Leftwich

Elisha 47
Mary 47
Leftwitch
Elisha 68
Legate
Ann 226
John 226
Leigh
John 38
Joseph 78
William 120
Leiper
James 126, 188
Thomas 126
Leman
Rachel 120
Lemon
Jacob 223
Lendrum
Andrew 130
Robert 130
Levan
Francis 224
Levell
William 21
Leverton
Isaac 5
Levins
William 73
Lewellin
John 65
Lewis
Clement 177, 208,
210
George 192, 214
John 27, 60, 116,
160
Jos. 210
Joseph 177, 208
Sarah 27, 60, 160,
192, 214
Light
Peter 136
Lindsay
Jane 16
Thomas 136
William 16
Lingan
Thomas 219
Lingo
Robinson 202
Smith 202
Link
Adam 94

Linn
Henry 192
Linsey
Thomas 113
Linthicumb
Hezekiah 129
John 129
Linzey
David 91
Thomas 91
Lister
Jesse 91
Little
George 133, 214
Mary 214
Robert 211
Litton
Michael 135
Llewellin
Ann 65
Justinian 65
Llewin
Richard 39
Lloyd
Ann 176
Lluwellin
Justinian 126
Locker
Elisabeth 36
Thomas 36
William 36, 126
Lockhart
Samuel 131
Loftice
Burton 40
Logan
Thomas 10
Lomax
John 68, 95, 208
Luke 68
Stephen 68
Thomas 68, 208
Long
Comfort 143, 196
David 95
Elisabeth 87, 144
Hugh 114
John 87, 103, 144,
205
Littleton 102
Robert 112
Solomon 95, 101,
143, 196
William 34

Lookery
  Arthur 175
Lorain
  Mary 207
  Thomas 207
Lord
  Andrew 122, 147,
    199
  Ann 147
  Cratcher 147
  Henry 147
  Susanna 147
Love
  Miles 175
  Samuel 9
Loveday
  Anne 43
  John 43, 189
  Sarah 189
  Thomas 43, 66
Lovell
  John 100
  William 55
Low
  Samuel 98
Lowe
  John 138
  Michael 222
  Samuel 187
  Saphanah 187
Lowes
  John 91
Lowndes
  Christopher 80, 168
Lownds
  Christopher 31
Lowry
  John 106, 131
  Margret 112
  Robert 106, 131
  Samuel 106
Lowther
  Francis 141
Lucas
  Anne 215
  John Baptist 215,
    216
Lucky
  John 68, 121
  Mary 68
Lucraft
  John 95
Luke
  Frank 109

Lumford
  David 186
Lumon
  Jacob 196
  Mary 196
Lunan
  Alexander 61
Lusby
  Baldwin 72
  Draper 36
  Jacob 185, 218
  John 185
  Robert 193
Lux
  William 107, 177,
    218
Lydia's Rest 184
Lyles
  Hilleary 127
  Marjery 80
  Marjory 31, 167
  William 100
  Zachariah 31, 80,
    167
Lynch
  Francis 162
  Hugh 92
  Jemima 162
  Jethro 10
  John 65, 125, 180,
    206
  Mary 15, 180, 206
  Nicholas 15
  Patrick 75
  William 15, 49, 83,
    88
Lynn
  David 184
Lyon
  John 37

Maccatee
  Catharine 24
  William 94
Maccubbin
  Nicholas 12, 51,
    52, 76, 85
  William 217
Maccubbing
  William 176
Mace
  Josias 104
  Nicholas 122

Macgill
   Thomas 6
Mackall
   Benjamin 72, 212
   James John 100
   John 100
   Mary 212
Mackatee
   William 42
Mackay
   James 192
Mackey
   Phillip 190
Macky
   John 115, 192
   Robert 192
Macnabb
   John 2, 10
Maddock
   Edward 121
   Ignatius 121
Maddox
   Benjamin 88, 122,
     165
   Edward 68
   Frances 88
   Francis 165
   George 215
   James 15, 215
   John 4, 41
   Notly 15
   Sarah 15
   Thomas 88, 165
Magdalin
   Young 109
Maglamary
   John 205
Maglamore
   John 106
Magrah
   Philip 1
Magruder
   Alexander 191
   Alexander H. 67
   Hezekiah 90, 110
   Jeremiah 126
   John Read 109, 126
   Martha 90
Mahafey
   Joseph 192
Makin
   William 115, 116
Malet
   Cathram 192

Mallendore
   Jacob 223, 224
Mallot
   Catharine 63
   Peter 63
   Ruth 63
Malot
   Catherine 1
Manfield
   Thomas 189
Manger
   Nicholas 37
Manjer
   Ann 211
   Nicholas 211
Mankin
   Charles 221
Manley
   John 194
Manlove
   Betty 108
   Emanuel 108
Manly
   Ann 216
   John 90, 195
   Thomas 216
Mann
   George Vansant 7
Manning
   James 12, 38
   John 12, 28, 77,
     100
   Joseph 28, 66, 77
   Margaret 12
Mansfield
   Richard 189
Manship
   Charles 136
Mantz
   Caspar 42
Manwaring
   Elisabeth 208
   Richard 208
Manycousins
   Michael 116
Marcer
   Ann 211
   Mary 157
   Robert 157, 211
Marling
   Francis 44
Marloe
   Ann 168
   John 31

Ralph 168
Rebecca 168
Marlow
   Ann 90
   David 90
   Ralph 90, 98, 127
   Rebecca 90
   Samuel Middle. 90
Marriott
   Augustine 218
   John 218
Marshall
   John 202
   John Drummond 102
Marten
   John 68
Martens
   John 221
Martin
   Ethelder 68
   George 33
   Henry 92
   Heny 189
   James 101
   John 221
   Nathaniel 160
   Thomas 92, 102, 117
   Zachariah 153
   Zadock 195
Mason
   John 196
   Mathew 38
   William 111
Massey
   Alexander 202
   Catharine 120
   Hannah 18, 52
   John 14, 94, 202
   Jonathan 2
   Joseph 18, 52, 143, 196
   Moses 211
   Peter 224
   Sarah 14
Masten
   Robert 210
Masters
   Mary 210
   Robert 210, 224
Mastin
   Robert 1
Mathews
   Bennett 201
   Elisabeth 164

Hugh 46
Maximilian 10
Maximillian 212
Samuel 171
Sarah 171
William 164
Matkin
   Solomon 198
Matthew
   Hugh 115
   William 120
Matthews
   Hugh 116
Mattingley
   Robert 65
   William 216
Mattingly
   Edward 125
   Luke 28
   William 125
Mattox
   William 2
Maulding
   Benjamin 210
   Fra. 117
   Francis 211
Maw
   Edmund 73
   Elisabeth 73
Maxwell
   John 99
   Robert 64
May
   Edward 93
   Sophia 93
Maynadier
   William 199
Maynard
   Daniel 199
McAllen
   A. J. 35
McCallan
   Arthur 34
McCann
   Timothy 210
McChanon
   Thomas 21
McClain
   James 42
McClaster
   Samuel 95
McCleland
   Samuel 197
   Thomas 7, 13, 44,

James 201
McLane
  Alexander 91
McLeod
  Alexander 41
McLoad
  Abraham 11
McManus
  Phillip 119
McMarlow
  Samuel 126
McMechen
  Alexander 112
McNamarra
  Levin 123
McNess
  William 190
McPherson
  John 38
  William 132
McSwain
  Dennis 173
  Mary 173
Mead
  Benjamin 187
Meads
  Thomas 222
Meaner
  Joseph 22
Meanor
  Joseph 56, 151
Meckie
  Ebenezar 196
Medcalf
  John 216
  Thomas 50, 84
Medford
  William 41
Medley
  Clement 46, 124,
    126
  Mary 124
Meeds
  Rachell 222
  Thomas 136
Meek
  John 3
Meeks
  Mary 99
  Robert 99, 194
Meglamere
  Anne 202
Meglamre
  Isaac 202

Melson
  Benjamin 34, 35
  Jos. 34
  Robert 142
Melton
  Richard 65
Melvin
  Robert 34, 35
Mercer
  John 3
  Mary 25, 58
  Robert 25, 58
Meredith
  James 191
  John 4, 124, 137,
    140, 222
  Margaret 124
  Sarah 4, 140
  Thomas 124
  William 93
Merine
  John 19, 54, 146
  William 19, 54, 146
Merrick
  Daniel 149
Merrill
  Lovering 99
Merritt
  William 64
Merriwether
  Reuben 39
Merryman
  Nicholas 43, 46
  Samuel 46
Merrywether
  Reuben 72
Messeck
  Covington 18
  Sarah Ann 17
Messick
  Coventon 109
Meyer
  Frederic 72
Mezick
  Coventon 213
Middleton
  Smith 165
Miffling
  Southey 108
  Walter 108
Milbourn
  Aaron 11, 12
  Caleb 204
  Michael 204

Solomon 35, 89, 205
Milbourne
    Ann 144
    Augustus 11
    Austen 12
    Caleb 45
    Jacob 200
    Lodowick 200
    Stephen 11, 12
    Thomas 103
Milburn
    Adam 37
    Henry 37
    Stephen 126
Miles
    Edward 68
    Elisabeth 216
    Hannah 7, 206
    Margaret 13, 31,
        80, 167
    Mathias 113
    Nathan 206
    Nathaniel 7, 35
    William 13, 31, 80,
        167
Miller
    Abraham 120, 135
    Agnes 59
    Agness 157
    Ann 25
    Elisabeth 117
    Jacob 63
    James 23, 90, 135
    John 202
    Micha 119
    Nathaniel 119
    Richard 82, 119
    Samuel 25, 59, 157
    Simon Stephens 87,
        190
    Simon Steven 55,
        148
    Thomas 25, 59, 157
    William 34
Milligan
    G. 115
    George 60, 160
Millington
    Alenbye 118
    Allenby 44
Millontong
    Mary 44
Mills
    Achsa 52, 182

Acksa 86
Andrew 124
Charles 125
Frederick 52, 86,
    182
George 125
John 65, 125
Joseph 123
Joshua 221
Justin 37
Levi 1
Nicholas 124
Thomas 1, 192
Milstead
    John 188
Milton
    Abraham 119, 120,
        140
    John 210
    Joseph 120, 210
    Sarah 215
Minor
    Betty 196
    Charles 196
    William 20
Mitchel
    Edward 140
Mitchell
    Charity 169
    Elisabeth 140
    James 169
    Jean 192
    John 214
Mobberly
    Thomas 61
Mobey
    Rachel 15
    William 15
Mock
    Catharine 31, 80,
        169
    George 31, 80, 169
Mockbee
    Lucy 42
Mokeall
    Valentine 94
Monk
    Mary 176
    Renaldo 50, 61, 83,
        176, 195, 219
Montgomery
    John 10
    William 113
Moor

Ann 146
John 132
Mary 69
Moore
  Alexander 27, 60,
    159
  Ann 89, 142
  Benjamin 185
  Ealie 224
  Henry 90, 134, 156
  Isaac 132
  James 111, 132,
    141, 178, 185,
    212
  John 91, 213
  Josias 54, 69, 147
  Levin 6
  Margaret 27, 60,
    159
  Patrick 54, 147
  Peter 185, 188,
    212, 223
  Rezin 131, 141
  Rudolph 90, 156,
    224
  Sarah 111, 137
  Thomas 6, 18, 90,
    114, 141, 142,
    146
  William 6, 141
  Zadock 185, 212
Mooth
  William 111
Morgan
  Avery 143, 196
  David 2, 16, 45,
    131
  Hannah 143, 196
  John 2, 125, 216
  Lydia 2, 16
  Moses 45
Morningholer
  John 68
Morris
  Catharine 169
  Isaac 97, 103, 207
  Jeremiah 101
  Luke 97
  Thomas 10
  William 169
Morriss
  Luke 207
Morry
  Richard 42

Morton
  Alexander 69, 107,
    207, 213
Moss
  James 51
  Leonard 42
  Richard 51, 62
Mostane
  John 104
Mullendore
  Jacob 70, 210
Mumford
  Catharine 35
  George 205
  James 47
  John 22, 35, 56,
    89, 137, 150,
    196
  Margaret 47
  Naomi 196
  Rachel 87
  William 87, 190
Mundel
  Robert 41
Mundock
  George 94
Munroe
  Pharahe 13
Murphy
  Charles 111
  James 95
  John 193
  Philemon 5
  Sarah 199
  Thomas 199
Murra
  John 3, 10
Murray
  John 220
  Josephus 187
  Nathaniel Hopkins
    206
  Philip 9
  William 200, 220
Muschett
  John 120
Musgrove
  Anthony 218
  Samuel 218
Myer
  Bulcher 96
  Catherine 223
  Frederick 96, 201
  George 2

Jacob 2
John 223
Myers
George 10
Jacob 2

Nabb
Charles 137
Elisabeth 22, 56,
150
John 22, 56, 150
Nail
Daniel 68
Nailor
James 1
Nairn
John 102
Nairne
James 6
Navey
Henry 198
John 198
Mary 198
Neairn
James 113
Neal
Raphaele 188
Neale
Bennett 37, 38
Edward 66
Elisabeth 13
James 95
Mary 37
Raphael 13
Robert 66
Samuel 66
Wilfrid 13
Neall
Edward 118
Jonathan 118
Needham
Sarah 219
Needles
Ann 188
Edward 188
Negroes
George 170, 184
Hannah 54
Jasper 54
Sam 170, 184
Nellson
Thomas 139, 188
William 121, 188

Nelms
Ed. 131
Edmund N. 97
John 146
Nelson
Aquila 10
Elisabeth 121
George 218
Thomas 11, 47
Nevett
John Rider 199
Sarah Ennalls 199
William 211
Nevil
Walter 93
Nevill
David 5, 22, 220
Newcomb
Martha 156, 211
Thomas 156, 211
Newman
Butler 67
Buttler 67
Edward 95
Elisabeth 88
Isaac 36
Thomas 36
William 88, 141
Newton
Ann 98, 110, 185
Nathaniel 109
Susannah 215
Thomas 215
William 215
Nicholas
William 149
Nicholls
Simon 128
Nichols
Jos. 209
Samuel 7
Simon 94
Thomas 226
Nicholson
Charles 34
J. 224
John 62
Jos. 63, 91, 98,
118, 119, 194,
214
Josep 103
Joseph 7, 35, 69,
71, 103, 105,
110, 190, 205

Mary 103, 105
Samuel 34, 103
Tabitha 34
William 133
Nicols
    William 117
Noble
    James 18, 52, 142
    Levi 18
    Levin 69
    Levy 52, 142
    Mary Ann 68, 107
    Robert 110
    William 68, 107,
        124, 199, 200
Noel
    Sarah 4, 45
    Thomas 4, 45
Noke
    William 73
Norman
    Esther 198, 208
    George 198, 208
    Joseph 130
Normand
    John 183
    Nicholas 183
    William 39
Norris
    Anastatius 161
    Annastatia 28, 77
    Benjamin 112
    Benjamin B. 113
    Catharine 32, 81
    Edward 96
    John 113
    Jos. 96, 112
    Joseph 96
    Mary 112
    Robert 86, 182, 218
    Susanna 112
    Thomas 96
    William 28, 32, 77,
        81, 161
Norriss
    Martin 139
    William 38
North
    Catherine 131
    George 122, 209,
        214
    Reb. 122
    Rebecca 209
Norton

Richard 64, 134
Norwood
    Edward 128, 217
    Nicholas 128
Nottingham
    Anne 46
    Athinasius 46
Nowland
    Benjamin 115
    Daniel 29, 81, 170
    Dennis 115, 193
    Henrietta 29, 81,
        170
Nunar
    Jacob 197
Nutrell
    William 111
Nutter
    Ch. 54
    Christopher 20
    Eleanor 20, 54
    William 8, 20, 54,
        70

Oden
    Frances 95
    Jonathan 95, 222
Offuth
    Alexander 63
Ogg
    George 140, 177,
        201
    Helen 140
    Hellen 177
    William 201
Oldfield
    Jane 40
    John 40, 69, 209
Oldham
    Ann 26, 59, 116,
        158
    Edward 116
    Richard 26, 59, 158
Oldson
    Abraham 136
    Thomas 136
Oneal
    Charles 129
    Felix 84, 175
    Frances 129
    Francis 218
    Lawrence 135
Oram

Ann Statia 33, 82, 173
Hen. 82
Henry 33, 173
Orendriff
C. 192
Orf
Ann 192
Orme
James 191
John 191
Lucy 191
Orr
Hugh 82
Orrell
Francis 222
Orrick
Carolina 89, 175, 212
Cornelia 84
John 72, 84, 89, 175, 212
Orrs
Hugh 33, 173
Osborn
Elisabeth 31
Henry 24, 57, 154
John 24, 57, 154
Robert 31, 185
Osbourn
Elisabeth 80
Robert 80
Osbourne
Elisabeth 104, 168
Robert 104, 168
Owden
Elisabeth 222
Owen
Edward 128, 210
Lawrence 210
Robert 135
Sarah 210
Thomas 41
Owens
James 67
Owler
Andrew 32, 48, 71, 81

Paca
Aquila 131
John 61
Mr. 185

William 54, 184
Paden
John 107, 146, 200
Padgett
John 105, 185
Pagan
John 14, 20, 54
William 14, 20, 54
Page
Aquila 7
Daniel 212
George 212, 223
Joh. 91
John 91, 118, 119
Pagett
Elisabeth 105
Pagon
William 69
Pain
Elisabeth 14
Isaac 97
John Baptist 125
Peter 126, 216
Sabina 126
William 14
Pallitt
Thomas 131
William 131
Palmer
Benjamin 120
Sarah 176
Solomon 197
Paltry
William 28, 77
Pamer
Sarah 176
Parish
Comfort 15
Richard 15, 70
Park
Andrew 48
Jos. 48
Parke
Jos. 89
Parker
Andrew 81
Charles 34, 202
Elisabeth 44
Elisha 102
George 15, 102, 208
Isaac 15
Jacob 102
John 15, 44, 96, 208

Page 275

Joseph 81
Mary 15
Schoolfield 97, 202
Parkerson
John 8, 199, 200
Parks
Joseph 71
Parnal
Stephen 86
Parnall
Isaac 187
Stephen 52
Parran
Benjamin 74
Elick 12
Elisabeth 3, 74
Elleck 141
Ellick 76
Phillip 3, 74
Richard 119
Young 3, 119
Parratt
Aaron 117, 188
Benjamin 117
Parrit
William 39
Parrott
Joseph 149
Perry 149
Richard 117
William 7
Parson
Edward 38
George 98
Parsons
Benjamin 36
Jane 11
Partridge
Ann 47, 49, 83, 87,
    108, 174
Daub. B. 87
Daubin Buckley 174
Daubne Buckley 45,
    83, 108
Daubne Buckly 47
Daubne Duckler 49
William 44, 47, 49,
    61, 83, 87, 108,
    174
Paterson
Wilson 189
Patterson
Sarah 189
Pattison

Jacob 197
Sarah 197
Patty
John 14
Powell 14
Pawnall
John 3
Payne
Basil 95
Daniel 199
Eleanor 83
Elisabeth 50
William 50, 83, 95
Payton
James 4
Peach
John 90, 127
Joseph 90, 168
Peacock
Robert 224
Peale
H. George 130
Pearce
Andrew 113
Daniel 185
James 63, 64, 133
William 24, 46, 57,
    58, 155, 207
Peasalle
John 166
Penington
Paul 107, 187
William Boyer 114
Penn
Joseph 129, 130
Pennington
Abraham 26, 59,
    105, 127, 158,
    195
Benjamin 196
Henry 193
Reuben 196
Sarah 26, 59, 105,
    158, 195
Thomas 137
Perdue
James 203
Perkins
Araminta 194
Frederick 120, 194
George 75, 106,
    133, 134
Isaac 91, 120
Mary 189

Page 276

Philip 189
Solomon 189
Thomas 24, 58, 62
Perkinson
    Edward 32
Perkison
    Edward 81
Perrie
    John 67
Perry
    Benjamin 63, 128, 184
    Elisabeth 63
    James 1, 89, 128
    James Owen 89
    Rebecca 89, 128
    Samuel 1, 135
    William 189
Peter
    Robert 135
Peters
    John 5
    Robert 90
Pett
    James 20
Pettibone
    Charles 51, 86, 182
    Philip 86
    Phillip 51, 182
Phelps
    John 42
    William 185
Philips
    James 10
    Rus. 134
Phillips
    Barton 187
    Daniel 6
    Evan 11
    George 93, 110
    James 11, 109, 186
    Lurana 46
    Mary 4
    Phillip 46
    Reuben 4, 41, 70
    Richard 4
    Sarah 109
    Thomas 41
    William 4, 107, 110, 200
Phillpot
    David 121
Philpot
    John 60

Phoenix
    Andrew 111, 222
Pickering
    Edward 124
    John 136
    Jonathan 129
Pigman
    Na. 223
Pike
    Daniel 202
    James 124
    William 45
Pindel
    Ann 182
    Phillip 182
Pinder
    Edward 93
    William 93, 191
Piner
    Ann 99, 194, 210
    Barbus 105
    James 99
    Sarah 90
    Susannah 105
    Thomas 90, 134
Pinkney
    Robert 129
Piper
    Chr. 9
    Christopher 9, 19, 206
    John 206
    Mathew 19, 206
    Rachel 34
Pitney
    William 207
Pitts
    William 97
Plowman
    Jonathan 96, 176
Plumer
    John 63
Plummer
    Christ. 17
    James 109
    Mary 109
    Priscilla 183
    Yate 183, 220
Pointer
    Thomas 101
Polk
    Alice 76
    Daniel 76, 107
    David 36

James 103, 200, 204
Josiah 131
Robert 69, 76, 107,
    108
Sarah 103
Pollitt
  George 113
  John 206
Pollock
  David 8, 75, 124
  Priscilla 75
Polston
  John 87
Pomphrey
  Lazarus 39
Ponder
  John 124
Pooley
  Elisabeth 42
  Mathias 42
Porter
  Ezekiel 102, 202
  Hugh 213
  James 113, 114, 205
  John 196
  Laurence 22, 148
  Lawrence 11, 56
  Richard 113
  Sarah Ann 213
  Stephen 113, 115
  Thomas 149
Posey
  Elisabeth 213
  John 213
Postlewaith
  James 179
Postly
  John 101, 102, 204
Pounds
  Comfort 85
Powell
  Elisabeth 117
  George 5
  Isaac 71
  James 71
  Samuel 102
  Thomas 117, 197,
    203
Powles
  Jacob 171
  Susannah 171
Pratt
  Benjamin 156
  Charity 11, 206

Esther 222
Henry Wright 222
John 5, 74, 219
Philemon 11, 156
Phillip 206
Robert 156
Pravat
  Margaret 38, 65
Presbury
  Thomas 178
  Will. Rob. 112
  William 112, 180
Preston
  Ann 137, 138
  Daniel 47, 137
  David 111
  James 43
Price
  Ann 38, 87
  Catharine 221
  Elisabeth 137
  Hyland 193
  James 39
  John 17, 150, 197
  Margaret 221
  Nicholas 222
  Sarah 22, 56, 151
  Thomas 94, 110
  William 22, 23, 56,
    87, 88, 122,
    151, 219, 222
Pridix
  Thomas 202
Priestly
  William 189
Prig
  Hyland 115
Pritchard
  John 149
  Richard 149, 190
Pritchet
  Jane 123
  Phumback 70
  Zebulon 123
Pritchett
  Jabus 11
  Phunback 11
Probart
  Yelverton 97
Pue
  Michael 217
Pullett
  John 113
Pullit

Thomas 186, 195
Pumphrey
    Rezin 129
    Walter 129
    William 129
Purdue
    James 102, 202
    John 202
Purnal
    John 140
Purnall
    Jephah 98
    John 143
    Stephen 182
Purnel
    John 53
    William 17, 191
Purnell
    Benjamin 13, 97
    Dennis 101
    Elijah 13
    John 105, 204
    Joseph 13
    Lemuel 101
    William 101
Purveyance
    Samuel 83, 174
Purviance
    Robert 131
    Samuel 131
Purvyance
    Samuel 49
Pusey
    James 18
Pye
    Henrietta 188
    John 188
    Walter 31, 79, 164,
       188, 216

Quaile
    James 193
Quartermus
    James 75, 207
Quatermus
    James 18
Queen
    Edward 31, 79, 164
    Marsham 68
Quynn
    Allen 73, 129

Rackcliff
    John 103
Rackliffe
    Nathaniel 204
Radney
    William 203
Railey
    John 136
Raisin
    Abraham 64
Raley
    John 37
Ralph
    John 156
Ramsay
    Robert 115
    Thomas 187, 192
    William 131
Ramsey
    Robert 116
    Thomas 42
    William 226
Randall
    Richard 218
Rapeir
    Richard James 65
Rapier
    Richard James 37
Rapour
    William 37
Rasin
    Philip 7
    Thomas 64
Ratcliff
    James 189
    Peter 214
    Richard 121
    Stephen 7
    William 189
Rauthin
    Paul 39
Raven
    Isaac 2, 43, 196
    Lettuce 138
    Luke 138
    William 138
Rawlings
    Ann 27
    Daniel 73
Ray
    William 67
Read
    Dean 155
    James 123

John 38, 65, 155
John Hatton 216
Record
   Sarah 139
   Thomas 139
Redue
   John 45, 94
   Sarah 45
Reed
   Abraham 123
   Amos 64
   Dean 25, 58
   Elbert 90
   Eleanor 217
   Hannah 98
   James 47
   John 16, 25, 58,
     64, 99, 194
   John Hatton 16
   Michael 118
   Rachel 47
   Samuel 98, 118
   Sarah 23, 57
   William 118, 217
Reeder
   Benjamin 3, 29, 41,
     78
   Conrod 63
   John 63, 163
   Margaret 3, 29
   Mary 78
   Simon 42
   Thomas 3, 29, 78
Regan
   Charles 114
Register
   Francis 117, 196
   Sarah 190
Reid
   George 219
Reitnauer
   Mathias 42
Rench
   Peter 192
Rencher
   Thomas 132
Resin
   Thomas 133
   William 133
Reston
   Henry 83, 176
Retter
   John 63
Reyner

Ebenezar 58
Reynolds
   Edward 31, 80, 100,
     166
   Hammond 102
   Thomas 31, 80, 166
Reynour
   Ebenezar 24
Rezin
   Susannah 133
Rhode
   Richard 131
Rhodes
   Mark 216, 217
   Richard 45
   Sarah 45
Ricards
   Thomas 6
Rice
   David 162
   Hugh 108
   John 195
Richards
   John 105, 205
   Jos. 105
   Thomas 187
Richardson
   Barbarah 127, 152,
     153
   Barbary 89
   Benjamin 226
   Isabella 32, 81
   John 101
   Levi 101
   Meriam 219
   Richard 214
   Samuel 103, 144
   Thomas 39, 61, 193
   William 32, 81, 144
Ricketts
   John 64
Ricords
   Thomas 43
Riddle
   Jennet 193
   John 193
Rider
   Peter 114, 115
Ridgaway
   Samuel 111
   William 111, 225
Ridgely
   Charles 138
   John 219

Joshua 39, 221
William 129
Ridgly
Westall 192
Ridout
Mr. 182
Rigan
Charles 116
Rigby
Moses 117
Rigdon
Alexander 112
Rigg
Thomas 121
Riggs
Amos 51, 85, 181
John 51, 85, 181
Mary 51, 85, 181
Right
Ann 95
Ringer
Mathias 63
Ringgold
Charles 25, 58, 155
Edward 56
Josias 156, 195,
225
Joyce 155
Sarah 156
Thomas 119
William 22, 56, 99,
154, 194, 221
Risiner
Tobias 223
Risteau
(N) 51
Riston
Henry 50
Roberson
John 109
Roberts
Abraham 110
Alban 99
B. 187
Benjamin 16, 87,
211
Dorothy 115
Francis 216
Jane 16
John 2, 149
Jonathan 99, 191,
222
Rebecca 149
Thomas 149

Robertson
Charles 226
David 23, 56, 151,
211
John 6, 20, 53
William 8, 10, 91,
206
Robey
A. 221
Alexander 41
John Alley 121
Robins
John Purnel 144
Robinson
Benjamin 96
Charles 112, 131,
195, 217
David 66
James 70
John 54, 109, 147
Joseph 8
Richard 112, 195,
226
Richard Garbin 189
Robert 131
Rosannah 8
William 112, 195
Roboson
John 20
Robson
John 113
Roby
James 95
John 95
Peter Harriot 121
Rock
Charles 9, 95
Fra. 116
Francis 116
Jacob 33, 82, 89,
172
Rodgers
Parker 34
Roe
Benjamin 191
Rogers
Benjamin 49, 82,
173
Jacob 204
John 204
Mathew 204
William 49, 82, 173
Rolle
Feddeman 118

Rooke
    William 110
Rooney
    John 100
Rop
    Jacob 32
    Margaret 32
    Nicholas 32
Rope
    Jacob 141
    Margaret 141
    Nicholas 81, 141,
        170
Roper
    Nicholas 224
Rosland
    Abraham 70
Ross
    Jacob 81, 170
    Margaret 81, 170
    William 198
Rosse
    John 101
Routh
    Chris. Cross 136
    Christ Cross 23
    James 212
Rowe
    Robert 17
Rudolph
    Hance 43
    Hans 3
Rumsay
    Edward 46
    Margaret 46
Russel
    John 8
Russell
    Henry 118
    John 208
    Josiah 203
    Solomon 203
    William 218
Ruth
    Christopher 48
    Elisabeth 209
    James 104, 129, 153
    John 209
    William 13, 48,
        140, 151
Rutherford
    James 66, 118
    John 217
Rutland

Elisabeth 40
    Thomas 51, 129
Rutledge
    John 96
Rutter
    Hannah 138
    Thomas 138
Ryan
    Ignatius 120
    James 140
    Sarah 140
Ryon
    James 185

Safford
    Abraham 197
    James 197
    Mary 197
Sailes
    Clement 54, 55, 189
    Elisabeth 55
    Gabriel 44, 54, 55
    Jane 55
    Susannah 54, 55
Sales
    Clement 20
    Gabriel 20
Salsbury
    John 214
Sanders
    Charles 29, 78, 163
    George 7
    John 120
    William 7
Sanner
    Nicholas 38
Sansbury
    William 100
Sappington
    Fran. 51
    Frances 86
    Francis 85, 182
    Hartley 193
    John 217
    Margaret 217
    Mark Brewer 217
    Richard 217
    Thomas 3, 86, 182,
        218
Sater
    George 128
Saterfield
    Mary 14

William 15
Saunders
    Charles 88
    Robert 2, 201
Savin
    Augustine 193
    Thomas 114, 115,
        193
Schartel
    Jacob 201
Schley
    Jacob 135, 223
Schneider
    John 73
Schoolfeild
    Joseph 102
Schoolfield
    John 101
    Thomas 101
Scoggin
    Richard 9
Scoolfield
    John 140
Scott
    Abraham 138
    Alexander 114
    Benjamin 6
    George 6, 14, 18,
        62, 191, 218,
        220
    Hugh 138
    James 27, 60, 65,
        115, 159, 193
    Jane 88
    Jean 21, 55, 149
    John 7, 27, 44, 60,
        149, 159, 182,
        207
    Rosanna 115
    Thomas 88
    U. 127
    Upton 119
Scotton
    Lydia 110
    Richard 110, 191
Screvener
    Jacob 81
Scrivenor
    Francis 218
    Mary 218
Scrogen
    George 95
Scroggen
    George 67

Sarah 67
Seady
    Stephen 205
Seale
    Leonard 65
Sealey
    Thomas 225
Sealy
    Thomas 25, 58, 155
Searce
    Catharine 222
    Shadrack 222
Sedgwick
    Mathew 157
    Nathan 25
    Richard 25, 59,
        117, 158
    Sarah 25, 26, 59,
        158
Sedwick
    Catherine 100
Seeders
    John 23
Selby
    John 103
    Jos. 61
    Joseph 130
    Kenelmn 188
    Samuel 31, 80, 167
Semmes
    Frances 139
    Francis 10, 188
    Henrietta 221
    Mary 221
    Thomas 1, 188
Semons
    Henry 91
    Solomon 91
Sennett
    Robert 9
Sergant
    John 33
Seth
    Jacob 92
    James 47
Sewal
    Charles 38
Sewall
    Nicholas Lewis 216
    William 90
Sewel
    Clement 5
    Vachel 218
Sewell

Charles 28
James 3, 50
Shaaf
  Caspar 42
Shadrick
  John 215
  Margaret 215
  Mark 215
Shanks
  John 75
  Robert 37
  Thomas 37, 217
Sharer
  Conrod 1
Sharp
  William 7, 92
Sharpe
  Edward 180
  John 99, 207
  Rachel 180
  Samuel 92
Shaw
  James 11, 147, 196, 209
  John 86, 183
  Josias 6
  Mary 11, 147, 196, 209
Sheckels
  Richard 61
Shehawer
  Dennis 107
Shehawn
  David 108, 199
  Dennis 211
  Mary 108
Sheilds
  John 112
Sheldon
  Henry 103
  Mary 18, 47, 52, 142
Shepard
  Samuel 114
Sheredine
  Thomas 83, 131
Sheridan
  Thomas 88
Sheridine
  Thomas 49
Sherman
  Benjamin 69
Sherwin
  James 8, 41, 70,

    200
  Stephen 11, 70
Sherwood
  Catharine 140, 152
  Daniel 54, 108
  John 20, 54, 140, 147, 152, 191, 222
  Thomas 20, 54, 55, 148
Sheypot
  Jacob 96
Shink
  Susanna 96
Shipley
  Benjamin 43
Shirly
  John 223
Shirmentine
  James 119
Shiviner
  Jacob 32
Shoat
  Christ. 63
  Christian 45, 63
Shore
  John 103
Shores
  Ellis 19, 53
  John 97
  William 6, 19, 53
Shortell
  Jacob 2
Showell
  Armvell 203
  Armwell 205
  Rebecca 203
Shrior
  Jacob 48
  Margaret 48
Shrivour
  John 218
  Lawrence 217, 218
  Mary 217
Shroyer
  Margaret 71
Shuter
  Christian 135
Sikes
  William 43
Silvester
  Andrew 110
  John 47
Simm

David 93
Simmonds
  George 51, 62
  James 51, 128
  Knighton 51
  Mary 51
  William 17
Simmons
  Andrew 123
  Bridget 123, 209
  George 85
  Knighton 85
  Richard 225
  Thomas 123, 209,
    214
Simms
  Thomas 132, 187
Simpson
  Ignatius 90
  Mary 47
  Thomas 47
Siner
  Henry 172
  Jacob 172
Sinklar
  Mary 96
Sisk
  John 198
Skees
  John 138
Skinner
  Benjamin 100
  Catharine 212
  Jeremiah 121
  Samuel 42, 212, 224
  Thomas 87
Skipton
  John 33, 82, 173,
    201
  Mary 33, 82
Slater
  David 211
  Hen. 42
  Jonathin 211
Slator
  David 100
Slay
  Edward 137, 210,
    222
  Sophia 210
Sleith
  Mary 148
Slice
  Garshum 43

Slicer
  William 73
Sligh
  John 96
Sliney
  John 5
Slipper
  Thomas 99, 118
Slivers
  William 130
Sloss
  Thomas 61, 185
Slubey
  Nicholas 35
  William 118
Sluby
  Rachel 25, 58
  William 25, 58
Sluth
  Mary 87
Sly
  John 108
  William 73
Slye
  Eleanor 30, 74, 79
  George 13, 37, 107
  John 72
Small
  Frances 191
  James 3
  Richard 3, 17, 137,
    191
Smallwood
  Bayne 29, 68, 78,
    86, 166
  Elisabeth 108
  Grace 107
  John 1, 31
  Priscilla 29, 78,
    86, 166
  Thomas 132
  William 29, 78, 79,
    86, 95, 166, 188
  William Manbury 107
Smiley
  Andrew 18, 52, 142
  Samuel 18, 52, 142
Smith
  Andrew 172
  Ann 3, 15, 106,
    144, 208
  Buchanan 43, 141
  Charles 91
  Clement 73, 100,

129, 168, 183
Sollers
  Benjamin 73
  James 33
Somervell
  James 73
Spadding
  Levin 117
Spaight
  Palmer 97, 207
Spaights
  Esther 46
  Palmer 46
Spalding
  Benedict 216
  Catharine 28, 75, 77
  Henry 37
  Thomas 28, 37, 66, 75, 77, 217
Sparks
  Absalom 93, 111
  Absolom 23, 57
  Benjamin 137
  Caleb 93
  James 111, 149
  Jos. 134
  Ruth 93
Sparr
  George Thomas 1
Sparrow
  Kensey 135
Spavold
  James 201
Speak
  Elisabeth 211
  John 68
Speake
  Elisabeth 9
  Hezekiah 41, 121
  John 9, 211
  Richard 41
Spear
  Henry 97
  John 97
  William 97, 138
Spears
  Henry 97, 101, 103
  John 101
  William 101
Specknoll
  John 100
Spedding
  Hugh 20, 54, 146

  Laurana 54
  Lurana 20, 146
Speek
  Theodosia 41
Spencer
  Isaac 7, 64
  John 64, 99
  Thomas 120
Spicknall
  Dorcas 104, 166
  John 104, 166
Spiers
  John 93, 94
Sprigg
  Joseph 128
Sprotsman
  Elisabeth 75
  Jacob 75
  Laurence 94
  William Laurence 75
Sprouce
  George 208
  Rachel 198, 208
Sprouse
  George 198
Spry
  Frances 88
  George 5, 88, 137
St. Clair
  Mary 43
  William 91, 133
Stainer
  Laurence 154
Stainton
  Benson 69
Staley
  Henry 192
Stallings
  Lurana 106, 171
  Richard 106, 171
Stamper
  Josiah 214
  Josias 69
Standforth
  John 100
Standifor
  William 130
Standley
  Sarah 193
Stanfield
  John 163
  Richard 163
Stanford
  Jonathan 186

Stansbury
    Daniel 128
    Mary 131
    Richardson 138
Stapleford
    Edward 197
    Raymond 197
    Thomas 197
Staton
    Nehemiah 103
Steel
    George 121
Steiniffer
    Daniel 104
Stenhouse
    Alexander 2
Stephens
    John 190
    William 189, 190
Stephenson
    Joseph 204
    Samuel 205
Sterling
    Hannah 18
    Joseph 18, 34
Steuart
    Adam 135
Stevens
    Benjamin 183
    Edward 122
    Frances 8
    Hester 120
    John 20, 119, 189, 198, 214
    Luke 68, 122
    Peter 92, 189
    Richard 15
    Robertson 54, 104, 147
    Samuel 189
    Sarah 189
    Thomas 7, 118, 189
    William 5, 9, 144
Stevenson
    Edward 186
    Henry 50, 83, 141, 174
    James 89, 145
    John 10, 44, 112, 193
    Samuel 89, 97, 145
    Sater 44
    Tabitha 144
    William 97

Stevett
    James 138
Stewart
    Betty 14
    Elisabeth 199
    J. Travilion 123
    John 14, 69
    John Travillion 14, 198, 199
    John Trevilion 123
    Joseph 199
    Stephen 218
    Steven 73
    Thomas 199, 214
    William 12, 18, 20, 214
Stigar
    Andrew 33, 82, 89, 172
Stoane
    Jane 226
Stockett
    Elisabeth 130
Stockley
    John 89, 205
Stoddart
    Kenelm 30
    Kenlem Truman 13
    Richard 13, 30
    Walter 13, 30
    William 30
Stoddert
    Elisabeth 89, 165
    Kenelm 79
    Lucy Herbert 29, 78
    Margaret 86, 188
    Richard 68, 79
    Walter Truman 86, 188
    Water 79
    William Trueman 133
    William Truman 89, 165
Stokely
    Sophia 145
Stoler
    John 96
Stone
    James 138, 226
    Jane 28
    John 28, 38
    Margery 67
    Marjory 107
    Samuel 68

Thomas 46, 67, 107,
    121, 188
William 67
Stoner
    Jacob 70, 210
Stonestreet
    Edward 67, 110
    Eleanor 67
    John 66, 212
    Thomas 66, 110, 212
Stoops
    John 115
Storp
    Peter 223
Strainer
    Laurence 24, 57
Stratford
    Teresia 65
Strawbridge
    Jane 13, 26, 60,
        105
    John 14, 26, 60,
        105
Stricker
    George 171, 211
Stromat
    Johannah 165
    Thomas 9
Strutford
    Teresia 217
Stuart
    Alexander 193
    William 53
Stubbard
    Phillip 192
Studdon
    Elisabeth 21
    John 21, 55
Studham
    Elisabeth 54
    John 54
Stull
    Adam 192, 223
    Christopher 192
    John 63, 172
Sturgis
    Joshua 101, 203
Sudler
    Emory 99, 137
Suite
    Thomas 65
Sulivane
    Daniel 216
Sullivane

Daniel 147
Mr. 147
Sunderland Josias
    80 1
Sunderland
    Josias 31, 166, 219
    Lydia 119
    Stocket 74
    Stockit 119
    Thomas 119
Sutton
    John 22, 56, 89,
        150
    Margaret 56, 89,
        150
    Mary 22
Swagler
    George 172
    Jacob 172
    Joshua 172
Swain
    Anne 203
    John 203
    William 204
Swann
    Edward 31, 73
    Rebecca 65
    Thomas 31
Swarmstead
    Nicholas 74
Sweaney
    James 214
Swearingen
    Lucy 184
    Samuel 94, 135
Sweeney
    James 24
Sweeting
    Edward 44, 226
Sweney
    Elisabeth 24
Swift
    David 69
    Gideon 5
    John 190
Swoope
    Michael 2
Swynard
    John 88, 131
Sympson
    Clear 1, 46
Syndall
    Jacob 72

Page 289

Tablor
  Milcor 135
Talbot
  Hen. 35
  Henry 36
  John 15, 43, 98
  Joseph 93
  Sophia 43
Talbott
  Joseph 93
Tanehill
  Ninian 172
Taney
  Elisabeth 216
  Francis 216
  John Frances 216
  Raph. 216
Tanner
  Teter 32, 42
Tanyhill
  John 138
Tarbutton
  William 5
Tare
  Edward 37
  John 162
  Mary 162
Tarlton
  Ann 161
  Anne 215
  James 215
  John 161, 215
Tate
  David 43, 208
  Robert 5, 137
Taylor
  Ann 100
  Christian 65, 206
  Daniel Jenifer 76
  Elias 109, 212
  Elisabeth 191
  J. 119
  Jeremiah 114
  John 65, 112, 126,
    206
  Richard 191
  Sarah 109, 122, 212
  Solomon 35
  Thomas 122
  Thomas Woodard 100
  William 65, 115,
    122, 162
Teare

Edward 126
Elisabeth 37
Temple
  George 40
Tennally
  Phil. 168
  William 80, 168
Tennant
  Moses 224
Tennely
  Josias 222
Tennison
  Jesse 162
  Jessee 215
  Thomas 162
Tennisson
  Elisabeth 65
Terry
  Elisha 27, 60
  William 27, 60
Tewell
  John 216
Tharpe
  John 64
Theobald
  John 77, 105, 133
  Prior 105
Theobalds
  John 27
Thilleson
  Robert 51
Thiphart
  Godfrey 1
Thomas
  Ann 50, 84
  Catharine 77, 161
  Catharine Wilson
    16, 28
  David 4, 43, 49
  Elisabeth 92
  Henry 4, 8, 45, 70
  J. A. 64, 124
  James 16, 28, 38,
    77, 99, 126, 161
  John 12, 38, 70,
    212
  John Allen 36, 215
  Mary 70
  Nicholas 147
  Notley 48, 94
  Philip 84
  Phillip 50, 212
  Rebecca 48
  Richard 193, 220

Henry 192
Tomlinson
  Grove 4
Tongue
  Robert 218
Tooir
  John 65
Tool
  Timothy 110
Tootell
  James 197, 198
Toup
  Jacob 42
Towers
  James 136
Townsend
  John 105
  Luke 100
  Mary 100
  Samuel 91
  Tabitha 105
  William Bartlet 13
Townshend
  Brickus 145, 204
  Jeremiah 145
  John 143, 205
  Mary 97
  Samuel 95
  Tabitha 143
  Thomas 176
Townslin
  Joseph 139
Towson
  William 187
Traverse
  Amelia 198
  Ann 20
  Henry 20, 62, 198
  John 198
  John Hicks 20
  Levin 20
  Priscilla 198
  Thomas 198
  William 198
  William Hick 198
Travey
  Lorando 135
Treaharn
  James 18
Tree
  Eleanor 104
  John 104
Trego
  Roger 199

Solomon 8
William 12, 70
Trehearn
  James 9
Trice
  Abraham 69
Tripolete
  Abraham 14, 45
  Magdalene 33
  Mary Magdalane 14
Tripolite
  Abraham 82
Trippe
  Henry 208
Tropolate
  Magdalen 82
Troth
  Henry 117
Trott
  John 86
Trotten
  Elisabeth 3
  Luke 226
Trout
  Jacob 223
Troutman
  Michel 70
True
  John 126
Truerdale
  John 63
Truit
  William 206
Truitt
  George 204
  Mary 34, 97, 204
  Reyley 34
  William 34, 97, 205
Trundel
  John 128
Tucker
  Elisabeth 195
  John 179
  Seaborn 179
  William 195
Tuckerman
  Ann 35, 90
  Joseph 35, 90, 133,
    134
Tuill
  John 126
Tuking
  Robert 189
Tull

Esther 9
Turbut
   Richard 190
Turbutt
   Sarah 190
Turner
   Abner 15, 20
   Ann 29
   Edward 21, 55, 106,
     149, 190
   Hannah 21, 55, 106,
     111, 149, 213
   Isaac 111, 191, 213
   John 73
   Jonathan 24, 58
   Jonathin 223
   Jos. 43
   Thomas 29, 39, 62
Turpin
   Elisabeth 91, 186,
     195
   John 91, 195
   Nehemiah 91
   William 42
Tury
   William 117
Tuttel
   William 218
Twelly
   Elenor 200
   John 200
Twyford
   Lovel 57
   William 57
Tyer
   Boles 221
Tyers
   William 132
Tyler
   Robert 6

Ubankes
   George 197
Ulrich
   John 1
Usher
   Andrew 194, 224
   Hannah 194

Valles
   Alexander 2
Vallette

Elie 39, 72, 129,
   217
Van Bebber
   Isaac 60
Vanbebber
   Isaa 14
   Isaac 26
Vance
   Adam 25, 59, 107,
     115, 157
   David 145, 202
   James 25, 59, 107,
     157
Vane
   David 101
Vanhorne
   Benjamin 44
   Martha 44
Vanhornel
   Benjamin 138
Vansant
   Cornelius 99, 115,
     224
   Eleanor 156
   George 156
   Isaijah 72
   John 89, 157
   Joshua 89, 91, 157
Vantcome
   Benjamin 201
Vantsaveran
   Cornelius 127
Vardel
   James 172
Vaudrie
   George 215, 216
Vaughan
   Charles 113
Vaughop
   James 37
Veazey
   John 193
Venables
   Charles 75
   Theodore 75
Venneman
   John 192
Vennemon
   Elisabeth 1
   John 1
Vicars
   John 8
Vickars
   John 69

Mary 8
Vickers
  William 8
Vine
  Thomas 110
Vineyard
  James 68
Vinson
  Betty 213, 214
  John 213, 214
Vowles
  Jacob 211
  Susannah 211

Wade
  Robert 9
Waggaman
  Mary 186
Wales
  John 133
  Jonathan 71
Walker
  Charles 199
  Cloe 104
  David 91
  John 110
  Joseph 37
  Robert 104
Wall
  Thomas 8, 69, 208
  William 8
Wallace
  Andrew 15
  Christiana 8, 70
  James 122, 213
  John 122
  Whitten 10
Wallis
  Henrietta 7
  Henry 7
  Hugh 90, 134
  John 3, 7, 71, 90,
    194
  Samuel 90
Walmsly
  Allethea 114
  Nicholas 114
  Robert 114
Walston
  Boax 146
  Joy 146
Walter
  Peleg 204

Walters
  Ann 111
  Frances 5, 23
  John 226
  Robert 111, 221
  Samuel 190
  Stephen 226
Walton
  Meredith 24, 57
  Solomon 103
Ward
  Benjamin 121, 132,
    188
  David Lindsay 11
  Hannah 15, 116
  Henry 15, 25, 59,
    117, 132, 157
  John 15, 25, 59,
    157
  Nathaniel 114
  Sarah 132
Warden
  Mary 208
  William 208
Warder
  Eleanor 9
  John 9, 41
  Mary 9
  Walter 9, 41
  William 9, 221
Ware
  Edward 68, 114
Warfeild
  Gerrard 129
Warfield
  Absalom 219
  B. Ridgely 72
  Bazil 110
Waring
  Francis 31, 62, 167
  Leonard 31, 167
  Marsham 44
  Mary 31, 167
Warner
  Charles 13, 57,
    111, 137
  Hovel 13
  Lovel 57
  Richard 13, 57, 61
Warren
  Elisabeth 1, 210
  John 107, 200
  Lucretia 124
  Notley 15

Paroah 101
Sarah 101, 205
William 46, 102,
    206
Warring
    Francis 80
    Leonard 80
    Mary 80
Wason
    John 136
Waters
    Daniel 199
    Edward 109, 186
    George 87, 209
    James 95
    John 87, 130, 209,
        220
    Peter 109, 186
    Robert 40
    Thomas 37
Wathen
    Leonard 125
Watkins
    Gassaway 218
    John 8
    Mary 24, 46, 58,
        155, 207
    Nathan 184
    Nathaniel 184, 185
    Richard 129
    Samuel 129
    Thomas 184, 218
Watson
    Charles 140
    David 32, 42, 47,
        71, 81
    Easter 195
    Esther 157
    John 157, 190, 195,
        221
    Jonathan West 204
    Robert 140
    Sarah 32, 47
    Stephen William 81
    William 32, 47
Watts
    Charles 90, 135,
        136
    Edward 118
    George 163, 183
    Joshua 11, 28, 47,
        77, 119, 161
    Rebecca 163
    Richard 125

Robert 78, 162, 216
Sarah 125
Thomas 11, 28, 47,
    77, 126, 161
William 125
Waughop
    James 37
Wayman
    Edward 50, 84, 180
    Mary 50, 84, 180
Weartime
    Henry 96
Webb
    Edgar 108, 191
    James 222
    Nany 108
    Solomon 34, 203
    Vernon 125
    William 110, 112,
        124, 222
Webster
    Hannah 48, 82
    Isaac 49, 201
    John 48, 82, 123,
        180, 206, 226
    John Lee 130
    Samuel 48, 82
    William 68
Wedding
    John 95
Weeden
    James 66
Weedon
    William 168
Weems
    John 30, 79, 166
Wells
    Alexander 83
    James 61, 84
    Mary 98
    Samuel 80, 168
    William 52, 98,
        223, 225
Welsh
    Andrew 12, 26, 60,
        159
    Benjamin 40, 220
    Henry Oneal 51, 85,
        181
    James 3
    Lydia 50, 84
    Milcah 3
    Richard 50, 84
    Thomas 39, 62, 220

Page 295

West
  Joseph 32, 42, 81,
    214
  Samuel 91, 106, 206
  Stephen 31, 168
  Steven 80
  William 44, 115
Westbay
  William 179
Wethered
  William 63
Whaley
  Benjamin 152, 213
  John 152
Wharton
  Charles 203
  George 92, 111
  Sarah 203
Wheat
  Francis 66
Wheatherly
  Joseph 9
Wheatley
  John 93, 126
Wheatly
  Elisabeth 163, 206
  John 163, 206
  Richard 216
Wheeler
  Bazil 62
  Benjamin 3, 4, 10
  C. 110
  Elisabeth 4
  Hezekiah 47
  Ignatius 47, 67,
    112
  John 8, 10, 11, 44,
    62, 87, 127, 198
  Mary 198, 209
  Rebecca 3
  Rebeccah 62
  Richard 217
  Samuel 44, 113
  Thomas 4, 10, 12,
    43, 69, 209
Whelch
  Richard 116
Whelsh
  John 219
Whetherspoon
  Thomas 159
Whichcote
  Martha 120
  Paul 120, 194

Whitacre
  Abraham 44
  Isaac 88
Whitaker
  Abraham 201
  Alexander 223
  Isaac 113
White
  Abigal 113
  Isaac 113
  James 62, 124
  Mary 207
  Richard 193
  Samuel 87
  Stephen 143
  Thomas 9
  William 190, 207,
    223
Whiteford
  William 113
Whiteley
  William 8
Whitely
  Arthur 69, 122, 213
  Massey 123
  William 200
Whitenhall
  John 107
Whitesides
  Rebecca 46
  Robert 46, 115
Whitherspone
  Thomas 60
Whiting
  Samuel 5, 40, 149
Whitister
  Isaac 130
Whitman
  Frederick 135
Whittaker
  Elisabeth 223
  Henny 223
  Robert 223
Whittington
  Mary King 144
  William 144
Whyatt
  Caleb 102
Wicks
  Joseph 71
  Simon 71
Wiggins
  Elisabeth 4
  William 4, 17

Wilcocks
   Daniel 40, 94, 207
   William 40, 207
Wilkerson
   Elisabeth 89
   John 89
Wilkins
   Thomas 35, 108
Wilkinson
   Barbarah 176
   Chris. 190
   Elisabeth 178
   John 131, 178
   Joseph 73
Will
   Sarah 105
Willcocks
   William 111
Willen
   Thomas 46
Willett
   Edward 135, 192
   Mary 225
   Thomas 126, 145
   William 97, 145,
     225
Williams
   Aaron 139
   Andrew 32, 81, 169
   Ann 27, 32, 47, 76,
     77, 78, 81, 160,
     169
   Baruch 192, 220
   Benjamin 62, 74,
     77, 126, 129
   Catharine 25, 58
   Charles 32, 81, 169
   Comfort 129
   Edward 69, 107,
     124, 200
   George 140
   Jacob 78
   James 88, 108, 129
   John 47, 94
   Jos. 39, 130, 220
   Nathan 210
   Rachel 69, 107
   Robert 15, 25, 58
   Thomas 6, 15, 25,
     48, 58, 98, 129
   Walter 222
   William 38
Williamson
   Alexander 128

   Elisabeth 30, 79
   George 16, 35, 194
   James 30, 74, 79
   John 16, 64, 140
   Thomas 112
Willin
   Leui 198
   Thomas 140
Willis
   Richard 70, 99
Willmott
   John 112
Willoughby
   John 66, 117
   Rachel 117, 196,
     197
Wills
   Benjamin 105, 146
   Sarah 146
Willson
   William 168
Wilmer
   John 194
   John Lambert 24,
     58, 140, 155
   Simon 24, 58, 118,
     155
   Thomas 140
   William 7, 36
Wilmot
   John 48, 180
   Rachel 48, 61, 82
Wilmott
   Rachel 173
Wilson
   Basil 67, 212
   David 186, 195
   Edward 90
   Elenor 186
   Elisabeth 6
   Hileary 166
   Hugh 6, 67
   Isaac 25, 35, 36,
     106, 194
   James 90, 109, 113,
     136, 138, 153,
     168, 178, 186,
     211, 225
   John 10, 111, 131
   Jos. 106
   Joseph 67, 166, 219
   Lancelot 67, 212,
     223
   Lansolot 110

Levin 61
Mary 35
Meredith 154
Thomas 8, 166, 218
William 90, 98, 118
Wimsat
Robert 36
Wimsatt
Richard 38
Winder
John 186
Windsor
Anne 97
John 97, 103, 205
Phillip 97
Wing
James 69, 199
Winsor
Ann 141
John 141
Winwright
Cannon 200
John 200
William 200
Wise
Bridget 64, 194
Samuel 97
Withers
Rosannah 105, 195
William 26, 59,
105, 158, 195
Witherspoon
Thomas 27
Withrington
John 37
Wolford
Charles 186
Wolston
Boaz 88
Boz 132
Joy 88
Wood
Benjamin 100
Edward 30, 73, 79,
100, 108, 138
Leonard 100
Levi 109
Mary 13, 68
Robert 23, 56, 151,
211
William 49, 61
Woodal
Thomas 35
Woodard

Benjamin 122, 198,
214
Thomas 100
Woods
Jonathan 150
Woolen
Edward 76, 209
William 76, 124,
200, 209
Woolford
James 198
Levin 41, 198, 214
Mary Mary Ann 186
Woollen
Edward 41
William 41, 69
Woolsey
George 96
Wooten
William Turner 14
Wooton
William T. 109
Wootton
Samuel 73
Singleton 126
W. T. 222, 225
William T. 98, 126,
185, 187
William Turner 18,
66, 127
Worrall
Priscilla 224
Worrell
Simon 224
Worrick
Arthur 19
Elisha 19
Worthing
William 86
Worthington
B. T. B. 72
Charles 50, 84, 85,
180, 181
John 50, 84, 85,
180, 181
Nicholas 72
Samuel 85, 181
Vachel 85, 181
William 39, 86, 183
Wrench
William 4
Wright
Abigail 186
Abraham 201

Daniel 11
Edward 92
Eleanor 50, 84
Francis 123
Jacob 199, 208
James 199
John 13, 29, 68, 78
Lemuel 199
Levin 109, 195, 199
Mary Ann 92
Nathan 96
Nathaniel 4, 16,
   92, 94, 136
Rezin 50, 84, 128
Samuel 61, 125, 216
Sarah 199, 208
Solomon 109, 186,
   195
Sophia 88, 96, 146
Stephen 196
Susannah 125
Thomas 4, 16, 40,
   92, 93, 110,
   124, 136, 190,
   221, 225
Turbutt 93
William 8, 199,
   208, 214
Zebulon 88, 132,
   146
Wroth
   Kinvin 99
Wyat
   Caleb 102, 207
   William 207
Wyatt
   William 102
Wyle
   Cassandra 104
   Luke 3, 104, 131
Wynn
   John 109

Yates
   Hellen 185
   Theop. 121
   Thomas 38
Yerby
   John 43
Yewell
   Thomas 23, 56
Yoe
   Thomas 153

William 110, 153
York
   Edward 202
Young
   Adam 210
   Andrew 70, 223
   Daniel 97, 204
   Ezekiel 97
   Jacob 42, 107, 135,
      220
   John 11, 94, 104,
      189, 209
   Rebecca 149, 195
   Rebeccah 43
   Thomas 149, 195
   W. 200, 225
   William 2, 10, 43,
      44, 71, 96, 111,
      130, 137, 187,
      212
Younger
   John 64, 108
   John Reeder 215
   Joseph 108

Zacharias
   Daniel 75, 94
Zuile
   Mathew 27
   Zarah 27

INDEX OF EQUITY CASES

Kirby vs. Clouds 22

Lane vs. West 168
Lawson vs. est. of Smith 180

Maccubbin vs. Bounds 51
Maccubbin vs. Iiams & Elliot 52
Martin vs. Baxter 160
Milligan, Earle, & Gordon vs. est. of McDuff 60,
    160
Minor vs. Stevens 20
Moore vs. Stevens 54, 147

Oneal vs. Kelley 84

Pett vs. Turner 20
Pounds vs. Maccubbin 85

Ruth vs. Baily 151
Rutland vs. Welsh 51

Sedgwick vs. Sedgwick & Boyd 25, 158
Selby, et. al. vs. Dorset, et. al. 31, 80, 167
Shaw vs. Davis 86
Stoddert vs. Smallwood & Smallwood 86

Tennally vs. Lowndes 168
Twyford vs. Warner 57

Vansant vs. Comegys 157
Vansant vs. Vansant 157

Williams vs. Williams, Bennett, Henley, &
    Williams 77
Wilmot vs. Carlisle 48
Worthington & Worthington vs. Worthington &
    Worthington 181

CPSIA information can be obtained at www.ICGtesting.com
Printed in the USA
BVOW11s0711280515

401932BV00009BC/136/P